Mark Townsend is Home Affairs Editor of the *Observer*.
won or been shortlisted for more than twenty
in a journalism career which began on the *Western
ing News*. His reports from Afghanistan, on which
t Man is based, were judged runner-up in the features
gory of the 2007 Foreign Press Association (FPA)
a ards. The following year he was part of the *Observer*
team that won an FPA award for their investigation into
I qi honour killings. Most recently his 2011 investigations
o human trafficking won several prizes and were shortl-
d for the Paul Foot award. Other awards include Press
tte Specialist Reporter of the Year and British Envir-
ental Journalist of the Year. He lives in London.

Praise for *Point Man*:

'A illiant must-read.' Rosie Boycott

'The best narratives are the ones that capture real voices
and al stories of humanity at its best and worse. This is a
sto y of war and hardship, but also how rage and trauma
sses through generations. An excellent book.' Janine di
Giovanni

'Mark Townsend tells a story politicians don't want to hear.
Wr en with elegance and compassion, this book should
ake you angry. Why do we send our young people to kill

and be killed in unjust wars? Why do we not care for them if they survive? Why do we tolerate the hypocrisy of politicians who parade at the Cenotaph but clearly don't give a flying fuck?' Ken Loach

Point Man

Mark Townsend

faber and faber

First published in this edition in 2012
by Faber and Faber Limited
Bloomsbury House,
74–77 Great Russell Street,
London WC1B 3DA

This paperback edition first published in 2013

Typeset by Faber and Faber Ltd

Printed and bound by CPI Group (UK) Ltd, Croydon, CR0 4YY

A CIP record for this book
is available from the British Library

ISBN 978–0–571–27243–3

2 4 6 8 10 9 7 5 3 1

To Shyboy, Morwenna, Juliet, Peter and Kerry

Contents

Illustrations

I

The Cornfield

Kenny usually knew when something was up. Now he recognised the unmistakable countdown to combat. The young soldier turned to his colleagues trudging behind him and noticed their tense bodies, faces creased with fear.

For half an hour they had shuffled in single file along the trail from the district's military headquarters at Sangin towards Waterloo, an isolated patrol base a kilometre away on the town's outskirts. The mission was straightforward enough: reach Waterloo, exchange intelligence with the Afghan troops stationed there and get back in one piece. They had set out in high spirits as they picked their way through Sangin's southern suburbs. They smiled at the children playing with dented cooking pots in the dust, nodded at the parents eyeing them anxiously as they marched past. Kenny, as always, grinned back. The features of the twenty-year-old private had somehow withstood the parched heat and choking dust to retain a flawless, almost pre-pubescent complexion. Just five foot seven, Kenny looked benign, a peaceful emissary wrapped in a warrior's uniform.

As the men of I Platoon A Company trooped onwards the land began to empty. By the time they reached Tank Graveyard, the overgrown clearing holding the corroded corpses of Soviet T-55 tanks, the surrounding streets were deserted. Now there were no dogs rooting in the heaps of litter. The squawking roosters and black-faced sheep padding the nearby fields had vanished. Even the rats had gone.

Kenny led the young men forward, scanning the terrain. It was just after 11 a.m. and Tank Graveyard was cleared for a shootout. He could tell from the silence. 'It was like those old Westerns, the bit before the bad hats ride in and everyone in the town scarpers before the gunfight.' They moved on, Kenny wincing at the crunch of his combat boots on the rocky ground. He paused; the silence absolute, save for the warble of a dove from the treeline to the right. In the still moments before battle he struggled to breathe properly. His heart would beat hysterically. He would grip his SA80 assault rifle to stop it slithering from his grip. Kenny sucked greedily from the tube leading to his Camelbak pouch, three litres of water strapped to his sodden back. It was a futile exercise. In the build-up to battle, Kenny had learned, all moisture leaves the mouth and swallowing becomes almost impossible.

They were being watched, he had figured that much. Five minutes earlier he had seen a 'dicker', a spotter monitoring the thin column of invaders. The dicker had appeared to whisper urgently into a mobile phone. There was no doubt in Kenny's mind that they would be attacked; it was a simple question of when. He squinted in the glare of the high sun, eyelashes heavy with dust, and studied the way ahead for traces of the enemy.

Private Kenny Meighan was the eyes and ears of the platoon. He was young but he was learning fast about death. One friend had already died and more were sure to follow. But Kenny had convinced himself he would survive. He hadn't even fallen in love yet. Not properly anyway. He wouldn't be allowed to die without having ever fallen in love. It would be too unfair.

He caught sight of a pile of rubbish teetering beside the trail: perfect cover for a booby trap. Beside the path he scrutinised the angular blocks of disturbed earth: loosened soil could betray a newly planted bomb. Further on there was a fresh deposit of human excrement – the crap of an enemy sniper? Close by, recent sandal prints led to a towering mud-baked compound. To his left, crumpled grass-blades suggested a newly laid trail – to a waiting assassin?

The enemy were close. Somewhere nearby, Taliban marksmen were keeping it tight, suppressing pre-ambush nerves as they willed the young foreigners into their sights. Kenny contemplated the silence, but his mind was jumbled. He later said that he recalled hearing his mother's final warning and his father's parting advice and then visualised the Taliban crouched behind the mud walls ahead, their beards fluttering in the draught that heralded the midday heat. He imagined the barrel of an AK-47 stalking him down the track.

The silence hung heavy. Below his Mark 6 combat helmet, Kenny's forehead trickled with sweat. His hands had started to tremble with the certainty of what lay ahead. Kenny drew hard from the Camelbak and choked briefly on a dry cough. Another attack of the fear; these days, nothing new.

Then it began. A rocket-propelled grenade, its tail spewing scarlet like a firework, sailed overhead. Even before it had shattered above him, the air rippled with a sustained burst of AK-47 fire. There were ten Taliban, maybe more. Up high, to the right. Another rocket, then another. Three, four, five of them. Kenny scrambled for cover and fired back. The brittle rattle of British SA80 rifles and machine guns dominated the soundscape until there was an abrupt tense calm. To his left, movement. The Taliban, about thirty of them, platoon strength, running fast downhill towards a distant cornfield. Kenny bounded forward in pursuit. Witnesses often wondered how the men managed to move so freely with so much weight strapped to their bodies. Each British soldier carried at least forty kilos of equipment: eleven magazines of ammunition plus a bandolier, two high-explosive grenades, two smoke grenades and one red phosphorus flare, in addition to a personal radio and five litres of water. They also carried doses of morphine, hefty compress bandages and two tourniquets – they had learnt you could bleed to death inside three minutes. Each had the weight of a newborn calf on his back. Private Matt Slater carried a St Christopher for protection; Scott Hardy had his lucky West Ham pendant. Private Fabio 'Olly' Olivero brought a pocket Bible because his mother said Jesus would protect him from the jihadists. Kenny carried only his instincts. He was already overburdened with responsibility for the lives of the men who followed him.

Below, the enemy melted into the huge cornfield, the size of five football pitches, as if they had dived headfirst into the maize. The nine-foot plants bobbed in the hot breeze, taunting the British soldiers.

Kenny entered the cornfield first, the crops rustling as he tiptoed forward. Whoever owned the land had defied the prospect of a mediocre harvest; the planting was dense and jungle-like. He stumbled on, the green leaves slapping his face, obscuring his vision. Above, he noticed the cornstalks jerking manically with his every step. Stealth was impossible. The most-prized military stratagem – surprise – was lost. He may as well have strapped a Union Jack flag to his back. It was dark inside the cornfield. 'The sunlight couldn't get through the plants. I remember blinking over and over trying to get my eyes to adjust to the light, it was horrific.' Several steps in and Kenny could barely see a metre ahead. Five metres in and it was almost black. Glancing down, he struggled to make out the shape of his boots. Kenny moved slowly, stopping every few moments to listen for the rustle of the undergrowth or the sound of the enemy's breathing. In his mind, he was making as much din as a silverback stumbling through brushwood. Please Dad, he prayed, please don't let them hear me. His headset crackled into life.

'This is Two One Charlie, affirmative. Over,' whispered Kenny, concentrating to keep his voice steady.

'The Taliban have regrouped in the field. We intend to flush them out. Keep your wits, it's going to get cheeky. Advance to engage. Over,' instructed his platoon commander, Lieutenant Nick Denning.

What followed was an order to chill the veins of young soldiers trained in the techniques of hi-tech warfare, the art of killing from afar. None of them had signed up expecting to gore a human being to death. 'Fix bayonets.'

Immersed in the suffocating jungle, the troops could literally stumble into the enemy. Kenny knelt down and unfastened his rifle sling, which would allow him to jab a twelve-inch blade into a man's chest with his full body weight. The action would easily slice through a rib. The real problem could be the time it took to lever out a bayonet wedged in the mesh of a ribcage. Kenny had heard of men forced to stand upon a dead man's chest as they extricated their blade from the carcass. The one positive aspect of their situation was that the enemy were petrified of the bayonet. You could pummel their positions with A-10 tank-buster planes, volley one missile after another into their bunkers and they would fire back all day, but approach with a sharpened rifle and the Taliban would run.

Kenny inched forward, groping in the gloom, spitting out the fronds that caught in his mouth. 'I cannot see a shitting thing,' he muttered and was seized by panic in his isolation. He span round, gasping with relief when he saw Slater behind him, blinking back through the twilight. They stared at each other, swamped in their corridor of corn. For a while they stood listening to the breeze in the leaves towering above their heads, wondering where the enemy lurked. Kenny listened for a clue to the Taliban's presence. Left or right? In front or behind? In the still moments before a firefight, the body struggles to control the spurts of adrenalin, the nerves flooded with fear. The mind switches between thoughts of death and the life you might soon leave.

Kenny was plunged back into the cornfield by a sudden noise ahead. Something heavy was moving through the crops. Kenny licked his lips and stooped forward. For a minute he squinted at the curtain of green ahead, wondering what might possibly be out there. Then again: the noise. This time it was indisputable. Footsteps. A column of figures was moving through the corn. They were headed right for him. Judging by the sound, Kenny reckoned at least seven bodies were weaving closer and closer through the foliage. Their angle of advance provoked a momentary panic. Whoever was out there was hoping to outflank the isolated British platoon. Kenny lay flat in the darkened depths of the cornfield. Down here, where wind or light never reached, he could smell the dank soil. The dense, unmoving air was heavy. Kenny strained his neck to peer through the vegetation, half expecting to glimpse strangers' legs shuffling towards him. Nothing. He checked his watch. Eleven thirty.

By now they were practically on top of him, no more than fifteen feet away through the dense jungle. He was convinced the Taliban could feel his pulse vibrating through the narrowing strip of ground that separated them. Maybe, Kenny remembers kidding himself, it was just some curious farmhands? Perhaps the mysterious figures were friends? But Kenny knew he was the furthest forward, out on a limb in a killing field.

Up to his right, there was a burst of commotion, as if the enemy were unable to repress their anticipation as the ambush reached its point of no return. Kenny held his breath and groped for the metal bauble that dangled off his webbing. Slowly he pulled the pin and lobbed it like a pebble in front of him. There was a loud hollow bang like the noise balloons make when they burst. The battle had begun. Instantly, the judder of gunfire erupted in front of him. A clump of corn heads burst above Kenny, showering him with fragments of shattered plant. Two metres to his right the corn was completely torn apart by gunfire, the tall stalks splintering. The bullets were close together. This was no random firing. Crucially, however, they told Kenny exactly where the unseen Taliban were gathered. He tracked their position along the axis of disintegrating greenery and took careful aim. He had to be spot on. The instant he returned fire the enemy would, in turn, know precisely where he lay. Within seconds it would be clear if Kenny had failed to subdue his target. He emptied the entire magazine – thirty rounds in four seconds – knowing that before he had finished shooting the enemy might be attacking his position. There was the briefest lull before bullets snapped back at him. Both sides were fighting blind, razing the corn with scattergun fire. Shrapnel sliced through the air, whipping the corn. Twigs and leaves rained down. Kenny recalled that at times he felt comforted by the thick blanket of maize that encased him. Some of his section told him later that they had kidded themselves it was a protective shroud which would save them from the lethal metal rounds.

So it went on. British soldiers shooting blindly through walls of green, thickets of corn exploding. The enemy seemed to be everywhere and nowhere. Taliban rockets whooshed through the green, scarlet tracers flashing past in the opposite direction. Large swathes of corn were burning, trapping them. Kenny was certain that he would die. Then, elation as his section pushed alongside him, a line of men all firing from their knees as another group pushed forward protected by their covering fire. It was a tried and tested manoeuvre known as the pepperpot. The men advanced steadily, moving with programmed discipline. In response, the Taliban intensified their onslaught of rocket-propelled grenades. The jungle of corn collapsed around them. A lone Taliban fighter loomed in the twilight. Private Slater clocked him first, but was too close to lie down and line up his machine gun. Slater was one of the coolest cats in the unit and even now, when his nerves might have betrayed him, the twenty-year-old from east London managed to balance his 12.5 kg weapon on his shoulder and take aim. A burning splinter of metal travelling at nine hundred metres a second struck the man between the eyes, slicing his forehead clean off and into the bushes beyond. Kenny's headset fizzed with urgent instructions.

'Two One Charlie come in. Watch your arc of fire on either side. Covering sections are on both flanks. Over.' In the chaos of the flaming cornfield it would be easy to lose your bearings and shoot your friends.

A deadly game began. The men from eastern England advanced and the enemy sank further into the gloom, lost in the maize. As they were pulled deeper into the corn, the soldiers' greatest fear was realised. In the maelstrom of battle, Denning radioed the news. They were alone. Submerged in the corn, his section had become separated from the rest of the company. Kenny and just seven others were cut off. Even before the latest update, Kenny had known he was totally isolated. Summoning attack helicopters or F15 jets was out of the question. From above, the fighters would resemble termites upon a smouldering patch of earth. Buried in the dim corn-walled battlefield, the superior weapons of A Company counted for nothing. Time stood still. It could have been 1880, a bunch of British regulars chasing turbaned Afghans across a southern province. And just like their ancestors, Kenny and his boys risked getting routed in the moments ahead. Just after 12.30 p.m. the Taliban made their last stand: a ferocious weight of fire forcing Kenny to slide for cover into one of the irrigation ditches that dissected the cornfield. For a couple of minutes – it seemed much longer – he crouched in the putrid brown water, sufficient time for invisible bugs to fasten themselves upon his body, time to aim at shapes among the leaves, not knowing whether they were real or imagined.

Out of the water, he almost stumbled over the body. It lay twisted in the twilight. Around it, the stalks were crooked and flattened; Kenny deduced the man's legs had flailed in agony against the corn. A faint gurgling came from his throat as though the man was issuing a curse. But it was his attire that caught Kenny's attention. He turned and nudged Denning. 'Sir, have a look at this. Look at the bloody kit, that explains a lot. He's no muppet.'

The dead man was clad head to foot in black like a ninja and wore full webbing complete with a chest rig laden with grenades and advanced radio equipment. His AK-47 was in good nick, unlike most of the enemy's weapons. This was no two-bit farmer paid ten dollars a day to take potshots at the infidel. Whoever had sent him had access to decent military hardware and no little cash. Kenny rifled through his pockets, taking a mobile phone and radio that might prove valuable for intercepting Taliban messages. There was little else of interest and nothing personal: no lucky charms, no football badge, no medallions of sentimental value and definitely no pocket Bible. No photographs of the family that would soon mourn him. Later, intelligence would confirm the man had travelled from Pakistan, one of the highly trained jihadi foot soldiers streaming into Helmand in ever greater numbers.

The British soldiers went on, creeping through the corn until they came to a small clearing hemmed in by a baked mud wall. An anxious scuffle of boots like the sound of a stiff brush on stone came from the other side. Kenny raised his hand and the section went down on one knee behind him, frozen. For a while they listened. They heard the familiar sharp click of a rifle's safety catch. Then a sound like the rasping wheeze of the dying Taliban fighter minutes earlier. Kenny listened to the shallow gasps of the enemy, reassured they too found fighting knackering. Again he reached down for a grenade. There was a muffled crump, startled screams and then, away from the wall, the scamper of boots. The chase had resumed. Orders came through to fight on the 'front foot', to track the Taliban once more through the twilit tunnels of foliage.

It became a lethal version of catch-me-if-you-can. Kenny ran, weaving through the brush, avoiding the patches where sunlight streamed through gaps in the canopy, a spotlight for snipers. They came to another mud wall, this time a ten-foot rampart housing one of the many citadels that doubled as a defensible home to the people of Helmand. The Taliban had slipped inside. They would be lying in wait, their weapons pointed towards the large wooden door, the only apparent entrance. It was Kenny's job to enter first. He had been here before, countless times, and instinctively rehearsed the risks. He knew that if you survived the freeze-frame of the first second or two of entry, you'd probably make it. This was the worst part, wondering what waited on the other side, the traps that had been set: the killers he might never see. But Kenny had learnt to dull the thought process. Too many ifs and buts and the body would fail to respond. Nerves would tighten and eventually, fatally, decisions would not reach the limbs.

Quickly an explosive was fastened to the door. The men retreated, curled into themselves and then – boom! – Kenny was off, rushing through the cloud of sulphur and wooden splinters as the door was torn from its hinges. He ran into the compound, rifle dug into his shoulder, finger on the trigger. Across the courtyard, barely discernible through the billowing debris, a shape scurried into the rooms at the rear of the complex. Kenny went forward, his breathing fast and shallow, his mouth dry, chest tight in his armour. He entered the murk, momentarily blinded as his eyes adjusted from the afternoon glare outside. From the corner of his gaze, he caught a figure disappearing through a doorway at the back. It was a ruse, surely? As if following bait pulled on a string, he was being lured into the enemy's bottleneck.

Voices. Definitely voices. From an adjoining chamber, he heard anguished muttering. Orders came over the radio for Kenny to hurl a grenade inside and move on. But something did not feel right to the young infantryman. To this day Kenny cannot explain what came over him, why he never pulled the pin. 'I had this feeling, a sixth sense, telling me to hang back,' he said. Rifle cocked, instead he slipped inside.

The room was dark and crammed with junk. Nothing stirred. Kenny heard voices again, this time a soft, mournful whimper. In the corner, obscured in the shadows, loomed the distinctive shape of a human head. The person appeared to be in terrific pain, as if they had crawled there to die.

The figure rocked gently backwards and forwards. It was holding something tight, a bundle wrapped in its arms. A suicide vest? A trap – but in the dark Kenny couldn't be sure and he had promised his dad he would never take aim at an unarmed man. As he advanced, gun raised, his heart leapt. It was a young woman. She sat cross-legged, mumbling in Pashto. In her grip two infants, each no more than four, clung to her chest. She gawped at Kenny, eyes pleading with the intruder in her bedroom. She was shaking, the infants trembling in her terrified embrace. For a moment they stared, entranced, at each other. Kenny tried to turn but he was held by her gaze. She wasn't hysterical like he would have expected. It was almost as if she was used to it – like she'd seen a lot worse than a man with a gun in her house. Then she pointed to the back of the room, where there was rubble and a hole in the wall through which the enemy must have escaped. At that point the room shook with an explosion.

On his knees Kenny scrambled through the mousehole at the back of the compound and into the lush cover of the corn. The section followed. It was pepperpot time again and so the fight raged on, the English occasionally stumbling on bodies in black outfits speckled with broken and powdered corn. At one point the men ran straight past the hiding Taliban, only realising what they'd done when the bullets began chasing Hardy, who was caught wide-eyed guarding the section's rear.

They fought on, buoyed by a tense conversation overheard by an Afghan interpreter on the enemy's communication system. A Taliban commander was barking orders to a comrade who, his voice faltering, said he had tried to stand and fight, but that it was futile. 'They are coming at me like rabid dogs. They keep coming.'

And then, after two hours of fighting, the end came. Soaked in sweat and twitchy with fatigue, they stopped shooting. The enemy was either dead or had fled. As the Englishmen surfaced from the cornfield and realised they had travelled only three hundred metres during the battle, a headcount confirmed the impossible. The entire platoon was alive. Shrapnel had scored the wrist of one teenager, making it look like he had tried to take his own life out there in the corn. Another limped gingerly where a ricochet had slapped the flesh above his knee. Nothing major, no need for a medevac, just the usual scrapes and bruises.

Everybody in the platoon was alive. That was all that mattered. After three months in Helmand, the truest measure of achievement was the number of men who could walk back to base. Euphoria washed through their bodies at the realisation that this outing had not been the patrol when their luck ran dry. Olly patted his biblical protector, Hardy slapped Kenny on the back and exhaled deeply. As the moisture returned to their throats, the men began to joke. As usual, everybody giggled a touch too hard, determined to conceal their terror out there in the corn. When they laughed, at times like these, it was easy to believe they were only nineteen or twenty years old. They were boys, smiling easily. But occasionally Kenny said he would catch his friends gazing at the mountains across the valley, burdened by the lethal consequences of the war.

He began to cry. The tears came easily, Kenny said later. 'I couldn't stop myself. Sometimes you can get really weepy after a firefight. It can happen days, sometimes weeks later, out of the blue. It's why a lot of the lads volunteer for guard duty afterwards, to be on their own, grab a Condor moment so they can pull themselves together.' He guessed it was the shock, the sudden subsidence of the noise and fear, the surprise of surviving. Normally the aftermath of a firefight manifested itself physically in bouts of nausea. Once the adrenalin abated, a wrenching urge to vomit overcame many. Kenny frequently threw up in the wake of battle. That afternoon as they left the cornfield no one mentioned Kenny's tears. Everyone understood.

They trooped warily to Waterloo, Kenny obsessing about the terrain. To his left a stream trickled through the fields. Wild flowers shimmered in the grass. He recalls a pulse of wonder at the unbroken blue sky and the sun-dappled trees, but the sensation faded as quickly as it arrived. This was no place to admire the view. Life on the verge of death required mental discipline; the mind could rarely deviate from what was essential for the platoon's survival. The one constant was that tomorrow, perhaps the day after, Kenny's fighting instincts would be tested again.

No public record exists of that day in the cornfield. Mention is made of it in a few paragraphs in the intelligence archives of the Royal Anglian Regiment 1st Battalion battle group's account of their time in Helmand. It warrants only a handful of statistics: 1 Platoon A Company experienced a 'contact' in a cornfield six hundred metres south of Sangin's district compound during which Kenny threw five grenades and fired more than ninety rounds, and a dozen or so Taliban were confirmed dead. But such figures meant nothing in the context of the wider war. It was just a patrol like countless others, erased from popular knowledge because no British soldier died.

As they marched further from the cornfield, Kenny tried hard to think of home – his Essex local, his young half-brothers, Andrew and Alexander, the family's Jack Russell, Rosie – but the images were vague. All he registered was the quiet returning to the land and the crumple of his desert boots on the gravel.

For now, this was his world. Only the present mattered. But Afghanistan was changing him. He no longer felt young. He was twenty years old and his dreams, his hopes, his fears, were being contorted by war. Kenny would never be the same after Afghanistan. Deep inside the maize fields that line the Helmand River, he was learning what man is capable of and that nothing stays the same.

Soon his world would change in ways he could never have imagined. Soon, that day in the corn would seem as unreal as home.

2

A Messy Tour

It was dusk and shadows were spilling across the courtyard of the British forward operating base in Sangin when I first met Kenny. He shuffled over meekly, olive eyes blinking in the fading light. He looked like a child soldier, yet his stories were those of an old warhorse. At first Kenny was reticent but gradually he warmed up, speaking matter-of-factly about the time he should have been a goner.

'I was pinned down on the domed roof of a compound getting smashed by the enemy. They had a bead on us, I couldn't move a muscle. I was trapped there for ages just waiting to be hit, RPGs, small-arms fire coming right up at me.' He made an exploding noise with the back of his throat and gestured with his hands to replicate rubble tumbling upon his body.

His twenty-first birthday was in nineteen days' time and Kenny wondered whether he would make it. 'It seems a long way off out here,' he mused before remembering it was poor form to be fatalistic. 'But I'll get there, don't you worry,' he said, raising his eyebrows. Only later did it become obvious that he was seeking reassurance.

Rivulets of grime streaked his face and his blond hair, clotted with dust, stood on end hedgehog-style. Kenny calculated that he had been shot at sixteen times since arriving in Afghanistan three months earlier. Rockets, mortars, Pakistani AK-47s, Russian PK machine guns, Chinese Dushka howitzers, Iranian explosives; you name it, he'd dodged it. Like his friends, Kenny was well versed in the idiosyncrasies of the weapons deployed against him.

He described the high-pitched whistle that bullets make as they fizz past your face. The pop of Kalashnikovs, the peculiar hiss of rocket-propelled grenades, the crack of a sniper round as it zips by your head. He could tell the distance of the shooter by whether he heard the bullet only after it had whooshed past. If the steel-jacketed slug was whistling above the speed of sound, the enemy was close. Further away and you could sometimes hear the 7.62 mm projectile spinning in the air as it lost velocity. Kenny whistled and ran his index finger past his left ear. Like all the soldiers in Sangin that summer, he had developed a grudging admiration for the enemy. The courage of the Taliban was acknowledged along with their discipline in battle. There was a trace of envy. Not because they had better equipment or were tactically superior, but because they fought for ideals they fully understood. 'In many ways they believe in their cause more than we do and that must help,' he said. 'The only thing that really lets them down is their shooting. I should have been waxed a couple of times, completely,' he grinned.

Even among the young soldiers, there was something particularly boyish about Kenny. Open-faced and glossy-eyed with a button nose, at times he had the look of a choirboy. Other things set him apart. He had the widest smile of all the troops. And he talked the quickest. Conversations would start and pick up in excitement until thoughts toppled out while his tongue tried to keep up. He smoked to slow down. After a drag his articulation became precise and considered, accelerating steeply until the next puff. He laughed at most things, his shoulders shuddering. And his size marked him out. He was a small, almost fragile figure compared to some of the other soldiers. It was hard to believe the weight he could carry unless you saw it for yourself. He whistled while he walked sometimes, giving the impression of nonchalance. But Kenny cared a lot.

'You love your men of course, but there is a wider responsibility to your country, the people at home, everyone who cares really,' he said, stamping out a Lambert & Butler and hurriedly lighting another. Practically his entire platoon smoked – not to do so was considered unlucky. Those who desisted because it might knock fifteen years off their life were asking to be killed in the months ahead. Even in the brigade headquarters fifty miles south in the town of Lashkar Gah, the urbane commander of the British forces, Brigadier John Lorimer, would chainsmoke Dunhills in the tented enclosure outside his office.

The base at Sangin straddled the constantly shifting front line and lay on the edge of a market town of fourteen thousand people that had been recaptured by British forces weeks earlier. Kenny had arrived, like all those that reached this, the deadliest outpost for UK troops in the war, wondering if he would survive.

Back then, when the war was young, Whitehall briefings in London indicated that progress in Helmand was tangible and growing. Those present heard lofty talk of civic re-building and empowerment. Reconstruction was the buzzword. But in Helmand province the reality was different. Visitors didn't have to do much digging to learn the disconnection between what Whitehall was spinning back home and events on the ground. Hollow-eyed teenagers described a frenzied, unrelenting battlefield. Entire districts would be cleared, only for the enemy to creep back in a few days or weeks. Talk of progress belonged to another world. Back there, newsdesks in London were grappling with an outbreak of avian flu at a Bernard Matthews turkey farm in Suffolk and new research indicating that long-term military deployments induced post-traumatic stress disorder (PTSD).

Here in Sangin, on 3 August 2007, no one dared think beyond the next patrol. Out of sight and largely forgotten, the nation's soldiers were sliding into the quagmire of a misunderstood, unrelenting war. Young men returned from manoeuvres and described lying face down in the shallow furrows of a poppy field as soil spurted beside them from enemy bullets. Others told how one hot morning they stuffed the guts of an Afghan soldier back into his belly, his hot innards spilling over their hands as they waited in enemy territory for a helicopter.

One night a sergeant played me some recent footage from his helmet-mounted camera. I had arrived in Sangin hours earlier to interview troops for a newspaper article and as darkness fell found myself among a group huddled around a small screen. The opening scenes are calm, almost idyllic. British soldiers can be seen trudging through a landscape like that of Provence. There is a sudden roar and the images start to jerk. Trees begin shaking and shedding leaves. Tiny figures appear – more British soldiers – screaming blindly among dense undergrowth. The sergeant gasps. 'Fuck. Fuck, fuck.' The picture wobbles, darting left, then right, spinning 360 degrees. By now the trees and bushes are vibrating madly, the trees look like they are shooting back. The roar is louder now. Off-camera, there is a dreadful scream. 'Man down, man down, get me a fucking stretcher.'

'Fucking hell,' the sergeant gulps and he tries to say something else but his voice chokes with panic. He moves through the foliage gasping. The camera is suddenly staring at ground rippling with the mushroom puffs of bullets. Ahead is a body on its back, twitching in the dust. Figures crouch over him. One is pressing the man's chest. Blood is leaking from his side and the viewer realises that his helper is pressing down to keep the organs from sliding out. 'It's all right mate, stay calm, just hold on in there.' A tattooed forearm lunges across the foreground and shoves more bandages to restrain escaping tissue. The sergeant is breathing heavily. His camera pans away, the bushes are shaking faster now. British soldiers are firing madly at trees but there is no one there. 'Who's down?' A name is uttered. 'No! No! Please. Fuck. No!' Above the cacophony, a man wails as if he has lost a child. You can feel the tears in his voice. The images stop.

Each evening, senior officers in Sangin's operations room studied satellite images of Helmand. Scarlet blobs denoted the latest skirmishes, spattered like a bloody trail along the length of the valley. There were a lot of blobs on the night I met Kenny. After a supper of boil-in-the-bag beans I had wandered around the base asking guys who they thought had a few stories to tell. A few names were touted, but one in particular kept cropping up. 'Kenny,' they said. 'Talk to young Kenny.' Kenny was point man, they said.

He was standing in the courtyard beside a cross made from used .50 calibre machine-gun cartridges welded together, a memorial to the fallen. Several names were etched into its wooden plinth, those of British troops killed defending the base the previous summer when relentless enemy attacks threatened to overrun it. 'They've tried it a few times since we've been here. They're never far away, you can see them watching us every time we step outside.' He dragged hard on his cigarette and gazed across the base. To the left lay the helipad where the Chinooks swept low across the Helmand River dodging the occasional enemy rockets. Beyond was the pomegranate orchard where, the summer before, the Taliban had breached the site's perimeter and a young soldier died among the fruit trees. Directly ahead, past the operations room, lay the wadi on whose banks Taliban snipers sometimes crouched and, behind, the treeline of Wombat Wood. Further along the dried riverbed, the remains of Sangin itself. The nearest buildings had been wrecked and were deserted. Against the sunset the silhouettes of watchtowers loomed; sentries stared into the shadows for enemy marksmen.

It was typical of Kenny that he had to be coaxed with the promise of a shorter interview before he agreed to talk about being point man during our first meeting. It was only when Lieutenant Denning ambled past and asked if I could imagine 'doing point' that the conversation properly turned to what it was like having the most dangerous job in Helmand. Even then Kenny was cagey. 'Well,' he finally said with a diffident smile, 'you switch off for a moment on point, you're probably already dead.'

Taking point means you are the lead soldier of a patrol, the figure who guides the unit through enemy terrain. The point man walks ahead, scanning for danger. It is the most exposed position in a warzone. Taking point guarantees you will be first to wander into an ambush, first to tread upon a hidden bomb, first to be framed in the sights of an opposing sniper. Those who take point accept a vastly reduced chance of surviving. Men can 'take point', 'walk point', 'do point', 'be point', but it all amounts to the same thing: high risk. It was no coincidence that the first Royal Anglian killed in Afghanistan was a point man. Private Chris Gray had been shot weeks earlier during a gun battle among the mountains across the river. Chris was Kenny's pal; they bonded over the role they shared. Both agreed that point was the patrol's most vital position. Reading the land ahead for tell-tale signs and deciphering clues to an imminent ambush, a good point can save the lives of the men who follow. The merest detail interpreted correctly is the difference between life and death for the rest of the unit.

Out here, Kenny had felt his senses sharpen until his instincts were tripwire taut, honed to notice the tiniest inconsistency. He could hear the crunch of loose rock across the valley, decipher scratches in tree bark and determine the anxiety of a stranger from the depth of their footprint.

Kenny compared himself to a great white shark, a creature capable of sniffing blood in water up to five kilometres away. Sometimes, Kenny said, it was as if the land talked to him. 'It's weird. Your senses become so highly tuned that you get all these subconscious instincts that start to read what's going on around you.'

As the weeks rolled by, Kenny had developed an understanding for the land, the way it dipped and rolled from the lush riverbanks to the bald crown of the desert. Patrol after patrol, the platoon would troop faithfully behind, knowing that Kenny would navigate the buried landscape of improvised explosive devices (IEDs), roadside bombs and booby traps. They had followed Kenny through enemy compounds, watching him creep through the maze of murky antechambers where, quite literally, he had bumped into the enemy. They had followed him across fast-flowing rivers, bug-infested ditches, swaying meadows of red-headed poppies. Hardy carried his West Ham pennant and Olly had his Bible, but for the soldiers of 1 Platoon A Company, Kenny was their real lucky charm. 'You just know when something is out of the ordinary, when something is wrong. Why is that rock there? That's a device; that's a Taliban ambush. I was point because I knew what to look for. The amount of times I would hold my section up and say: "Listen, I don't think we should come this way because it looks like a bottleneck, we're gonna get smashed," so we flank the area and, well, what's waiting ahead?' He arched his eyebrows: 'An enemy ambush, sat there, waiting for us. You have the weight of the soldiers relying on your judgement. Where to go? What to do? Switch off for a moment and it's all over.'

The unique pressures of point can overload the mind. Accordingly the position is usually rotated frequently between the most alert and agile of soldiers. Officers often insist on an individual taking point for a determined number of consecutive patrols before relinquishing the role. Kenny was not one for abdicating responsibility. He was there to lead from the front, viewing point as a coveted privilege that should not be surrendered. Kenny called point the 'star prize' of soldiering, like a centre-forward. The platoon operated in the same way as a football team, he said. Without a decent midfield behind he was useless up front. The midfield in turn relied on a solid defence which depended on the good judgement of their keeper, Platoon Commander Nick Denning. But in football a striker can afford to fluff a chance. Not here. 'Everyone is jostling for that position and so you have to keep scoring to make sure you do not miss any opportunities. You can't afford to; miss an IED and the game's over.'

Kenny had convinced himself he had secured the most coveted position on the team. Before leaving, he had promised his father he would be the best infantryman he could possibly be, a man whom future Meighans would be proud to call their own. Point provided the platform to be the best. It was completely unimaginable to Kenny that others were not vying for point. For some, however, there could be no harsher punishment. Point slashed the odds of making it home and represented the military equivalent of a death wish.

But Kenny's enthusiasm for the position was unswerving. The twenty-year-old approached it with a purist's fervour. He scorned any technical devices. When offered the metal detectors that might save his life, he turned them down. If he was going to die, Kenny reasoned, he ought to be out front on his own. After all, he would have missed the clues. 'I just learned to look at the ground. You learn the signs. Our company did have metal detectors but I was having none of that bullshit. And I wasn't going out with an IED man either' – a bomb-disposal expert – 'because you have to learn how to survive and I thought, "Well, if I'm getting slugged I'm getting slugged on my own."'

It was not in Kenny's nature to consider himself different from others or worthy of special favours. One evening, I offered my satellite phone so he could call his mum, let her know he was OK. Kenny looked offended. 'It wouldn't be fair on the rest of the boys,' he said, thanking me for the offer. His one request was that the article should not glorify him or his platoon. 'I get sick of all that "our boys" and "heroes" shit, brave squaddies fighting against the evil Taliban – it's bullshit.' He looked more serious than at any point since we'd met. 'We're not fucking heroes, we're ordinary soldiers.'

He was only a boy himself, but many of the younger soldiers looked up to Kenny. He rejected the culture of 'beasting', the traditional roughing-up of new recruits by older troops. Instead he looked after them, guiding them through the difficult first few months. 'The first rule in the army is that you get called names, you get treated like shit. I didn't see the point in bullying so I took the young lads under my wing. I'd try and encourage them as much as possible. My dad taught me that. You bring the best out of people by showing them a bit of love.' Senior officers rated him for different qualities. Kenny was never told by his superiors to pull back from doing point or to take it easy. They knew his men trusted him with everything they had: their dependable guide. With Kenny at the tip of their spear, the men of 1 Platoon A Company felt they could make it through.

Kenny John Meighan was born in Colchester General Hospital shortly after 6 a.m. on 21 August 1986 and weighed 7 lb 8 oz. Like many born in the town before and after him, he was soon touched by its military legacy. By the time he was five, Kenny was fixated on tanks, warplanes and various other means of destruction. His dad, John, was a serving soldier and Kenny begged to watch the troops perform drill in their combat fatigues. Aged six, he was marching around the kitchen table – left, right, left, right – in his dad's kilt and wellington boots. 'Attention Corporal Meighan,' he would bellow at his father. 'Yes sir!' said Meighan of the King's Own Scottish Borderers as he snapped upright before saluting the most junior officer in the British army. Soon, Kenny had his own set of infantryman's fatigues and together they would visit military bases dressed in near-matching uniform. Once, on holiday in Cyprus in 1992, his dad took him to the battalion barracks and Kenny had his picture taken sat astride the huge gun barrel of an Iraqi anti-aircraft gun that the regiment had seized during the Gulf War months earlier. His grin was almost too big for his face. No kid could have looked happier.

As a child he had asked his dad what it was like to get shot at. Kenny would re-enact the answers by recreating various military campaigns on the carpet, swiftly deploying infantry units to outflank the enemy massed behind the sofa. Infantry figurines guarded his bed at night and, from positions within his satchel, protected him on the way to school. He examined sepia photographs of past conflicts and the uniformed portraits of his father. Aged seven he received his first soldier's camouflage kit for Christmas and begged for them to be photographed together. Father and son: infantrymen.

The military became his obsession: its protocols, codes and creeds captivated him. At primary school, among the aspiring spacemen, supersonic pilots and deep-sea divers, Kenny told teachers he was going to be an infantryman. Aged twelve he joined the local cadets in Harwich, persevering through the monotony of the school day before climbing into uniform to perfect his drills. School held no appeal. Already he was convinced that being able to march in time was more impressive than being good at sums. Besides, had Kenny wanted to be a chief economist or civil servant, it was probably already too late. Aged seven, he had been diagnosed with acute dyslexia. The written word meant little to him. Yet he loved one kind of learning and weekends provided good cramming time. War film after war film was scrupulously digested. He concentrated on the old classics, the ones that showed a redoubtable and menaced but fair and decent army. Soldiers became moral guardians, defenders of faith and humanity. His favourites were easy to guess. *A Bridge Too Far, Zulu, Battle of Britain, Dambusters* and, of course, *The Bridge on the River Kwai.* He developed an intricate knowledge of military hierarchy and tactics. More importantly, he learnt what was expected of men in battle. He enquired about joining the army when he was fourteen.

'When I was in the army careers office I asked what exams I needed to join up and they said you don't need none. Nothing. That was the worst thing the army could have said to me because I went back to school and I didn't try.' He graduated from Harwich School with GCSE C grades in physical education and drama. Despite his dyslexia Kenny was given no special treatment or tuition. Not that it mattered to him. He wasn't even planning to wait for his grades. Shortly after his sixteenth birthday he returned to Colchester's army recruitment centre. He remembers a bright crisp morning and being so excited he was literally trembling after a sleepless night.

Inside the recruitment office, he notionally studied the posters that promoted the other armed forces. Rise above the rest. Sail the world. Kenny ignored them. He knew exactly what he wanted. The teenager turned to the image of a foot soldier crouching in some godforsaken bog. Have you got what it takes? Be the best. The infantry. Kenny was going to be a combat soldier for his local regiment, the 'Vikings', the 1st Battalion of the Royal Anglian Regiment. The recruiting sergeant seemed delighted with his career choice. A choreographed chat ensued and Kenny's Body Mass Index was calculated, confirming him as a slip of a lad, a tad on the scrawny side perhaps. Soon the task of moulding his unpromising frame into a five-foot-seven-inch fighting machine would begin. Later, the sergeant would make him sit an aptitude test. He remembers staring at the words melting, but he had learned to keep cool and slowly deciphered the hieroglyphics shifting before him. He managed to respond to the written demands. Finally, the sergeant asked whether he had considered any armed forces options other than the infantry. Kenny shook his head.

The Meighans were born to fight. For more than three hundred years his ancestors had fought as infantrymen for God, king, queen and country. It began with Captain James Meighan standing among the Jacobite ranks as they peered anxiously through the heavy morning mist towards the River Boyne below. It was July 1690 and the family had entered battle for the first time, fighting furiously but ultimately defeated by King William's forces on the banks of the river north of Dublin. A century and a half later, family lore had it that Kenny's great-great-grandfather had died in the Battle of Balaclava, the Charge of the Light Brigade in the Crimea. The doomed advance of more than six hundred British horsemen against heavy Russian artillery was interpreted by Kenny as a symbol of heroic failure, self-sacrifice and devotion to duty. He marvelled at sketched drawings of the headlong race towards the Russian guns, the wild-eyed horses carrying courageous men resplendent in their red uniforms. Despite his dyslexia, Kenny was familiar with Alfred, Lord Tennyson's poem and his account of the 'Valley of Death'.

The first of the world wars reinvented the scale and

scope of mass killing and again the Meighans were out at the front. Great-grandfather John and his brother Hugh went over the top in March 1915 to take the French town of Neuve Chapelle from the Germans, Britain's first large-scale offensive of the war. They followed the kilted bag-pipers, skirling like never before, towards the enemy's machine guns. Hugh went down as they raced towards the German bunkers. As John stooped to pull his brother from the cloying mud, he was struck by six bullets that pierced the entire right-hand side of his body. But Hugh couldn't be saved, one of 11,200 Allied casualties from an advancing force of fifty thousand, five for each metre of land recaptured. He died aged nineteen from unspecified wounds; a russet-haired Highlander whose body now rests in the nearby village of Armentières.

The Meighans' next call to arms arrived twenty-five years later. John served as an RAF gunner, helping London repel the Luftwaffe throughout the Blitz. 'Jesus, Jesus, what a man,' Kenny's father would say when recalling what his grandfather had done in the two wars. 'You've got to be proud of your grandpa; he stood up to be counted.' On his grandpa's forearm was a tattooed heart with an arrow passing through it; in the heart's centre was a bulge of scar tissue from one of the German bullets. The wounds he received at Neuve Chapelle would claim him decades later, acute arthritis gradually stiffening the right half of his body until a fatal stroke in 1959. But Hugh's death was also never forgotten. Kenny's dad would often recite the fact that Uncle Hugh died on 12 March, the same date on which he was born forty-four years later. For the Meighans the coincidence had assumed an otherworldly significance. Fate had bound the dead to the living. 'There's something in that. Spooky, isn't it?' Kenny's father would say.

Kenny and his dad bonded over their ancestors' bravery, at the unbroken lineage that proved the family would never shirk or surrender. The Meighans, they agreed, were born to lead from the front: the first into battle and the last to leave. Kenny's father had proved that. Eleven medals hung in his hallway, one for each operational tour during his service with the King's Own Scottish Borderers regiment. Northern Ireland ten times, Iraq. From an early age Kenny knew that he too would fight for his country. It was an inherited duty, a continuum of patriotism and courage. For Kenny it was the family's collective history that mattered; the cause was secondary. 'Kenny would say to me, "Dad, it's in the blood, right?"' said John. The eagerness to embrace whatever fate would throw at him was undeniable. And now, in late 2002, another young Meighan arrived at Colchester's military recruitment centre and offered himself to his country.

Kenny's father, though, experienced mixed emotions that day. He couldn't have been prouder of his excitable cherub-faced son, but inwardly John was deeply anxious. He had begged his son not to join the army. The price was too high. 'You'll see things you wished you never saw. Carry them around too long and you'll end up praying for a lobotomy,' the forty-three-year-old told his son in his dense Glaswegian brogue. John had seen the world, known bravery and sacrifice, inspired unflinching loyalty among men. But he could not escape the drumbeat of his past. The things he had seen were destroying him.

Like Kenny, John had also been unable to sleep the night before. But that was normal. For the past twelve years, Kenny's father would lie in bed and wait for the memories – the torso of his friend Big Jim Houston, twitching on a South Armagh road after being gunned down by the Provisional IRA. Houston had a chin like Bruce Forsyth and hours before his death John had stroked it teasingly, just like he always did. Now in the night, Big Jim's long face lay staring back, pale and wide-eyed on the Irish tarmac. Later, the dead Iraqis would gather around John's bed. They had lips that moved but their eyes were gone and it was their hollow sockets that asked him why – why did they have to die like this? Then he would be back on the Highway of Death, the road that wound north to Basra, during the 1991 Gulf War. There, the columns of retreating Iraqi troops had been annihilated by US gunships.

During our first meeting, I was struck by John's capacity to recount his military career with candour and wit. But fifty-seven minutes into the interview, his previously animated persona suddenly disintegrated. The conversation had turned to the Highway of Death. 'Heads were lying everywhere, there were twisted lungs and intestines hanging out of their bodies . . . dogs were eating the dead, even children . . .' The tape recorder captures him swallowing hard, his voice starting to falter. Then he begins sobbing, so hard that it sounds like he might forget to breathe. He apologises and tries to carry on, trying to force out the words until there is only a rasping noise on the tape as John gasps for air. After a minute or so, he manages to control his breathing and just stares at the floor. Finally he looks up and his expression is so utterly dejected I say sorry for dredging everything up. 'It's not your fault. I was a soldier, I was paid to see that shit. But,' his voice loud as he leans closer, 'there were babies reported among the dead. They were not all combatants, know what I mean?' He is angry now and I nod even though we both know I cannot imagine such slaughter. John could never comprehend that his own side was capable of such brutality.

For fourteen years and forty-seven days, Corporal John Meighan served his country with distinction. But he had seen what most could never imagine. He left the military because he couldn't risk seeing another corpse. Once out, he repeatedly tried to kill himself. The images of big-chinned Jim and the mutilated Iraqis grew more real over time; they began visiting him in the morning, when he woke, in the afternoon and on the way to bed, gradually eclipsing everyday reality. John tried to obtain psychiatric help – counselling, medication, anything – to shoo away the dead but no one wanted to know. As a young man he eschewed drink in favour of physical fitness and a clear head, but now a litre of supermarket vodka might be drained before the lunchtime news. His torment grew. His overdoses failed, so he upped his drinking. He fought with strangers in the hope they would deliver a fatal blow and, when that didn't work, moved on to picking scraps with people who knew how to hurt. But all that was child's play compared to what would follow.

Shattered by his procession of awful memories, John felt

he would not be able to bear it if his easy-going boy – the most sensitive of children – were to suffer the same. Kenny was such a benevolent, caring kid. As a child he had taken in a friend whose dad had left and whose mum had run off to New York with a new bloke. Kenny offered his room, sharing his bed, his clothes, his meals, even his favourite Nike trainers. More than anything, John wished he could spare Kenny the trauma, the knowledge that the country you serve so diligently can cut you off when you need it most.

The eleven tour momentoes that hung in the hallway were reminders from another life, a time of camaraderie and unity of purpose, a time when he could never have dreamt he would end up like he did. But they also took John back to a time when, five years old, he too had dreamt of emulating his grandfather's wartime heroics. He under-stood how his own service had bred a longing in his son that could not be denied. In a way, his father's suffering had only intensified Kenny's obsession. What force could exist that could so ruthlessly break a man like his dad? Only something utterly magnificent could be responsible, something so compelling that it rendered life afterwards en-tirely bleak.

From the start John knew his warnings to Kenny were futile. As far as Kenny was concerned, had his father been able to attend, he would have turned up at the recruitment centre that morning with a national hero for an escort. His dad was Britain's best living soldier, probably the best it had ever had. He would have half-expected the recruiting sergeant to bow down in awe had Corporal Meighan of the

King's Own Scottish Borderers entered. Kenny believed in his father more than anything else. Even if he could be just a bit like him then he would make a proper Meighan. To make the friends he had made. To experience derring-do. To see the things he had seen. 'I was so proud of him,' said Kenny. 'I thought when I was a kid looking at my dad that he was God. I loved the fact he was part of something so special.' He only wished his dad had been able to make it to the recruitment centre that morning. But he understood: his dad was having 'problems'.

After leaving the recruitment centre Kenny wandered into Colchester, past the towering winged figure that guarded the city's castle. He stared at the war memorial and imagined the hidden casket engraved with the names of the First World War dead buried within its huge plinth. Perhaps, one day, his name would be similarly immortalised. Even then, Kenny fantasised about the war stories he could tell his children.

In 2002, his dad's conflict in Northern Ireland was winding down four years after the Good Friday agreement; the IRA were under increasing pressure to destroy their arms dumps and cease operations. Now talk was brewing of invading Iraq while units of British troops had been deployed to Afghanistan in the wake of 9/11. Afghanistan seemed pretty tame to Kenny. He wanted action, a land where the enemy were everywhere, where only the best might survive.

Now it was his turn to step up to the plate. The war in Afghanistan had soured. It was 21 March 2007 and in seven hours' time he would be leaving for Helmand province. The night before war felt like standing on the edge of a high diving board. Kenny just waited, controlling his nerves, trying not to look down, knowing that once he jumped there was no turning back. He was terrified and exhilarated. The hours passed slowly in Pirbright barracks in Surrey. Kenny's section ordered in a Chinese takeaway but found digestion difficult. No one could sleep so they just sat on their mattresses – Olly, Slater, Hardy and Denning – trying to keep things light and easy. They took it in turns to phone home. Kenny spoke to everyone he could think of: long-lost cousins, obscure relatives; grans and grandads; his young halfbrothers, Andrew and Alexander, from his father's second marriage. He had to speak to them all, just in case. He made daft promises to everyone. He said anything he believed might ward off death for the next 180 days. His mum, Susan, said how much she loved Kenny and then put down the receiver and cried. His dad shared his pride and some last-minute tips: make sure you shoot them in the nuts, they go down quickly if you get them in the bollocks. John reminded his son that he was a Meighan and told him not to worry. On the bright side, the weather was good out there and he always suited a tan.

When the conversation ended, John later admitted, he felt sick. He remembers studying the pictures on his lounge wall. Him in his regalia alongside a grinning boy in camouflage fatigues. Now his son was private 25162300 in the British infantry. Please God, he thought, please do not let him see the things I saw. But there was no pretence in the final military briefings given to Kenny and his company before they headed out. No one dared shirk the horrors. They were off to war.

'The army didn't lie to us. They said, there is a high possibility you are going to get hurt or you might not come home. Everyone knew what we were going out there for – to kill the enemy and that they are going to try and kill us. There was no bullshit. We were told from day one that this was going to be a messy, messy tour.'

3

Bait Platoon

Something big was brewing. In the hinterland north of Sangin, huge numbers of Taliban forces were said to be massing. Intelligence had intercepted talk of the enemy moving south in an offensive to drive the invaders out. The British senior command were planning a decisive counter-attack, an event they hoped would define the conflict. High on ambition, it was fraught with risk. By night, a unit of infantry supported by Afghan troops would march eleven kilometres into the enemy's heartland. Caught off guard, the Taliban would be routed in their own backyard.

But there were doubts. Unknown to Kenny at the time, some officers felt the undertaking was overloaded with danger. If it went wrong, the repercussions could be catastrophic for the young soldiers. Isolated in enemy terrain, few might survive. But war, the commanders argued, was about risk and on 29 May 2007 the order came to go. Operation Ghartse Gar would take Kenny and his platoon deeper and further into Afghanistan on foot than any British unit had gone for more than a century. Had anyone correctly guessed how long and how far, the more cautious officers at battalion headquarters might have won the debate.

They slipped beyond the perimeter wire of Sangin forward operating base in the dead of night. Within two minutes they had entered the shadows of the nearby treeline. Submerged in the undergrowth, they were effectively invisible to the supporting artillery systems and air power. Now they were on their own.

Sangin lay like a rock on the edge of a whirlpool. Upon leaving the base, Kenny had entered its calm outer waters, but already, groping in the dark, he could feel the undertow, its suction pulling him steadily inwards. Kenny led the men, slowly and deliberately, careful not to trip over hidden tree roots and twist an ankle. Behind him, the column of men concentrated on following the same footprints as the figure in front. Starlight bathed the undergrowth in a silvery sheen, the landscape held its breath.

They carried everything they would need. Five litres of water, forty-eight-hour ration packs and a spare pair of socks. Kenny's small frame, bent almost double, carried a hundred-round link of 7.62 mm machine-gun ammo slung over his shoulders. Several bandoliers were wrapped around his chest and another hundred link in his Bergen daysack for Hardy's GPMG – general-purpose machine gun. In his Bergen he also made room for a spare radio battery, to stay in touch where they were headed. But what they would find when they got there, no one really knew. The intelligence, as always, was vague. A battalion of trained Pakistani fighters or some 'hocus-pocus' potshooters – anything was possible.

They pushed on, surrounded by an enemy they had yet to see. The radios monitoring the Taliban had gone quiet, but in the dark the vegetation seemed alive. Kenny heard odd noises in the undergrowth. Unseen creatures, lying low in the sticking heat of the day, began to roam.

Behind him, he could make out the shadows of the other soldiers, at times silhouetted against the sky. He recognised Lieutenant Nick Denning, platoon commander, six months out of officer training. At twenty-four he was considered an old-timer among the men. He used to joke that his ambition was to become a news anchorman. 'Good evening, world, and I'm Nick Denning,' he would say in a mock television-presenter voice.

Close by was Slater, sauntering along as if they were out picking strawberries. Then Olly, his Bible close at hand, and somewhere in the strung-out column was Hardy cradling his machine gun like a 12.5 kg infant. He saw Badger, so-called because of a white spot on his scalp corrupting an otherwise jet-black barnet. Kenny had christened him Badger and it had stuck so completely that no one could remember what his real name was.

Kenny led them across narrow bridges above irrigation channels, chest-deep through ditchwater and down dusty trails. They passed a graveyard, where the branches of the trees held prayer flags. Past the desert hillside where forward operating base Inkerman would soon be built. And up high to Kenny's left, across the river, loomed the brooding mass of the mountains where the enemy gathered.

The communications net came alive at dawn. As grey light spread across the valley, the enemy appeared to be in a peculiar mood. Usually the Icomm system that eavesdropped on the Taliban radios overheard the bombastic chatter of men busily swapping audacious plans for attack. Yet now the enemy were whispering, murmuring secrets to one another. They soon realised why. 'Shhhhh, they are coming,' an Afghan voice hissed. Orders travelled down the line of British soldiers: the enemy were ahead. Kenny was told to keep moving. Cautiously, he guided them towards the inevitable ambush. Their bodies stiffened, minds psyched for the impending mayhem. A cluster of mud-baked compounds appeared above a dip in the trail. Kenny remembers feeling the place had a bad vibe. Real bad. He raised his hand. The column slowed. A mutual anguish settled over the men. Kenny examined the patch of open ground that separated them from the compounds, an ideal ambush point. This was it. He felt it with a certainty that drained the moisture from his mouth.

He was still scrutinising a possible passing point when the enemy began firing. Bullets ricocheted off the rocks. Rockets poured down from medieval slits in the buildings. The men fired back, the chaos immediately dispelling their anxiety. Across a field, Kenny saw figures darting to a second complex of compounds. Beside him Scott Hardy chased the runners with bullets until they disappeared inside a doorway. Kenny trained his rifle sights on the entrance. He could see shapes hovering inside. Suddenly one stuck his head out as if checking the weather. Hardy began spraying the doorway. He was a decent shot. He laid down almost one hundred rounds and the door disintegrated.

The fighting lasted all day. Bouts of frenzy, then calm as the enemy engaged with B Company who had been ordered to offer support from the northern flank. By late afternoon, the Taliban began retreating rapidly towards their flimsy boats to navigate the channels of the river, two hundred metres wide, back to their hilltop hideout. The British gave chase, lungs bursting, wide-eyed. They had already decided on a harbour area, a safe haven, by the river where they would regroup, but in the enemy's heartland nowhere was secure. As they sprinted down into the designated safe zone, Kenny heard Badger right behind. There was a sudden terrible popping noise and the surrounding air began snapping. Kenny could feel the bullets, the air warping and sucking as the projectiles flew by.

They had been outmanoeuvred. A line of fighters were waiting for them in dense foliage just fifty metres away. Several steps ahead, to Kenny's left, a group of Afghan army soldiers attempted to storm the enemy position. One by one they fell. They simply fell. One, two, three men down. Gone. It was a kind of no-nonsense killing that Kenny later said reminded him of the opening sequence of *Saving Private Ryan*, when US marines are matter-of-factly mown down on Omaha Beach.

There was a grunt behind him. Badger collapsed. He was holding his chest. 'Man down!' screamed Kenny.

The enemy's firing intensified. The British soldiers were being targeted in their chosen safe zone. Kenny knelt beside Badger. A 7.62 mm bullet had been directed at his heart, but Kenny knew his friend was going to survive. The Kevlar slab of his Osprey body armour had hollowed at the point of impact as if a scoop had been taken from a tub of ice cream. The bullet had deflected from Badger's chest, pinging into his wrist which now dangled limply.

Badger seemed delighted with the development. He was going home. He might even get laid. 'Yes! A war wound. I'll get some ladies with this,' he shouted, holding up his crooked limb. Amid the maelstrom came another cry. Denning was down. Kenny crawled over to his platoon commander. 'All right?' he asked and Denning, grinning, explained that he'd tripped up. It was Denning's first cartoon fall of many. Steady during battle in every aspect except his balance. The fight carried on into evening until the bent bodies of the enemy lay still in the treeline.

They settled down for dinner by the river. Lumpy beef stew with unidentified vegetables, dumplings lying part-sunken in congealed gravy as dense as chocolate sauce. For afters it was chocolate pudding with sauce the consistency of gravy. Ration pack B. It was always ration pack B. The quartermasters must have had a job lot. Kenny wondered what was in ration pack A. He doubted it was line-caught lemon sole with hand-cut chips.

Badger had been taken by Afghan troops back to Sangin for treatment. Kenny wondered how he was getting on, and why his friend and not he had been shot. Badger was right behind at the time, right up his arse. The bullet must have passed straight through him. The margins of war; sometimes they worked for you.

Kenny, like every soldier, was dependent upon an immeasurable chronology of lucky breaks. He understood the importance of chance. He recognised that he could be squashed flat by a mortar bomb as he dozed or he could survive ten hours being shot at without a scratch. 'You could trip over and break your ankle, or you could find

cover when an RPG explodes and a bit of shrapnel rico-
chets and gets you in the neck.'

The men prepared for night. It was a gorgeous evening,
a red glow behind the dark mountains. Kenny had never
ventured so deep into the valley before and viewed the
landscape as if he was an explorer; it reminded him of pic-
nics in the old days when he and his dad camped by the
River Colne on summer nights and bragged about how
many perch they would catch in the morning. But the tension returned as the light faltered. Kenny knew the enemy
would stay close, biding their time.

Night fell quickly, draining the heat from the land. The
moon hung low. To Kenny's right the far bank of the
river was black and beyond, rearing straight up, towered
the hulk of the mountains. Beyond the ridgeline lay Musa
Qala, the enemy's stronghold. Word had it that two thousand fighters had regrouped there in preparation for a
climactic, winner-takes-all scrap.

Kenny remembers feeling shattered, but restless with the
thought of what lay ahead. He lay on his back, in rigid
body armour, listening to the drone of nearby crickets. He
craved a cigarette, but he was worried about the enemy
watching from above. It was a daft idea; the smouldering
tip would double as a sniper's beacon in the dark.

The night wore on and things got spooky. The crickets
intensified their screeching, ratcheting their shrill chorus
up another octave. Dogs squabbled in an unseen village
somewhere inland. In the darkness creatures seemed to be
shifting, scuttling about in the dust. From the corner of
his gaze a large spider inched forward. Silhouetted against

the starlight, its hairs stuck up like a pin cushion. Kenny banged his foot on the ground and it froze. In response, the crickets cranked it higher. Trees shuddered in the dark. Kenny remembers thinking of the dead Taliban lying in the nearby bushes and imagined them jerking upright and, zombie-like, joining the spiders creeping through the undergrowth towards the riverbank, bent on retribution.

Another hour and a new sound emerged. Noises, floating across the river. Kenny sat up, eyes trained on the black shoreline across the water. He thought he heard the clanking of machinery, the noise of men preparing an offensive, but he couldn't be sure. Hushed voices, men willing each other on, but again he wasn't certain. Maybe it was just the breeze. He could feel the eyes of a silent army on him.

In the morning the river looked solid. The men were still cutting deals over whose turn it was to make the brew when a dull boom ruptured the dawn air. A moment later the river erupted and a fountain of water reared up. A sequence of overlapping thuds rang across the banks. The water churned as the enemy mortars flopped short of their targets. Another series of bangs. The white water towers crept closer. Spray hit the men crouched on the far bank. The enemy were finding their range.

Machine-gun fire stitched across the river surface like skimming stones. Puffs of dirt appeared as bullets slammed into the bank behind where Kenny lay. He peered at the wall of greenery across the water. Figures winked and waned in the foliage. Denning gave urgent instructions to return mortar fire. 'Incoming friendly,' he yelled. The salvo looped short, sploshing sadly into the water. The British began firing back, shooting steadily across the river as the mortars found their range. Hardy was in his element, squaring off a hundred rounds at the shapes gathered on the opposing bank.

The Taliban melted away. There would be other fights. Talk of a cup of tea was abandoned as the men moved out, radioing co-ordinates of enemy bodies that would be collected by a unit of supporting Afghan soldiers. It was a grim task. Already the corpses were blackening in the building heat, hunched and rigid as flies settled on them. The dead enemy were, like them, young and enjoyed a smoke. Before leaving, the soldiers filleted the corpses for reserves of Pine cigarettes. Kenny had always liked a tab, but out here, coping with the hair-trigger tension of point, his intake had climbed above forty a day. He would need every cigarette he could carry. They moved up the riverbank, scouting the waters for possible Taliban crossing points. But the land was empty.

They carried on, zigzagging back and forth across the floodplain for around twelve kilometres, looking for signs of the enemy. Lieutenant Denning noticed their water supplies were running low. By late afternoon, the company was reduced to sharing a few litres. Kenny waited in turn for the precious fluid to be passed around. He took small steady sips the temperature of bathwater that he studiously swished around his mouth. The moment he swallowed it was back to counting down to the next mouthful. Swigging with discipline was the key. No loss of self-control. No gulping. His cravings for Irn-Bru, profound even when he had a ready supply, became almost intolerable. 'I would pour that shit on my cornflakes if I could; I was so thirsty I began dreaming of it.'

Night was spent in a deserted compound, sleeping on straw, smelling the dung stored for winter fuel. Even before dark, Kenny realised they had visitors. The place was crawling with fleas and lice. His skin shimmered with parasites. Long before dawn, the men sat in twos and threes chasing black dots, trying to squeeze the carapaces between their fingers.

They were up at sunrise. Sucking the ciggies of the dead, finishing what was left of Menu B, the bits you normally avoided eating. Kenny had just finished checking the firing mechanism of his SA80 rifle, replaying the rituals that had kept him alive the day before, when the order came through. There had been a change in direction down at headquarters. The original plan had them heading back to the comparative safety of Sangin in several hours' time. They were now told to stay out in the field until further notice. 'We only had kit for two, maybe three, days as part of the original mission. Something had obviously changed,' said Kenny. The Taliban were out there somewhere. Their job was to find them.

They spent the day moving north through hamlets looking for the enemy, but the enemy could not be found. Even the locals had vanished. The land was hot and empty. Maybe it was the pervading stillness of the land but Kenny remembers sensing an uncomfortable presence in the valley. It still felt like something was watching them.

They started calling themselves 'Bait Platoon'. Later Kenny and his pals even had T-shirts specially made emblazoned with their unofficial moniker. Tactically, it felt pretty straightforward. They were sent out to lure the enemy into the open, where they would try and kill as many as possible. But the Taliban weren't biting. The only movement was the mechanical plodding of the platoon.

One by one they passed through the land, up through Gerday, Mazak and Myan Roday, following the kalays – villages – that dotted the lush floodplain. On they went, past the ragtag hedges, the mung-bean plots, apricot orchards, conical piles of dung, the stench of faeces wafting in the heat. But still nothing moved. The sun beat against their helmets. Their thirst grew. Dust coated their cheeks like brown flour. Sweat ran down their soiled faces. Kenny looked like a weeping chimney sweep. But it was the bites of the parasites that drove the men half-crazy. Red welts, clustering on the skin beneath their body armour where they were impossible to reach.

Lieutenant Denning admitted that by this stage he was wondering what they would do if the enemy didn't show up soon. Rations were almost out and the platoon was down to sharing the last mouthfuls of water. If the Taliban appeared, the men would be so enfeebled with dehydration they might collapse during a firefight, especially if it was the type that dragged on past nightfall. Kenny said later that his focus had started to narrow right down; he thought only of the cracked earth ahead, what lay behind the next bend.

The men had heard the rumours about the local creepy-crawlies that infected the water supply, the invisible bugs that swam down your throat and expanded inside until your stomach popped open. They called them 'belly creeps'. But they didn't care about belly creeps any more and the men stopped beside the next village well they found. Purification tablets were popped in the water. Kenny termed them 'screech' because of the way they made you wince. When they were mixed with the caustic residue of fatigue and fear the body shuddered. 'But I don't think I've ever enjoyed a drink as much, though we were concerned that the Taliban might have poisoned the well like they kept promising.' It transpired they were bluffing, as usual. But the men got poisoned in a different way. Rolling waves of nausea and diarrhoea cut them short. D&V: diarrhoea and vomiting, came quick, announcing its arrival with a sharp cramping of the stomach. Within minutes, the spasm had bent its victim double and the patrol would hold up as a soldier, arm aloft as if asking a teacher for permission to go to the toilet, staggered off the trail and squatted down before gingerly walking back into line. Onwards the men trooped, moving unmolested along the deserted mud paths. Kenny wondered where everyone was. It was quiet, way too quiet. He recalls a latent tension, a sensation that something was about to happen.

Left. Right. Watch your arcs. Straight ahead. Look down. Scan the dust for the slender coil of a wire, a booby trap. All clear. Keep moving. Compound. Check. Cornfield. Check. Possible ambush points. Check.

The land remained stubbornly still. Yet all around were signs of life. Bundles of farmed opium, rotting in the heat, lay stacked by the trail. Packs of emaciated dogs grovelled in the shade. A herd of sheep was spotted trotting along to their right. They moved towards the flock, but could find no shepherd. Kenny was troubled. Sheep were precious commodities in Helmand. It was inexplicable that a flock would be allowed to roam untended. Something had frightened the owner away. The enemy had been here. Confirmation arrived when they uncovered a bomb-making factory, its detonators, rolls of wire and pots of fertiliser dust-free. Someone had recently touched the equipment. Later they found a cache of 7.62 mm ammunition alongside a stash of mortars and rockets. Then another, this time alongside what appeared to be half-eaten bowls of rice. Clearly a significant force had camped here, but again the same question: where the fuck had they gone?

The platoon followed the point man, his small hunched frame like a crab against the vast, muted landscape. The men behind noticed how his head jerked from side to side, instinctively as an antenna. Every so often Kenny would stop and squint through the dust. His head would tilt as he inspected some peculiarity in the terrain. Often he would lean forward as if the extra inches afforded a much improved angle. Moments later he would turn, give a quick thumbs-up and the trek would start all over again. Sometimes they heard him say 'Fuck' over and over, but he seemed to be talking to himself. Mostly, though, he never said a word, just kept his head moving, scanning the scorched land.

Kenny reasoned that no foreign soldiers had walked here before, not even the Russians decades earlier. The prospect troubled him; he had a fundamental fear of unexplored ground. But the men never questioned the route he chose.

They never doubted him even when privately they may have doubted themselves. Silently they continued north with the river to their left. Still, the enemy refused to show itself. The day grew hotter. Denning radioed headquarters, requesting word on a helicopter resupply, but the reply was emphatic. Landing a chopper in the green zone, the band of dense vegetation that lined the river, was considered way too dangerous. Weeks earlier a US Chinook had been shot down just north of their position, plucked out of the sky by an unseen enemy as it banked steeply towards the foliage. All four of those on board had died. Unconfirmed reports indicated the Taliban had acquired Stinger surface-to-air missiles.

Strange things had started to happen to Kenny and the rest of the men. Deprived of fresh supplies, they had started to disintegrate, unravelling from the outside in. Their clothes had begun to rot from their sweat, fragmenting around the armpits, fraying apart at the seams and where perspiration ran down the spine. The first set of socks had disintegrated and the second were well on their way. The number of irrigation ditches they waded through ensured that their feet, perpetually wet and crushed inside boots, had begun to corrode. White wrinkled flesh rotted at their sides, their soles crinkled as if after a bath. Fungus grew between the toes. The base of the neck, where the collar chafed, became shiny like buffed teak. Deep lacerations, lined with pus, cut into each shoulder from the weight of their rucksacks.

In the morning, before the day's march, their uniforms would be streaked with tributaries of salt that would gradually blacken with sweat as the hours passed. Getting going each morning became harder. Kenny would start gingerly, his thigh muscles stiff, blisters raw until the pain fused with fatigue as he forced himself into the monotonous rhythm of the march. Each time they paused to regroup, Kenny would brace himself for the pain of fresh movement. Often it seemed easier just to keep marching, moving stiffly from compound to compound, village to village.

They were getting hungry. They had started out with enough rations for forty-eight hours; already they had been in the field for almost double that. They were reduced to eating the once brittle, flavourless brown biscuits that had softened in the heat and moulded into mulch at the bottom of their bags. Kenny promised he would never complain about Menu B again. There was nothing he wouldn't trade for a serving of meat stew and its side order of floating veg.

The heat affected everything. Headaches exploded with each step. By noon the light turned so stark that the valley became bleached, without definition. As the mercury topped fifty-two degrees Centigrade in the early afternoon, the land itself became a mirage, tantalising the men with fruit orchards and small ponds that receded when they approached. The patrol became nightmarish. Their packs bit deeper. Backs ached from the weight. But they continued, following the narrow trails that wound through the fields and alleyways, wondering where the men who wanted to kill them were hiding. Kenny later said that he sensed they were out there, somewhere, watching them traverse the massive landscape like bedbugs crossing a duvet. A deeper silence seemed to spread over the land.

Four days had passed by the time the odd local started to appear. Random potshots occasionally whistled through the air above them, but they were from lone farmers, not the assembled enemy ranks they sought, and so they kept on moving. Afghans stared at the bedraggled intruders filing past as if they were life forms from another planet. What civilisation had sent these humpbacked figures with their hollow eyes and decaying shirts? The Taliban called them donkeys. Kenny had heard them on the Icomm, laughing at the lugging weights they strapped to their frames. But the description contained a more disturbing meaning. The weight meant they were more likely to die. The enemy had carefully calibrated the hidden pressure plates of their booby traps to be activated by a vehicle or the weight of a mule. A farmer might survive a hidden bomb, but the mass of a foreign 'donkey' was another matter.

The cornfields reminded Kenny of those he played in with his first dog, who would become lost and force Kenny to leap up and down to spot him within the planted rows. Now Kenny stopped. He had seen another crop which reminded him of home. Urgently, he summoned his section. The reaction of the men was manic. Some sprinted towards the bush, hugging its leaves as if the plant was their own mother. Others started jiving. A couple sniffed the air, grinning. The war, suddenly, disappeared.

Kenny remembers some of the men adopting a Jamaican drawl, talking about the 'erb and the need for the 'brothers' to take it easy and start 'chilling'. A few of Bait Platoon turned towards the direction of Musa Qala and gave the V sign. 'We come in peace, love and peace,' they said. The marijuana plants towered over them, infusing the air with their sweet aroma. Most of the men recognised the famili- ar serrated leaves from home. There they had been shoved into cramped plastic pouches that dealers demanded £15 for and which tended to be either piss-weak or too potent. Here the leaves were out of scale and huge buds hung like feathered fruit. 'The lads couldn't believe it, an outdoor cannabis factory in the middle of a warzone,' said Kenny.

The men pressed the leaves close to their nostrils and inhaled. Some stuffed leaves greedily into their webbing, mementoes of Essex. But no one dared smoke it. There was no requirement for mind-altering perception out here. In any case, Kenny detested the drugs that flooded the port of Harwich. To him, users were 'crackheads'. Wasters. Drugs were a sign of weakness. Besides, he had the dead men's Pines.

They sank back into the repetitive slog of the search. They did not come in peace. They were here to kill, but still they could not find the men they should shoot. Yet again, though, they found fresh signs that the Taliban had been around not long ago. Inside an abandoned compound, they came across several rocket grenade launchers and AK-47s with their butts, oddly, removed. They radioed the co-or- dinates of the weapons cache back to headquarters and said the enemy had hotfooted. The answer remained the same. Keep looking, flush them out, they're out there some- where. And so Bait Platoon went on looking until the light began to fade. By now the men had given up picking fleas off each other. There were too many.

They moved off early, stiffly picking their way through

the kalays. As always, the initial leg of the march was excruciating. Joints creaked as they willed their bodies forward. Even with hardly any food or ammunition their Bergens felt like bags of cement. Kenny felt he would levitate if he could prise the dead weight from his back.

As they marched, single file and ten feet apart, most men battled an instinct to walk closer for protection. They knew the tighter they bunched the quicker they would all die when the ambush came. Kenny had no one to shuffle closer to even if he wanted. Instead he strode ahead purposefully, knowing he could betray no weakness. The men behind depended on him. But as the days crawled by he found himself sliding into automatic mode. He was becoming more pack animal than human. His neck had stiffened to the point where it was painful to look from side to side. His legs felt wobbly-kneed. His hands trembled from a state of chronic fatigue. The exhaustion combined with the heat meant he began to lose feeling in his hands. It was like holding his rifle with a pair of oven gloves.

From the hills, the snaking file of men must have looked chaotic. The sky was cloudless and still, the air loaded with expectation. Kenny felt that anything could happen. He had no choice but to keep marching, sucking the cigarettes of the dead. Even they had started to taste sour, as if their owners had somehow contaminated the cigs they needed for the journey to the afterlife. Plucked from the packet the Pines were white and innocent, but once lit the filter turned ink-black and gloopy with the tar that slid down Kenny's throat like treacle. 'It was like the way the desert pumps out oil, but the Taliban loved their Pines,' he said.

The days felt the same. Compound. Ditch. Poppy field. Meadow. Repeat. The enemy had gone and in their absence the land turned against them. Even the lower creatures of Helmand started behaving as if they resented the British soldiers. Scorpions came right at them. At night they scampered to where the men lay, tails poised ready to strike. Boggle-eyed camel spiders with bodies the size of tennis balls crawled over their prone forms. Above, crows circled the thin column of men, looking for food. Their black shapes troubled the men of Bait Platoon, who kept mistaking them for vultures.

The sun, too, felt threatening. Each day it seemed to burn hotter, its rays slamming against their helmets with mounting ferocity, scrambling their brains. Hour by hour the heat intensified; it felt to Kenny like some brutal experiment was being played out to see how long they could last before they melted. By mid-morning the temperature was thirty-five degrees; around midday it passed forty-five and from there, inexorably, it pushed beyond fifty, where it stayed for three hours straight. Three of the platoon did succumb, retching by the trails with jelly legs. Kenny had no truck with those who couldn't take the heat. He replayed the grainy footage of 1940, his forefathers trudging through the malarial jungles of Malaya and Burma. They had kept going without whinging. 'You can't sulk about the heat because the British troops have done it all before,' he said.

The remainder carried on, trudging up to twelve kilometres a day. The sun burnt Kenny's throat, sweat stinging his eyes. The heat played tricks on his mind. Reality became blurred. He remembers the distant trees, so still they looked plastic. Later, wobbling in the rising heat, they would morph into sentries, impassively observing his approach. Often Kenny imagined enemy lookouts in the fields ahead, sometimes rigid, on other occasions frantically body-popping in the afternoon heat. When he looked closer, they vanished. Silhouettes would appear high up on the distant ridgelines jerking madly in the ferocious up-draught. He blinked through the sweat and again, nothing. The shaded creases of mountains sheltered enemy sentinels who would magically dissolve under inspection.

Even the very ground he marched upon seemed to resent his presence. Intelligence had warned that the soil was sown with unstable Soviet mines and freshly planted Taliban devices. The thought tormented Kenny. If anyone was going to tread on one he knew it was likely to be him, out there on his own. Some point men became too traumat-ised to continue and no one ever blamed them.

Reports at the time warned an IED was exploding around Sangin every couple of days, usually wounding and killing locals. Bait Platoon had found covert bomb-making factories dotted throughout the area. Weeks earlier Private Matt Woollard from Westcliff in Essex had lost his lower right leg after stepping on a landmine. For days afterwards, the eighteen-year-old was plagued by a terrific itching pain in his right foot. He would reach down every time, imagin-ing the blast was a bad dream, only to grope thin air.

The utter randomness of IEDs terrified them all. The men following Kenny carefully pressed their heels into his exact imprints. Kenny despised the hidden bombs for more esoteric reasons. They contradicted his concept of war.

Kenny believed in a moral code that stemmed from assuming the ultimate responsibility: killing. He believed soldiers should risk their lives to help comrades who needed rescuing, that the bad guys should be vanquished and the vulnerable protected. To Kenny war was as much about restraint as aggression; only the bravest could hold their fire. One of his favourite scenes was in *Zulu*: outnumbered and isolated, the British redcoats keep their nerve as the massed enemy forces advance upon the ranch of Rorke's Drift in 1879. 'Hold, hold, hold.' They were almost on top of them, spitting distance. 'Fire!'

Kenny was familiar with historians who denigrated the soldiers involved as imperialist puppets mowing down spear-wielding savages with superior weaponry. But he chose to ignore the broader geopolitics, concentrating only on the minutiae of the battle itself, the courageous naivety of the attackers, the defenders' maintenance of discipline. The men who planted hidden bombs didn't, in Kenny's mind, understand honour or discipline. They were cowards prepared to kill without discrimination. They also corrupted the land that Kenny needed to trust. The cracked topsoil was the stuff a point man depended upon more than anything. It was the stuff he fought on, guided others across and, when the bullets began flying, the stuff he pressed his face into when he wanted to stay alive. The hidden bombs fucked up everything.

But still the donkeys plodded on, waiting for the earth to erupt, wondering if, in an instant, they would be left scratching phantom itches for the rest of their lives. They walked knowing that each step was confirmation they had survived the step before.

Kenny took to repeating over and over the mantra of his combat training to sustain his wits. Left. Right. Straight ahead. Watch your arcs. But the truth, as Kenny later acknowledged, was that he was in danger of losing his senses. They all were. He tried to read the land, but the column of men had started to resemble the walking dead. His head had begun nodding forward as he moved, his chin resting on his helmet straps. 'You're almost falling asleep while you're patrolling, you were that knackered,' he said. When they paused for a break, his head would tilt to the ground and he would drift off, still standing, gun in his arms. But it was better than sitting down. Those who did found themselves pinned to the floor by the weight of their Bergens. They had to beg their friends to help them get on their feet.

They were bait without a rod. They had come adrift, maggots floating woozily downstream. The men were good soldiers and were trained to be the best in the world, but now such facts no longer mattered. Even if they managed to put up a fight they wouldn't last long. Most of the men, Kenny reckoned, were down to a couple of magazines each, a few seconds of shooting time on automatic. If the ambush were a boxing match, they could muster the equivalent of a tentative flurry of body jabs before they were trapped on the ropes.

But it was the lack of food that occupied their thoughts. They had left the gates at Sangin expecting to be in enemy territory for two days. Almost a week had passed and the communal leftovers of Menu B were barely sufficient to propel the men forward. 'It was borderline starvation. Between us we had just about enough for your body to tick along, but mainly you moved through adrenalin,' Kenny said.

In desperation they began scavenging. One evening, Kenny found some abandoned hens' eggs in the dust, which he carefully carried to the compound where they would spend the night. With great ceremony, the eggs were delicately laid in a pan of bubbling water. Boiled eggs! With soldiers! Kenny's responsibilities as point man were all-encompassing and it was agreed he would be the man to try them. To applause, he flamboyantly fished the eggs from the bubbling pan and cracked one with his bayonet. There was a gasp. Instead of a runny yolk, a beady-eyed animal stared back at them. The dead chick, its smooth skin knotted by the heat, spilled out onto the dust.

They consoled themselves that there were beds in the compound they had commandeered. But the sheets were crawling with fleas. The stench of the men was awful. A smell Kenny described as 'stale piss in a public toilet': ammonia. With their fat reserves depleted, their bodies had started breaking down muscle. They were effectively eating themselves to stay alive.

A change had come over the men. The sentries who nodded goodbye from the gates of Sangin a week earlier would have surely wondered what horrors they had confronted. Bait Platoon gazed at the world through hollow eyes framed black with fatigue. Their faces were gaunt and skeletal. Their hands were swollen, ravaged with flea bites. 'We'd lost a lot of weight and we were covered in bites,

I had nits and bugs everywhere. We must have looked a right sight,' said Kenny. Physiologically, he had changed more than most. There was precious little of him in the first place, and now he resembled a small package of sinew. His face had tightened. He looked older. The restless nights, the pressure of taking point, the omnipresent fear had accelerated the impact of time. All the platoon looked like they had been on patrol for months. A combination of the awful Pine cigarettes and no toothpaste meant that their teeth, though young, were coloured like the ditchwater they sometimes crouched in. A fine film of the valley's soil, a reddish dust, plugged every pore of their skin.

Another, less obvious, change had come over the men. They seemed less approachable. Their bodies may have shrunk, but their expressions had hardened. Yet when they looked at each other, it was with a unique comprehension. Kenny felt an overwhelming love for his platoon: 'By that stage I began to look upon each of them as a brother.' The demarcations of background, upbringing and opportunity evaporated. Most of the men had come from England's sink estates and eastern seaports and almost all were taken from the battalion's recruiting counties – Norfolk, Suffolk, Cambridgeshire and Essex – looking for a way out.

Nick Denning, their commanding officer, was relatively privileged. He was from Colchester, like Kenny, and their families shared proud military achievements – Denning's grandfathers had fought in the world wars and his father was a senior admiral. Denning had graduated with an honours degree from the Department of War Studies at King's College London. There he studied strategy, but also theories that seek to explain premeditated acts of killing and the battle tactics that ensured men like the Meighans had fallen in their thousands. He went on to the Royal Military Academy at Sandhurst where he studied the strategies behind the battles of el Alamein, the Imjin River and Normandy.

Kenny left school with essentially nothing except the words of his dad and his library of films. Both came from the same place, just different worlds, and both realised that out here in the dust there was no structure, only chaos. The war defied convention; there were no preordained battlefields, no frontline or rear. To the young officers of Denning's generation, elements of the shining new doctrine of counter-insurgency already seemed archaic, too rigid in the face of Helmand's myriad, formless threat.

Aged twenty-four, Denning had been trained to lead men like Kenny, but he quickly figured that theories didn't count for shit out here. He knew that all he could do was win their trust. And when the chance came, he had taken it. Weeks before this march, early on in the tour, they had been pinned down, trapped in a ditch on Operation Silicon, the large-scale offensive against Taliban positions north of Sangin. The platoon dared not move for the volume of metal hurtling above them. They just lay there, suffocated by the noise. Denning looked down the line, examining the young faces beneath the bullets. They looked back. So he went for it. Up over the top he scrambled, careering headlong into the line of fire. 'He just got up and I went, fuck it – if he's doing it, I'm doing it, and I followed him. My dad said you can only go into battle with men you respect. He was a legend,' said Kenny.

Days later, another incident cemented the men's respect. A picture of Denning appeared in a tabloid newspaper, his face creased, pointing at a battle map with a fag. The article claimed that officers were under so much stress they needed to chainsmoke on operations. Rumours propagated afterwards that Denning was rebuked for unprofessionalism by senior command. His platoon knew better. He was one of them.

When the resupply helicopter was finally sent in for Bait Platoon, God knows what the pilots made of the specimens screaming below, darting like savages towards the boxed provisions dropped inside a huge net. Fresh socks and toothpaste and water. Cigarettes, Lamberts not Pines, and lots of ammo. And there, piled high in shoebox-sized containers, a stack of Menu B rations. The richest, most glutinous beef stew topped off with delicate sponge pudding and the most luxuriant of chocolate sauces. Moments later the Chinook rose unsteadily and the troops watched it straining for height before banking steeply and dipping south. A familiar sense of isolation descended upon the men.

With the arrival of sustenance and bullets, the mission's objective changed. It was agreed the enemy had indeed vanished and senior command identified an opportune moment to demonstrate they were a force for good. They were ordered to begin work on a dam to divert water from the river to the Jusulay irrigation ditch, nine kilometres north-east of Sangin. The ditch was the most crucial channel between Sangin and the British outpost at Kajaki forty kilometres north, supplying water to thousands. Days were spent helping an influx of Royal Engineers scrape away the land, shovelling the earth into artificial barriers that would guide the replenishing waters. They set up camp in a nearby compound and were told they would be allowed to leave when the work was complete. Time disappeared; there were no Mondays or Sundays, no working week. They became simple labourers in a land that felt as familiar as if they had been born there. The air-conditioned headquarters of Camp Bastion, the main British base in Helmand, belonged to another place; Essex belonged to other people. But one night the other world came flooding back to Kenny. He had suppressed his imagination for nearly two weeks and had almost forgotten women existed, but in the middle of the night he felt the caress of soft skin and a lingering touch. When he woke, he returned to the awful smell of himself, the creatures nipping at his leathered flesh. He looked different and felt different. He thought of the dead men and their stolen cigarettes, the graceless death of the Afghan soldiers who had sacrificed themselves trying to protect their safe area. He wondered if any of his friends would die. More than anything he hoped they would all make it. But he knew they wouldn't.

Yet even then, before any of Bait Platoon had died, Kenny remembers feeling that the war was starting to touch him in a way that might be irreversible. He knew that he had gone through nothing compared to the horrors his dad had seen, but he also knew that was likely to change. His father had withdrawn to a place where the recollections of war were more real than the moment he occupied. Kenny wondered if he would be similarly affected. It was apparent, even back then, that combat hardened the heart and screwed up the mind. He truly hoped not: there were so many things he still had to experience. 'I had always wanted to be in the infantry, but there was other stuff like having kids, getting married, meeting the right woman, love at first sight, all that shit, they were important too. You do worry that you might never get the chance.'

4

Crocodile Smiles

Some called it the most dangerous job in the world, but Kenny never saw it like that. To judge point by its riskiness cheapened the role, he said. To Kenny it was simply the convergence of all he had hoped for. It was a position that required exacting skills: some that could be taught, others mastered only through experience. But ultimately it was a job and like most jobs, most people could make a decent fist of it if they wanted it badly enough. You just had to learn the ropes.

First, you had to learn how to walk. You had to move with the delicacy and grace of a cat. Kenny learned to move on the balls of his feet, head darting from side to side, toes sniffing the dust, sensing the ground's rise and fall. It was as though he was tentatively stepping onto a frozen pond, but quickly, his weight suspended. Witnesses said that he seemed to hover above the ground. You had to glide through water as if it was not there, effortlessly negotiating the irrigation ditches that criss-crossed the terrain, overriding the currents tugging you downstream and the sucking mud that dragged you deeper. Their oozing beds were devious, seemingly calibrated to take you down the instant the enemy appeared. Kenny learnt to dab the river bottoms lightly with his toes so the cloying mire could never take hold of his ankles.

He felt safest in the water. He admitted kidding himself that the brackish fluid would gobble up incoming bullets. The narrow bands of water were everywhere, turgid trenches where he felt strange things drift past his legs. Most people assumed Kenny was locked in desert combat until they saw his pictures. 'Look at my feet! See!' he said. There are few images where his boots are not darkened with ditchwater.

You also had to learn to crawl on your belly like a lizard, especially when the bullets came in close. Kenny quickly mastered the knack of face-down movement, an awkward forward wriggle as the surrounding land erupted. He found shelter in the shallowest ditches on open fields. Knowing how to vanish on exposed farmland was a vital skill. You push your nose deep into the soil. You hug the ground and close your eyes, yearning for the earth to pull you down.

Then you learnt to read people. Specifically, you had to recognise a false smile. You had to differentiate indifference from hostility, dislike from diffidence. But the crocodile smiles were the ones to watch. The soldiers had all heard the rumours of the smiling shepherd who guided men into a minefield. Kenny admitted he would have done the same had the roles been reversed.

The smilers destroyed what trust was left to destroy. After a while Bait Platoon had no idea who they could believe. Kenny's father had learnt that lesson in Northern Ireland. Days before his son left for Helmand, John told his son: 'Make sure you are a hundred per cent switched on at all times, but more than anything – absolutely anything – trust no one. No one.'

The brittle pubs and estates of Essex had served Kenny well. They had taught him to recognise hate. Out on patrol Kenny stared into the gazes of the insolent groups of men who watched them pass because he knew that it was difficult for eyes to disguise hate. Back home, he had discovered you can sense the loathing of those who mean you harm well in advance. 'You can always tell. You're in a pub and some geezer doesn't like you, he's looking at you and you can sense that prick wants to take a pop at you. You can feel it coming, feel the hairs standing up on the back of your neck. You look into his eyes and you know he don't like you. You know he wants to kill you.'

Kenny could sense the hatred of the bearded men in black, but that was about all. He did not know or understand the people. He could only guess what they dreamt of at night, their hopes for the future. When the fighting got serious and no one came forward to reveal where the enemy were hiding, Kenny began to be unsure if the people of Sangin wanted peace, but he presumed they must.

To win over the local people they would have had to understand them. But the soldiers could not master the language. True, they had interpreters, but the relayed messages were simplified, coded, filtered, subjective. To really know the people, to build proper trust, they would have needed to shoot the shit over a forty-eight-hour poker game, or an all-day bender perhaps. And that was never going to happen, Bait Platoon agreed, even if they did succeed in bringing Western-style democracy and its attendant excesses to town.

Disconnected from the people, they carried a gnawing discomfort that the enemy were everywhere. They searched faces for traces of hate, but the inability to discriminate combatant from citizen generated a pervading paranoia. For a brief period, senior command thought they had the answer. Identifying the Taliban was easy, they said – they've all got tattoos on their hands. It was soon evident that there were more tattooists in Helmand than in Camden Town. Half the province would have had to be arrested. They went back to staring at faces.

Deciphering who wanted to kill them became a genuine obsession. Some of the locals fidgeted nervously when Bait Platoon approached, others ran. Some genuinely smiled because that was what people sometimes did. There was no pattern. Instead, the perceived enemy became those who could smile and straight-bat Kenny's hate-seeking stare. Over time the suspicion solidified that the more brazen the smile, the greater was the danger. In hindsight, they had known that from the start.

They had been in Helmand three weeks when they were despatched to guard the far-flung outpost at Now Zad, stranded among the mountains towards Farah province. The golden rule at Now Zad was that you never crossed the wadi, the fissured riverbed five hundred metres east of the garrison. The US Marines before them had been, if nothing else, dedicated in their adherence to the rule. Cross the wadi, they said, and you'd never come back. But on 13 April 2007 Kenny led A Company across the dried riverbed and into the unknown. The far side was quiet, an absolute quiet that didn't feel right. It was Friday the 13th and the troops were jumpy as they entered the town of Now Zad.

No one was at home, the place utterly deserted. Kenny remembers actual tumbleweed rolling down its derelict streets. Even the insects seemed to have fled by the time they began ferreting among Now Zad's labyrinthine alleyways. For five hours they forensically searched its empty thoroughfares, steadily moving away from the wadi, deeper into uncharted territory. Carefully they progressed eastwards, moving from the Sorkhani district into a quadrant of dense foliage known as the Parks. Nothing stirred.

Then a lone figure materialised from behind a wall. The apparition began walking straight towards the dust-smothered soldiers. The men shouted out and raised their weapons in warning. But on he came, half-smiling. Kenny stepped forward: '*Salaam? Salaam?*' But the man was either deaf or a decent actor and kept on coming closer. His step never faltered. When he finally reached them, the man simply smirked and walked right through the platoon. Kenny remembers the unit actually parting to allow the guy through.

He watched the man make a call from a mobile phone and duck down an alley. Kenny recalls thinking his movement was too fast. 'It'd been like a ghost town, and this bloke appears out of thin air and you're trying to work it all out.' Time, said Kenny, seemed to decelerate in the moments that followed, as if he knew something was about to happen; he just didn't know what. 'You can feel the tension building like a thunderstorm.' Then it broke.

Now Zad went mental. All around, the enemy popped up from nowhere. In the ensuing gunfight, A Company fired 19,400 rounds trying to stay alive. At one point Kenny was trapped chest-down on a compound roof, smothered in masonry as rocket after rocket thudded into the wall behind. He survived, but the point man of 3 Platoon, Kenny's friend Chris Gray, was not so fortunate. A single bullet struck him five centimetres to the left of his body armour's front plate. The round travelled almost straight to his heart. It would take another two years for the Ministry of Defence to improve their body armour, attaching protective side plates that covered the area where Gray was hit. With this he would have probably survived. He was nineteen.

But Friday the 13th didn't teach Kenny it was OK to shoot people who came towards you. It simply served notice of the need to watch the smilers. 'You have to weigh it up because there will always be a natural curiosity with some people, particularly when these warriors with their strange webbing and their awesome weapons appear. Does that guy deserve to die because he's curious? Personally, no, but is it curiosity? Your average farmer will ignore you, he'll carry on with a job, but then a random geezer with a pitchfork will walk straight through the centre of you. Then what do you do?' You wait and watch for the smile.

You had to get inside compound walls, not knowing who waited on the other side. That was probably the most fraught part of the job. The compounds were usually two storeys high with a single pair of massive wooden doors. 'Every time you come up to the doorway, you're thinking,

74

is someone going to be in here? Once in, am I the only one inside?' There was no easy method of determining what lay within. Sometimes, especially if he was short of ammo, Kenny would toss rocks over the mud ramparts, hoping the enemy might believe they were grenades and release a giveaway yelp. Often, though, you knew when the enemy were inside and you knew the only way to get to them was to follow them in.

You could knock on the door and hide, wait for a response. But you would normally be ignored. Two options would present themselves. Preferably, you'd blow the doors off the hinges with a bar-mine, but sometimes you'd be operating without suitable explosives and you'd be told to storm the building with an element of surprise. In that scenario you'd have to kick at the locks, karate-chopping the rusting bolts until the doors snapped open. Kenny found the first kick almost intolerable. Rumours were rife that the enemy had begun booby-trapping the entrances, priming the locks with touch-sensitive explosives. Burp too close and they'd go off. To navigate such a predicament, Kenny had repeatedly asked senior command for a shotgun to blast the locks. But two years would pass before the specially-designed 12-gauge combat shotgun was issued to point men in Afghanistan. The weapon made close-range killing a formality; no man could get up once a 12-gauge shell had ripped through him.

Inside the compound, Kenny likened the walled courtyards to a gladiator's pit. Men squared up to one another, face to face. You saw the enemy's wide stare, their rapid eye movement, how kohl runs with sweat. Three times Kenny burst into a compound and found them there, waiting. Each time, the sequence of events ran broadly the same. A figure looming through the dust, eye contact, the clatter of gunfire, screaming. Once Kenny confronted a bearded young man and carried on firing even after he went down. His dad had told him it was important to make sure. 'Keep tapping him, even when he's down, until he cannot get up.' So that's what he did: 'tapped' him until the man stayed down. Entering the compounds became harder, not easier, over time. The more Kenny saw, the more he learnt what could go wrong.

He was taught to enter compounds in the make-believe enemy strongholds on the regiment's training grounds in Surrey and the teaching had never left him. Years later he would re-enact the moves in his Essex living room, holding an invisible rifle wedged into his shoulder as he stormed a fictional fortress. Down on one knee he went, rolling quickly to the side as the enemy tried to fix a bead on him. 'Duff, duff, duff,' he cried as imaginary bullets came down. Kenny raced forward, almost knocking over the coffee table, stretching for cover by the sofa. 'Duff, duff, duff,' he shouted, spittle foaming at the corners of his mouth. He raised his weapon, a faint smile playing on his lips. Got him! In an instant he was above the guy, finishing him off.

Duff, duff, duff. Tap, tap, tap. Keep tapping. Make certain. You were taught to ignore the rifle sight because there was no time for scoping; you just shot like you did when you were a kid. Eye to muzzle. Duff, duff. 'We were trained the SAS tactic, not to look through the sight. As soon as I've entered the building the weapon is on the shoulder. I'm always looking over the top of the barrel. As soon as my eye matches up the barrel with a person's chest he went down,' Kenny said. Tap tap, tap until they stop twitching.

Of course, you also had to read the land. Kenny decided to go one step further. He learnt to *feel* the land. He sensed the power of rock and water, intuitively grasping how ancient forces had shaped the troughs and scarps of Helmand's river valley. He never bothered with geography at school, less still geology, yet he could decode actual landscapes. If not able to explain the science, Kenny could deduce when a meadow was likely to turn into swamp or where a stream's nearest passing point could be found. He stored every detail: the way soil crumbled in the sun, how channels ate through the desert flats.

He recognised Helmand's wild beauty. 'Once the fighting's over it'll be packed with tourists,' he would say. 'It's a hell of an adventure holiday destination.' But as the number of patrols mounted, Kenny found the land lost its scenic charm. Instead it became defined by its opportunities. Every landmark, he said, offered the chance to either succumb or survive. A knoll above farmland was simultaneously both an exposed target and a vantage point from where they could 'smash' the enemy.

He noted, too, how the land developed a habit of funnelling him towards an ambush. Trails would steer him into choke points, killing areas where the enemy waited. Choke points could be anything: narrow gaps in walls, threadlike passages which even Kenny had difficulty squeezing through or slender bridges that left the soldiers frozen above streams like fairground puppets in a shooting gallery.

At times, it felt like the land was an elaborate maze designed to usher Bait Platoon towards the next ambush. Kenny never forgot that the terrain belonged to an enemy who knew its every indentation. 'They had the advantage. It was their patch. As soon as you underestimated them, even for a split second, the enemy would punish you. If the Taliban were invading Harwich it'd be the same principle. I'd know exactly where to hit them: where the best killing areas were, the best way to trap them in a bottleneck.'

The trick was to move from cover to cover. Every large boulder, pomegranate orchard, muddy ditch became vital. Kenny made a mental note of each, just in case. He learnt to find cover on ground that would have seemed barren to most. 'You are always observing for cover as well as assessing places of vulnerability. Constantly looking at the ground, every twenty or thirty yards you are picking a place for cover. Every time we came under contact we were never caught out in the open. You memorised the location of that big boulder, the little divot, bomb crater. Anywhere you could get your head down.' No one quite knew the source of Kenny's aptitude for topography. Perhaps it was innate; perhaps it stemmed from his dyslexia. Kenny guessed so. 'Maybe my brain developed differently to compensate,' he said.

Kenny rarely spoke when he sensed the enemy were close. Instead he would drop onto one knee, turn and raise his left palm, signalling for the column behind to stop. Then he would point in front and turn his thumb down. Trouble, dead ahead.

Sometimes it was Kenny's turn to lay an ambush. He

would hear a dull thud approaching, footsteps of the enemy. Slowly he would turn to Denning and break an invisible twig in his hands – a snap ambush. On cue, the platoon would creep behind the nearest cover. The thudding came closer. One by one, the enemy filed past. All eyes turned to Denning, waiting for the signal to attack.

Yet the most constant fear was not the men they faced, but what they couldn't see. Kenny constantly scoured the dust for the worm-like wires that snaked across the pathways to hidden IEDs. Eventually, one morning, he found one. But it was not how he had imagined.

They were patrolling up from the main base at Sangin, passing the water fountain that marked the entrance to the bazaar, when from the corner of his eye Kenny saw something fluttering from a pile of garbage. A plastic bag, partially covered with junk, was flapping like a prayer flag in the hot breeze. It was hard to explain exactly why, but the bag's positioning didn't look natural, as if it had been placed instead of discarded. Kenny and his platoon sergeant, Larry Holmes, walked over and delicately sliced open the bag. Both gasped at the sight of its innards. It was a 'spider'. A large battery lay at an angle with a coil of eight coloured wires connecting it to a detonator. They had been briefed on the arachnid device: a sophisticated bomb thought to have originated in Iran and operated by remote control, usually a mobile phone. A call or text would activate it. If the bomb-maker was watching, they were dead. Kenny remembers kneeling beside the bag, looking down the bazaar, searching the crowd, the watching faces, for a sign. A smile. But the crowd just stared.

Then he ran, a flat-out mad dash, waiting for the shock-wave to carry him. He hid behind the first thing he found, a foot-wide concrete pillar that protected barely half his body. It was ten metres from the device. If the spider had detonated, the blast would have neatly removed his arms and legs. 'But hell, I would have kept my looks.'

You also had to learn to control the mind. War requires a total absence of imagination. The good soldiers were those who could suppress any thoughts beyond their immediate reality. But the nearness to death bred an obsession with events they could not hope to manipulate. What if the spider had gone off? Why had Gray, not me, been shot in the heart? Men with lively imaginations were prone to the 'what ifs'. The what ifs, like the whys, drained a soldier's sanity. A vivid imagination could torture you with the nagging feeling that something dreadful was forever about to occur. If unchecked, such thoughts could turn a man into that most selfish of soldiers: a coward.

Kenny learnt to narrow his thought process by focusing on his job. He learnt to feel fear only when there was good reason. His mind only tended to wander at night, when he relaxed and thoughts of home and hopes of love flooded in, and then a sense of foreboding.

When morning came Kenny strangled his imagination by constantly repeating his drills, focusing upon the prosaic. The twenty-year-old had quickly realised that normal cognitive processes were too slow in the heat of battle. Reactions that were totally instinctive, subliminal and instantaneous were required to juggle the chaos while making life-defining decisions. Over several months, Kenny developed what he routinely referred to as his 'sixth sense'. 'You are on such a constant high alert that you start processing everything much quicker. Physically you're leaner, fitter than you've ever been, but your mental reactions are like lightning, everything is clearer, sharper. Your brain feels faster than it has ever been,' he said.

Liberated from the sedating effects of booze and cast into a natural amphitheatre where he could be killed at any moment, Kenny's synapses, his clarity of thought, acquired an exceptional awareness he never thought possible. His sight evolved to detect shifting dust patterns in the distance; he became able to decipher the grunts of strangers across the valley. He reckoned his nerves themselves could decode danger beyond the next bend. Kenny said that eventually he could detect the scent of the enemy. 'In many ways I was like a sniffer dog.'

You also had to learn the machinery of death, the weapons of war. From the crack of a rifle Kenny could deduce the type of weapon, its condition and the direction it came from. He would listen to a mortar pop and know its barrel size, how far away it was mounted, and the angle of the shell's descent. He knew the grumbling burr of a Degtyarev DShK 12.7 mm anti-aircraft machine gun, the roar of a PG-7VL 93 mm warhead moving at 295 metres per second, the honking of the PK 7.62 mm machine gun. A sound so deep, the reverb got caught in your chest.

Some sounds became harmless: the clouds of AK-47 bullets that pinged off targets eventually sounded like the buzzing of flies. The tired wheeze of an RPG as it ran out of steam before exploding, sending shrapnel scything harmlessly through the watching trees. Sometimes rocket-pro-pelled grenades looked so weary, so fed up with the fight, you could actually see them limping like hand-thrown black spears before they burst. But the same weapon still held the capacity to terrify. Kenny would shake his head when recalling the first time a volley of RPGs shrieked over his head, in Now Zad on Friday the 13th. 'I was up on the roof of a compound and suddenly – voom voom voom – and I thought, "What the fuck is that?" and the next mo-ment I'm covered in plaster and dust and shit.'

And there were other things you mastered, like dressing the wounds of friends. You learnt to tie expedient tourni-quets to stumps, how to react when their blood pressure begin dropping like a stone. You have forty-eight seconds before the critical organs began shutting down. But you need more circulating volume. You need more saline fluid. Where are the fucking reserve supplies? How long?

Obviously, you must learn how to kill. This requires ma-jor reprogramming. A month before Bait Platoon landed in Afghanistan, they were sent to Kenya to fine-tune their combat instincts. East Africa replicated Helmand as closely as senior command considered reasonably possible. Its fifty-degree heat, exotic animals and wild terrain were a slap in the face to the young men, a taster for what would follow.

For three weeks on the scorched Kenyan plains they engaged a vicious, fictitious foe, suppressing them with full-on mortar barrages and attacking where they least expec-ted. They burst into empty compounds, searched dry soil for fake IEDs and negotiated make-believe choke points.

They finessed the art of taking out men. They were told it would be guerrilla fighting, warfare that demanded quick judgement and faster reflexes. The men were instructed what to do if they were taken hostage and how to withstand interrogation. Kenny excelled in defying his captors. He would never spill the beans.

East Africa also introduced them to strange, crazed creatures. Wild-fanged baboons attacked their convoys, leaping onto their all-terrain Pinzgauers and thrashing the windscreens with their fists. One guy was bitten by a black mamba and his arm puffed up like a football. Another woke up to find a termite had crawled inside his ear. Wedged inside, the insect began chewing through his eardrum. The guy went so mad the rest of the section had to sit on him. Men who lost both their legs screamed less, Kenny said.

Kenny took a shine to the praying mantis because it didn't seem to know fear. Regardless of its size the creature was prepared to pick a fight with anything it came across. For the diminutive private, it was an attitude to be admired. But the giant centipedes that crawled across the floor of their huts induced genuine terror. If anyone had asked Kenny before Afghanistan what scared him most in the world, he wouldn't have paused. 'Those fuck-off centipedes in Africa, all those tiny legs,' and he would shake his shoulders as if someone had tipped a bucket of iced water down his back.

Kenya welded a bond between the young soldiers. Most recruits had been drawn from uncompromising backgrounds. Many came from broken families and had been raised by single parents or spent a childhood in foster homes. In Africa, their upbringing started to feel irrelevant. They had found a new family.

Bait platoon had become a well-oiled engine, its men mere components. To Kenny, who had failed to sparkle in the tedious rituals of barrack life – the 'crappest camp soldier ever' – the pre-tour training stirred his soldiering instincts. Years earlier he had signed up inspired by a romantic military ideology, but found himself unmoved by the dry language of war, the theorising, the peculiar terminology and attendant acronyms. A gunfight became a TIC, 'troops in contact', a battleground was a TMA, a 'troop manoeuvre area', and a PONTI was a 'person of no tactical importance', someone you didn't shoot. The redcoats of Rorke's Drift never bothered with any of that, said Kenny.

Only later would he learn that war is the maddest thing there is. It was not like any of his films, no heroic poses, no cavalry to the rescue. Only in Afghanistan would Kenny learn what true fear feels like, the emotions of killing, the ramifications of imposing pain on another human, the spectacle of young British men dying.

The three weeks in Kenya changed Kenny more profoundly than all his twelve years of schooling. By the end he felt invincible. The officers had also learnt much about the men and how they might react under the pressures of combat. As the training came to a close, section commander Corporal Brooks took Private number 25162300 aside for a quiet word. 'Private Meighan,' he said, and Kenny remembers wondering what he had done wrong. 'I want you as my point. Well done.'

The first thing he did was phone his dad. 'It was the proudest moment of my life, I couldn't wait to tell him.' The latest in the long line of Meighans to have served the country would be leading men into battle. Their lives would depend on Kenny.

But the one quality soldiers need more than any other is luck. The best soldiers often died. The luckiest lived. Men could be killed, they realised, moments after disembarking from a helicopter on their first patrol. Others dodged bullets for six months straight and bounced home without a bruise. Kenny, who had learnt so much about how to survive, grew to appreciate that luck was the key variable. 'War's ninety per cent luck, ten per cent good soldiering,' he said. His dad, when asked what was the most important factor in combat, said the same. 'It's ninety per cent down to luck. The rest is hard fighting and you can control that, but luck will generally decide when your time's up.'

The vagaries of chance became crucial to rationalising the war. Without the existence of luck, you could end up blaming absolutely anything for a man's death. Equipment, the patrol route, the heat, senior command, Downing Street, even the manufacturer of the bullet. But you learnt not to blame anything but war itself. The dead were unlucky, that's all. 'You look back when Chris Gray was killed and everyone is wondering what they could have done different, but it was our first major battle. No one was to blame.'

5

First Love

He was practically jogging by the time he reached Yates's Wine Lodge on Head Street. Moments earlier Kenny had been dropped off in Colchester town centre by taxi straight from RAF Brize Norton. He was back in Essex for his fortnight's R&R and the only thing on his mind was his first pint of lager in ninety-six days. Giddily, he recalls entering Yates's around 2 p.m., dropping his bag by the bar, a puff of Afghan dust settling upon the wooden floor. He asked for a Foster's, but the barmaid shook her head. Kenny began scanning the pumps for a fallback option, assuming his lager of choice was off. 'We don't serve soldiers here, sorry,' she said. He demanded to see the manager. 'I am the manager.'

He had returned to Harwich from Helmand on 15 July 2007 bursting with stories to share. But it was not only the manager of Yates's Wine Lodge who failed to conceal her indifference. Kenny felt the entire town could barely disguise its apathy about the war. 'You're walking through town and hours earlier you'd been in Afghanistan, but nobody asks you, "What's it like?" Maybe it was my fault for thinking it would be different, but I had expected people would want to know.' In those first hours home,

Kenny remembers feeling overcome with nostalgia for Bait Platoon. He would find himself looking at the time and calculating what the lads might be up to. Midday meant they had probably just returned from patrolling the bazaar, possibly a quick recce to the cemetery near Route 611. Maybe they were gearing up for night manoeuvres. Were they all still alive? He pictured Denning sprawled on his backside as the rockets came in.

The following evening Kenny encountered the woman who would change his life. He was, he admits, 'half pissed' beside the bar of the Stingray Tavern in Harwich when around 8 p.m. he remembers looking up and seeing Sam.

At first he barely recognised her. He hadn't seen Samantha Sayers in ages. They had been in the same year at Harwich School and hung out for a while but she'd headed off to college and Kenny had joined the infantry. Five years had passed since they'd last met, and as far as Kenny was concerned she had blossomed. 'I couldn't take my eyes off her.' Later Sam would say that Kenny had, too, changed beyond belief: she was 'shocked' by his appearance. His puppy fat had fallen away to be replaced by a gaunt, sunken-eyed appearance, a confident gait supplanting the gawky adolescent. He looked much older, a man.

She couldn't believe he was a real combat infantryman fighting in a real war. Kenny remembers being touched that Sam seemed proud of him. She asked him what it was like out there, but he felt unsure how to describe the war. Otherwise, they got on famously. 'We clicked from the word go, we couldn't stop talking,' said Kenny. They joked about growing up in Harwich and the class of 2002. A decent proportion of their school year had offspring, most had stayed local. Some were making ends meet and quite a few weren't.

Kenny was drawn to Sam in a way he had never experienced and, that night, was anxious about whether she felt the same. Last orders arrived and outside, in the warm summer night, they held hands and later kissed. When Kenny first described to me how he met Sam he played down its significance in favour of a blokey account. 'We kind of saw each other across the bar and that was it. We started talking, had a hug and just went from there. I suppose you could say she was very interested.' But over the following years, whenever Sam was mentioned, it was obvious Kenny could still not believe his luck that night.

Combat induced a heady intensity that Kenny had assumed was impossible to match. But that was before Sam. In her company, he felt more alive than he could remember. His career choice ensured that their time together was infused with a sizzling potency. They were halfway through their first date when Kenny suggested a second. The following day they strolled down to Harwich's harbour and watched the procession of ferries setting sail for the Hook of Holland. Sam had never ventured abroad, not even to Wales. Now her boyfriend worked in a place called Sangin. By their third date Kenny knew he had to see Sam every day before he returned to Helmand.

The war was still being fought, but in Essex life seemed to go on as usual. Kenny admitted that, for the first time, he felt dislocated from the civilian world of his upbringing. 'You're at home and nothing has changed but you feel really weird. Part of you is still in Afghanistan because you know the lads are out there fighting for their lives, but here no one else feels the same.' He had even contemplated returning straight away, boarding the next flight to Afghanistan. His dad had talked him out of it. At least his dad understood, thank God. But his real saviour was Sam. She pulled him away from the war. Meeting her, Kenny said, altered everything. With previous girlfriends he had quickly accepted things might not last and, usually, that suited him fine. With Sam there were no imponderables, no doubts. She was the one. He would die for her. He just didn't want to die without her. He began to feel comfortable, in love with life. In love.

It didn't matter to Kenny that Sam had never heard of Lashkar Gah and would hesitate to locate Afghanistan on the world map. What mattered to him was how she cared about the war and those caught up in it. Sam's brother had also signed up to the 1st Battalion of the Royal Anglian Regiment and in fact had been on Kenny's 2005 tour to Iraq, opting to leave the infantry before the Afghan deployment. 'She was interested in what was going on, that meant a lot to me,' he said.

Soon, Kenny's time was up. On 3 August he was due to report back to RAF Brize Norton and board one of the Lockheed TriStars constantly shuttling personnel between Oxfordshire and the vast airbase at Kandahar in southern Afghanistan. Kenny had been devoured by the exhilaration of first love. 'Meeting Sam felt a bit like a dream. Going back out was like being woken up, it was over,' he said. They said goodbye as if nothing else could ever matter.

Heartfelt declarations were exchanged. They pledged not to falter in their feelings for each other. Kenny promised Sam he would return, knowing that he might not. But they never spoke of death or what ifs. He just held her tighter than he had held anything in his life and said farewell to his first love.

Kenny joined the ranks of the soldiers who carried a memento of a woman wherever they went. A letter was neatly folded in the pouch on his webbing, a keepsake Sam had written before their last day together. But he struggled to decipher its contents and had to enlist Lieutenant Denning to read key passages out loud. 'Slow down,' he would ask his platoon commander, 'repeat that bit.' He learnt the letter by heart and kept it close to his chest, taking it out when he sought proof that she did in fact exist. He examined the careful swirls, the spacing of the letters. He recalls running the paper through his fingers, wiping away the dust and becoming annoyed when the sheets became smudged with rifle oil.

Kenny thought it was a hell of a letter. It hardly weighed a thing but contained more than three hundred words. The paper itself felt posh, proof that she cared. The writing itself was typical girl's handwriting, big and loopy, but also deliberate, confirmation that what she wrote she meant.

When Kenny repeated the letter to himself, he said it triggered snippets of their conversations, what they would do when he got back. They might get a dog, or even start a family. It was weird how he sometimes forgot how she sounded. Of all the things Kenny wished he had done, he regretted not having taped her voice. That is, apart from not bringing a picture of Sam to Helmand. 'It was her idea not to, she thought it might jinx things.' Sam reasoned they could wait because they would have all their lives to look at each other.

Over time, Kenny also began to lose her face. The more he strained to remember what she looked like, the more she disappeared. Random fragments of Sam – a wrist, an eye, her mouth – would suddenly emerge but as soon as he tried to assemble her, the parts would begin receding. He could remember that she was beautiful and had brown hair, occasionally the troubled look when she had said goodbye, but that was about it. Try as he might, Kenny could never quite piece her together.

His inability to see Sam in her entirety helped fuel an anxiety that he might never see her again. He prayed that he would survive and that she would wait for him as she'd promised. Kenny said that often he imagined his homecoming, Sam jumping up and down with uncontained delight as he dropped his Bergen and ran towards her open arms. Eighty-four days to go. He had Bait Platoon to guide, but Kenny realised that he had also acquired fresh responsibilities. From now on, he would read the land to protect the soldiers but also to keep alive for Sam. Kenny had more reason to live than he had ever known.

Denning became their go-between. Kenny would recite his thoughts, rambling, emotive notions that he would write down and carefully craft in time for delivery on the next military flight home. It became a well-drilled operation. Kenny described standing outside Denning's digs chainsmoking while, inside, his platoon commander jotted down proclamations of desire to a woman he had never met.

Kenny trusted Denning. At twenty-four, he saw him as considerably wiser and more experienced in matters of the heart. Inevitably, though, choice lines from the letters would end up circulating around the base. Some of the soldiers blew him kisses; others puckered their lips when he passed. At nightfall, cries of 'lover boy' and the occasional wolf-whistle would float across the base whenever he passed.

Kenny's love life became a topic of mild banter. Not because he'd gone on R&R and met a girl – there was nothing new in that – but because in the confines of a combat zone it was unusual to meet a woman and admit that you didn't want to lose her. In the forward operating base, Kenny was one of the few self-confessed romantics. Falling in love in a warzone was tough. Each of the men, though, when pushed, had his own idiosyncratic love story. Almost everyone carried photographs. In Denning's pockets were pictures of a young woman from west London to whom the young lieutenant, when not producing letters for Kenny, wrote home. Kenny's offer of returning Denning's favour was promptly rejected.

A few of the lads clung on to flash-in-the-pan affairs that would probably have faltered already had they not been sent to war. Some, though, were deadly serious; teenage crushes that had lasted the course. Bait Platoon's GPMG operator, Scott Hardy, was typical of those. He was twenty-four but already had spent his entire adult life with Charlene Byrne whom he had met at school in Chelmsford.

Hardy, a bricklayer by trade, had completed basic infantry training only three weeks before arriving in Afghanistan. He'd signed up in tribute to his grandfather, who had been involved in the 1942 Cockleshell Heroes raid of Bordeaux harbour in Nazi-occupied France. Out in Helmand, the carrot-topped soldier rarely missed an opportunity to share how much he missed his childhood sweetheart. Scott and Charlene; but unlike Jason Donovan and Kylie Minogue in *Neighbours*, they were designed to last.

Bait platoon often debated the best story to tell each other's wives or girlfriends if they were killed. Kenny contemplated giving strict instructions to Denning, suggesting a riff on the theme of fate and how he would never forget Sam. Many of the men had written letters to be read in the event of their death, with the instruction: 'Not to be opened unless deceased.' Ultimately, though, Kenny decided not to leave a message from beyond the grave: there was no way he wouldn't see Sam again.

As the weeks passed, the men admitted they grew wistful for the touch of a woman and filled their head with misty recollections. At night in their beds they encouraged visitations from women they had known. Some tried to remember what it was like to be held; some escaped the boredom of camp life by immersing themselves in extravagant seduction scenes where they always got the girl. Others talked candidly about the unswerving frequency of masturbation. Magazine pictures of women in bikinis were plastered upon some of the scarred brick walls above where they slept. In places the shiny material was concave where it had been stretched above bullet holes.

War exacerbated love. The proximity to danger re-
awakened or strengthened feelings for those they had left
behind. There was no internet, just a primitive text system
that broke down almost every time Kenny tried to use it.
The letters they received assumed huge significance. Kenny
realised that in a war a soldier's happiness was determined
by the kind of woman he had left behind. And there were
two kinds: those that always wrote back and those that
never did.

Several serious relationships crumbled in the dust, an oc-
currence that greatly pained Kenny. His mum and dad had
split up in 1989 when he was only three. John was doing
rolling tours of Northern Ireland at the time and things had
just fizzled out. They tended to do that in the army, Kenny
could see that. He loved them both equally and was glad
they remained friends, but he still remembered the confusion, the incomprehension of parents parting. When he got
married it would be for ever.

Some of the men became resentful when the flow of letters began to slow and they could do nothing but wait
for the inevitable confirmation of a suspected infidelity.
Kenny remembered their torment, the inquest into what
might have been had they not been in Helmand; whether
they'd forced a fragile dynamic too far by leaving when
they needed to work things through.

They would be fine, everybody agreed on that. Once they
returned from the front, women would be queuing up. Em-
barrassing chat-up lines were open to committee, but the
consensus formed that simply mentioning the war should
suffice. If they got hurt, a couple of shrapnel scars, say,

then so much the better. Badger had it best, Bait Platoon decided. He had pulled off the perfect coup, a war wound that didn't leave you crippled.

Some of the men had already found the perfect match in Helmand. They had found relationships that could never be trumped. In many ways it was the purest love they would ever find. They had found people willing to die for them and the feeling was mutual. They watched each other's back, helped carry the weight on each other's back, shared their last rations with whoever was most needy. 'You'd do anything for them, anything,' said Kenny. It was the ultimate relationship, impervious to the drudgery of everyday life. Men died trying to rescue wounded friends, lost their legs as they ventured back into a minefield to pull a pal to safety. None of Bait Platoon was surprised when they heard the stories; it was what you did.

Denning understood the value of love for the young soldiers under his wing. 'I could never have asked for a better boss,' said Kenny. 'He wasn't interested in hierarchy and authority but he knew you needed to have that love. Denning hugged us a lot, made sure we felt loved. You might be stone-hard war fighters, fighting to the death, but you've got to have love.' Now Kenny had Sam, he said it felt like he was conducting an open affair with the platoon.

With Sam on the scene, the war changed. For a start, doing point felt more difficult. Trying to juggle the position's demands without thinking of Sam was in itself a challenge, Kenny admitted. The instant he arrived back in Helmand, Kenny recalls that things felt different. Even aboard the Chinook, before its steep rollercoaster descent into Sangin, he says he sensed a changed dynamic. As the chopper throbbed east above the Dasht-e-Margo, the 'desert of death', he remembers all his thoughts routing back to the girl he had left behind, her memory already starting to become swamped by the fumes and filth. 'I couldn't get her out of my mind. I couldn't believe my luck in meeting her and when I got back to Helmand it felt like even more of a weird dream,' he said.

Three months earlier, when he had first landed in Afghanistan, Kenny had found it easy to drive away fatalistic thoughts. Upon his return to Helmand, he recalls a sense of foreboding about the months ahead. Love, he later said, seem to act as an omen of terrible events to come. 'Before that it was just me, the lads and the Taliban. After I met Sam the tour was a lot harder to deal with.' Kenny remembers being suddenly awakened to endless possibilities; old age together, children, happiness. A future with someone he loved. Life, he learnt, was more straightforward when you didn't carry hopes for someone you loved. But then, life was more straightforward when you weren't doing point.

At night, Kenny recollects lying beneath his mosquito net on the top floor of the three-storey building in Sangin where he slept, its walls pocked by the scars of the enemy rocket fire that routinely peppered the base, holding letters that he couldn't read. Sometimes he held the letter close to his face or simply stared at the bubble handwriting under the light of his head-torch. He said he imagined her holding the pen. At quiet times like these, the softer, tender memories of Sam would float back, their first kiss, the hazy chronology of their courting in Essex, and finally the overwhelming gut-wrench of their goodbye. Her letters were signed off with four kisses, not an ungenerous amount, Kenny had gradually concluded. Spot on, in fact. Five might be over the top, three would have been one too few for comfort. It was signed: 'Love Sam'. It must be true if she had written it.

He knew it was down to chance whether he saw her again. He remembers trying hard not to worry too much.

6

Bonfire Night

There was a dull boom from the valley to the right and then from the ridgeline a sheet of tracers like splints of lightning flashed over the tower block. Interlocking explosions reverberated across the city and, directly above, an eruption of white phosphorus washed the streets in a silvery glow.

Orange streamers arced over the city skyline, followed by a salvo of high explosives; yellow, purple, red and green. Jesus, John thought, this is some bombardment. The living room seemed to rock as the bangs came closer. A rocket screeched past, glaring scarlet. Somewhere, from the night sky, the gunships would be coming in low any minute now, fanning the streets with fire. Ground troops would inevitably follow, picking their way down from the hills to the north. The city was under attack. Boom, boom, boom. The bombardment was relentless. The place couldn't hold out much longer, John was convinced of that. A rocket whined overhead. They were getting nearer, slowly finding their range. Take cover!

Behind him, the guests sat sipping tea and chatting, but John was not listening. Instead he remained crouched by the bay windows, monitoring the unfolding invasion. Below him, Glasgow's east end was cowering under the starbursts of high explosives. 'Fuck,' he thought, 'this is it, they're coming in.' He took a deep breath and walked unsteadily to the sofa. He remembers feeling that something was growing inside him.

It was Saturday evening, Bonfire Night 1995. John Meighan and his second wife Beverley had invited his brother Paul and his wife over to their place in the city's Carntyne district. John had been out of the army for almost twelve months and was trying to get used to nights like these, the way normal people behaved. But he felt far from normal. He just sat there stupefied, unable to hear a word his guests were saying. All he remembers were the rockets outside, the cacophony of the building offensive. They were getting closer. John feared it wouldn't be long before they scored a direct strike.

He tried hard to follow the conversation, but his focus kept turning to the dazzling trails criss-crossing the night sky. The thing inside him was beginning to bubble up, shifting from the pit of his stomach to his chest. Now it was pressing down on his ribcage, squeezing his lungs, making it hard to draw breath. He reached for his mug of tea on the table, but the brown liquid sploshed over the side. His hands were shaking uncontrollably. 'I could feel this thing inside, raw fear. I started to panic.' John forgot how to breathe. He remembers looking across at Beverley, watching her shout at him, her face falling at the sight of him. His eyes were bulging, his face pulled tight into a pale mask. His knees had started clacking together like a hyperactive child's.

Later he learnt Beverley was calling his name, asking

her husband what was wrong. But John did not answer. The thing inside him had burst. His shoulders started shaking, his entire body twitching. His wife screamed for help, but it was too late. John remembers sliding from the sofa, his throat gurgling, fingers grasping the rug on the carpet, reaching out for his brother, his wife. Anyone who could save him.

Things were never the same after that. At first John tried to pretend it had never happened. Only much later did he acknowledge it, referring to the incident as the 'start of the onslaught'. He had left the King's Own Scottish Borderers the previous November and, on paper at least, had made the transition from soldiering to civilian life seamlessly. Thirty-six years old, he was the owner of a nice new pad, had bagged a decent job with Group 4 Security and had even married again that summer. Now Beverley from Blackpool had given birth to their first son, Alexander. Meanwhile John's firstborn, Kenny, would come to visit every school holiday and he was the loveliest nine-year-old you could wish to meet. John Meighan was a success story.

Those who met him were invariably charmed by the articulate, thoughtful former corporal. Even his deadpan stare and jitterbug energy seemed endearing where in others they would invite caution. He was wiry and slight; Kenny had inherited his physique. John had an opinion on most things, politics certainly, and a dim one at that, combined with an inquisitive nature that made him hungry for differing views. The first time we met, in the spring of 2009, John had no sooner offered me a seat than he launched into a rapid-fire sequence of questions until he remembered who was meant to be doing the interviewing. He then embarked on a four-minute monologue that encompassed the varying psychological impacts of several global conflicts, the political disconnection between parliament and the poor, the Geneva Convention, the culture of celebrity and the unrelenting virtues of owning a Jack Russell. Like Kenny, sharing was in John's nature. His most striking characteristic was a preoccupation with the welfare of others. Once it would have been the young soldiers under his wing, now it was his family. 'Everyone has responsibilities. A good man makes sure he fulfils them,' he said.

But in the aftermath of Bonfire Night 1995, something profound had shifted inside him. He began to feel foreign to himself. Overnight, he sensed the city closing in. He became furtive and paranoid. He felt watched by shadowy figures, the spies he once imagined had stalked him as a soldier. Trips to the centre of Glasgow became fraught, furtive affairs. He sensed the crowds of Buchanan Street and Sauchiehall Street slowing to gawp as he passed. People whispered into their mobile phones. The dickers were everywhere. Kids, grannies, blokes in suits; they were all in on it. They watched him leave the house. They watched him return. They followed him far and wide. And somewhere up the line, they waited for him.

'Hyper-vigilance became the order of the day,' he said. Sudden movements heralded the onset of an ambush. Once, he remembers, an old man appeared too quickly from an alley near Argyll Street; John leapt and ran. Loud noises induced a neat shot of fear so pure he sometimes shrieked on the spot. A child's holler or an exhaust backfiring sent him racing for the nearest cover. 'People started calling me "the cat" because I was so jumpy,' he said.

His languid stride was gone. By the start of 1996 John found himself practically scurrying along Glasgow's streets, frantically looking over his shoulder, scanning ahead for choke points. One winter's afternoon he found himself in Renfrew Street, his back to the wall, anxiously looking for exits. A passer-by asked if he was all right, but John knew kindly faces could not be trusted. He felt trapped.

From his bay windows overlooking the city, the clouds seemed to be stained a different shade. Glasgow's skyline appeared flatter, grubbier. The city darkened and became full of shadows. And when darkness fell, they really came for him. Nighttime took him along the roads of his nightmares, the thoroughfares littered with broken bodies and the corpses of friends. John had no idea why but every time the journey was the same.

It begins in the pissing rain outside a sewage works at Mountfield, near Omagh in County Tyrone. Thomas Irwin is lying on his back, a quarter of his face gone, staring up at the storm clouds.

Private John Meighan, twenty-seven years old, is a rising star in the intelligence unit of the British army and about to be a father for the first time. Kenny will be born three months later, but for now the young soldier is preoccupied with a tip-off that the IRA are going to target a local part-time UDR officer, and his team are shadowing Thomas Irwin on his journey to work. They know little about him except that his brother was shot dead by the IRA seven years earlier while travelling to work, and that he is fifty-two and married with four kids. Just after 3 p.m. on 26 March 1986 Irwin's sewage truck turns down a slip road towards the sewage works but the patrol carries on, climbing a hill above the village of Mountfield for a better vantage point. And that's it; that's all it takes.

John looks back, knowing they are suddenly too far away. He watches as a car speeds furiously towards Irwin. His truck pulls over. Three men climb out of the car. They are wearing balaclavas. Irwin climbs out of his cab as if he can explain that it's all a terrible misunderstanding. But he sees the machine guns and John watches his expression turn to dread. The young soldiers begin racing downhill towards the IRA men, but still they are not close enough. Irwin says something, as if remonstrating might save his life, but their guns are raised and the men are close. John watches the sewage worker stagger backwards. He appears to lift a hand towards his missing cheek.

John stands guard beside Irwin's corpse outside the sewage plant for the next six hours. When night comes the rain falls harder. The stench of human faeces, the smell of death, is overpowering. 'The guy was lying on the ground and a whole part of his face had gone, the bullets had just cut a whole quarter of his face away.' Then the circus arrives, the forensics team, the police, the media, the photographers, the rubberneckers all hoping to catch a glimpse of the Troubles' latest victim. It feels like all of nearby Omagh has come to look. The rain falls harder; Irwin stares up, his skin shiny in the pissing rain.

Then onto another road, this time an arrow-straight

highway, stretching like a string of liquorice through the deserts of northern Kuwait. Its tarmac surface wobbles in the furnace-like heat. It is 26 February 1991 and as far as the horizon the charred husks of hundreds of Iraqi tanks are burning on Highway 80, the Highway of Death. On the horizon a storm is brewing. The black cloud approaches and settles upon the road and John sees it is made up of a billion flies.

Littered beside the tanks are odd-shaped matchstick figures. The sky is turning dark with smoke. John, floating above the scene, swoops down for a closer look and he can see the crooked figures better now. They are burnt people. Their faces have melted. Dogs pick their way among them, snapping their necks back as they twist charred meat from bones.

Further along, John sees an Iraqi soldier lying partly buried in the sands. He is looking up, wide-eyed at the billowing sky. A British tank approaches and with a belch of exhaust smoke thunders over him and the body ripples as it is pressed deeper into the desert. Another tank appears, following its tracks in case the surrounding land is mined. Then another. The body spreads sideways, its features wiped away on the tank tracks. The procession of tanks keep rumbling forward until, finally, the body becomes wafer thin, lost in the sands.

It is raining again, the westerlies tugging grey clouds across the Fermanagh border like a speeded-up film. A narrow lane bordered by wiry hedges winds down to a remote British army checkpoint at Derryard, two miles from the border with the Irish Republic. It is only 4.20 p.m., but night has set in. It is twelve days before Christmas 1989, the month he splits up with Kenny's mother. The outpost looks lonely, helpless. John sees a lorry edging towards the small base, stopping as it nears the checkpoint. Private Jim Houston walks over. His step is hesitant. The clouds are moving quicker now, tearing across the turbulent sky. The truck is large, dwarfing the six-foot-two frame of Big Jim. The driver is staring bug-eyed at the young soldier. Jim leans forward and asks for his identification. The driver shifts in his seat. Jim examines the paperwork and makes towards the back of the vehicle, his booted steps slow now, the sky flashing faster and faster above. Something is wrong. The driver starts rocking manically backwards and forwards. He is grinning. Then the truck's horn sounds twice. Big Jim knows immediately, because any soldier would, that things have gone wrong. A hooded gunman rears up from the back of the truck. The masked figure shoots Jim once in the head and twice in the chest. Big Jim is dead. The truck lurches forward; John watches it reverse and smash into the checkpoint compound. Twelve armed men stand up in the back of the lorry. Two 12.7 mm DShK machine guns are mounted on the back alongside a brace of rocket launchers. They begin firing and a couple of RPG7 rockets shriek into the base. A flamethrower engulfs the desolate outpost. Another man, Lance Corporal Michael Patterson – 'Squeak' to his mates – is killed.

Rewind six hours. John is standing before Big Jim in the regiment's briefing room. It is 10.10 a.m. and John is sharing intelligence suggesting the IRA is planning an attack on a remote border checkpoint. The problem is they don't know which one. Big Jim, who has a two-year-old son, Daniel, and a wife from Essex, Shirley, looks apprehensive. John cheers him up by scratching the underside of his chin and calling him 'Brucie', as in Bruce Forsyth. Big Jim breaks into a smile. John wishes his friend luck and sends him on his way to Derryard. He sends Big Jim to the checkpoint. The attack was of a scale and sophistication never previously witnessed in Northern Ireland, but John sent his pal to his death.

In his nightmares he sees Big Jim lying face up on the road, still creased with concentration, but now his brain lies beside him. He was a father. He was twenty-two.

The road trips of his nightmares always end in the desert, among the mounds of corpses piled high like ragdolls by the Highway of Death. John watches as molten figurines are scraped from the tarmac and heaped into funeral pyres by giant bulldozers. He can smell the anticipatory pungent wafts of kerosene. Night falls and they are torched by hooded men. Ten thousand bodies burn by the road, casting a yellow glow into the surrounding desert. He can hear the bones crackling like kindling, the popping of organs like empty crisp bags, the smell of burning flesh. Screams pierce the desert night. The British commanders said it was to stop the spread of typhoid, but this is no way to go. Is there no better way?

Finally, the wretched spirits of Highway 80 gather by his bed. John sees them, vapour-like above him, faces blackened from the inferno. They gaze down with sockets that have no eyes, smiling with teeth stripped of lips.

At that point John would wake. 'I'd scream and hurl

myself out of bed, often with such force I'd hit my skull on the bedside cabinet,' he said. 'Shit, shit, shit,' he would gasp, groping on the carpet as he felt his way back from the roads. Beverley was becoming worried. They'd only been married five months before the incident on Bonfire Night. They met in a Blackpool bar one Sunday night in August 1994, courting for several months before John left the army and headed home to Scotland. Three months later, out of the blue, Beverley called to say she was pregnant. 'She says, "What we going to do, John?" I says, "I know what I'm not going to do. I'm not going to leave you on a fucking limb. Come on up to Glasgow, let's make a go of it." Such a lovely girl.'

On Bonfire Night, her husband changed from the man she met. He never used to awaken bolt upright on the floor, gasping for air. Now it was routine. Their marital bed was frequently so sodden with sweat that Alexander might as well have wet the sheets. Beverley had tried asking what was wrong, but John would not say. It was a phase, he thought. He'd be all right, he convinced himself; just sit tight and ride it out.

But it got worse. John found the streets he walked by day gradually morphed into the roads his nightmares travelled during darkness. 'I would be out walking down the streets and it was as if I was back on patrol in Northern Ireland.' In broad daylight, out shopping, he became lost in his visions. The waft of drains transported him outside a sewage works in the pissing rain. The smell of meat from a butcher's would make him freeze, incapacitated by the stench of death. During this period he stopped eating bacon because it smelt like burning flesh. The simplest things felt beyond him. Buying baby food for Alexander became a harrowing ordeal. His taut nerves failed him during the most mundane tasks. John overcompensated, planning trips to collect the morning milk with military precision. Even then mysterious figures would appear from behind, forcing him to cross the road until the mother and child or the dog walker passed. Navigating the city grew increasingly terrifying. 'Parked cars became a particularly big battle in my mind.' John would rather negotiate an elaborate detour than walk ten yards past a stationary vehicle.

The fear of parked cars stemmed from another road that had started to appear in his nightmares. He had first walked down it three years earlier in Crossmaglen, the notorious town deep inside Northern Ireland's 'bandit country', the most treacherous posting for British troops during the Troubles. His daytime illusions became dominated by memories of this rat-run in South Armagh. By its kerb, at an oblique angle, was an ageing blue Vauxhall Victor. As if he was back there, John remembered gingerly approaching the old banger. His unit had been notified that a remote-controlled bomb was planted in the town, but as usual no one knew where. But the Victor, the way it appeared to have been hastily abandoned, stoked his suspicions. Had he seen the figures watching above, his fears would have been substantiated.

From their vantage point, the IRA men watched the young Scottish soldier approach. One of the men pressed the remote firing switch. The Vauxhall Victor didn't twitch. They fired the detonator again, but still there was no explosion. Below, the young soldier – his son Kenny seven years old last month – kept on approaching the vehicle until he was six feet away. John's electronic countermeasure device had intercepted the detonation signal before it reached the car aerial, the bomb's antenna. He had no idea that, as he stood surveying the vehicle, his life was literally being contested in the surrounding air.

Only later did he learn the IRA had planted a claymore mine in the rear wing of the Victor and covered it with papier mâché. The claymore contained 680 grams of plastic explosive and seven hundred ball bearings designed to be spewed in a fan-shaped killing arc. The device was deadly up to fifty metres. Anyone up to 250 metres away would have been maimed by the onrushing metal balls.

Nearly a decade later, John saw parked cars lurch sideways in a white flash and then a cloud of silver baubles, the size of marbles, drifting towards him as if suspended on strings. 'Years later in my nightmares I'm patrolling down that alleyway and that bomb goes off in my face. It was the final straw, I left the army after that tour.'

Everywhere he looked, every corner, he saw blue Vauxhall Victors.

John called it 'self-medicating' but it was most popularly known as heavy drinking. He had never been a big drinker, practically a lightweight in the hard-drinking British army. He had seen what drink did to people he loved. Deep down, he resented alcohol. The distorted face of his mother after a bottle of afternoon gin had seen to that. He never forgot the night in January 1991 before he left for the Gulf, when he visited his mother to say goodbye. She was in the lounge, plastered as usual. 'Lend me a fiver for a couple of gins. If you ever come back I'll give you your money then,' she said. Another time, on leave in 1989, he turned up at his mum's with young Kenny in his arms. She was a hostile drunk and immediately John knew there would be no pleasantries. 'I says, "Ma, don't start," and she went, "Aaaah fucking soldier boy, fucking soldier boy."' So they left.

A good woman, John would say, but the worst kind in drink. She changed abruptly after suffering a miscarriage when John was eight. In the wake of the trauma she demanded they move back to Glasgow to be with her family and in 1970 they left Northamptonshire where her husband, a gentle, placid man, held down a good job at the Corus steel works. The family moved into a filthy tenement block in Parkhead in the city's east end and John's childhood was over almost the moment they arrived. Until then his mother was virtually teetotal, the conventional moralistic matriarch. But John would come home from school to watch *Scooby Doo* and find the entire floor of the tower block hammered on booze in the living room. The family money went on drink. 'Drink strips away all the goodness in people. Once it takes hold, once it becomes medicine, it becomes poison. She couldn't cook when drunk and all the family money went on drink.'

John and his brothers were left for three days at a time with no food. It was the period of so-called social emancipation and the council had started tearing down the neighbouring tenements. John, aged eleven, spied an opportunity. He began bunking off school, spending days stripping out the lead, copper and brass piping from the abandoned flats, stowing the scrap in an old pram piled with rags and sneaking it to the local scrapyard for money to buy tea.

His two brothers were taken into care. This didn't arrest his mother's bingeing. She got worse. John moved out, sleeping in the derelict highrises, living inside a squat with no windows and no running water. He drank from a mains water pipe in the nearby street and in 1973 spent several days in Duke Street Hospital with severe dysentery. His schooling became secondary to survival. When his education officially expired at sixteen he couldn't read or write.

By then, he only wanted to join the army. He had watched the classics – *A Bridge Too Far*, *The Great Escape* – and his grandfather's exploits in both world wars had stoked his curiosity. And in the army you got three square meals and a clean bed. Signing up meant he could escape poverty and make his ancestors proud. But the recruitment centre couldn't accept the emaciated sixteen-year-old who turned up begging to join. His illiteracy was one of the worst cases the recruiting officers had seen. He couldn't even attempt the entrance exam. 'I'd been perpetually malnourished for so long that food had become my sole priority.'

Undeterred, he joined the local TA and enrolled at the city's Cardonald College, mastering the basics of grammar and spelling and ending up with four O levels. After five years he returned to the recruitment officers. They were impressed. John's command of grammar and mathematics was way above the required standard. They told him he could choose any path he wanted. But there was only one option – the infantry, the regiment for which his grandfather had fought the Germans. The King's Own Scottish Borderers.

John became one of the leading lights of their intelligence unit, a meritocratic leader regarded for possessing an acute emotional sensitivity. Those who served alongside him said John could sense when someone needed help; privates who had initially struggled blossomed under his command. He was also a man of method and reason, able to instil unflinching loyalty during operations in Northern Ireland and Iraq. But now, nine years later, he was drinking alone, turning into his mother. He drank to deaden his nightmarish road trips, but it didn't work. He began drinking longer, faster, but the procession of horrific memories became more intense.

On 21 August 1996 he reached breaking point. He was drunk as usual and by the time he tottered to bed Beverley was asleep. That night was worse than any other. Big Jim, his brain like a grey cauliflower hanging from the side of his head, asked why? Why did you send me to the checkpoint that day? The Iraqis, too, wanted answers: was there not a better way?

He went downstairs and hit the vodka. He apologised to Jim, to his sons, to his wife. Beside the bathroom cabinet he calculated how many paracetamol tablets he might need. Thirty was medically sufficient to kill. He took sixty.

Beverley found him two hours later, weeping in a foetal position on the lounge floor. She drove him to Glasgow Royal Infirmary. She didn't have long. Even if he survived, he might have permanent liver damage.

The following day John was referred to a psychiatrist at

the Royal Alexandria Hospital in Paisley who questioned him for forty minutes. For the first time he told someone about the roads, the stuff he saw. Afterwards, Beverley was invited to speak to the specialist. She emerged distraught. 'She was crying and says, "Why didn't you tell me half the shit you've been through?" and I said, "How could I?"' He could not admit to anyone, not even his wife, certainly not his twelve-year-old son, that the things he had seen had weakened him. He was a soldier of the KOSB. He was a Meighan. He could handle it. Admittedly things were tricky at the moment, but he was convinced he just needed some time.

John was diagnosed with extreme post-traumatic stress disorder that day in August 1996. 'P-something,' he called it when people asked what the doc had said. John suspected he was the first British soldier to have caught such a thing. He'd never heard of it. He never remembered anyone mentioning it in the army. The psychiatrist informed John that he had been traumatised by a series of events and his battle to bury the memories had ultimately failed. Instead, they had been stored up like some poisonous backwash against the barrier of his conscious mind, the equivalent of a dam holding back a rising sea of toxins. The dam had burst on Bonfire Night, triggering an intense emotional rush.

Studies in the US suggest that severe post-traumatic stress disorder can actually alter the chemical composition of the brain. The amygdala, which deals with emotional memory and is thought to store recollections of fear, was found to be unusually active in sufferers. Other research has even detected a loss of ten per cent of the brain's grey matter, as if the mind is willingly shrinking to protect itself from the memories. Although changes to John's emotional state had been officially diagnosed he was never offered any psychological treatment. He is adamant that if he had received help in that summer of 1996 then he would have never gone on to commit the terrible act that would change everything. 'It would have stopped the downward spiral, that's for sure.' But the NHS wouldn't help veterans who needed intensive rehabilitation. It didn't do anything. He didn't even receive advice on where to get help. He was on his own.

For a time things improved. Just talking briefly about his nightmares gave John a slight release from their torment. It reminded him that he'd never had it so good. He had his position with Group 4, driving cash transit vans across the city, paid £26,000 with reasonable prospects. In addition, Beverley was flourishing as a self-employed hairdresser, developing such a loyal client base the couple had a joint income greater than £40,000. She'd given birth to a second boy, Andrew, and they had a first step on the housing ladder, a council flat bought under the right-to-buy scheme for £10,500. Things were going so well, in fact, they could afford three cars and a caravan to take the boys camping in the Trossachs as a treat. And Kenny, too, when he came up to visit his dad and was allowed to drink as much Irn-Bru as he wanted. What a terrific fella Kenny was turning out to be, John thought, such a thoughtful gentle character – although he remained insistent on joining the infantry and that was a worry.

The family carried on, grateful for what they had. But

eventually it became too much of a pretence for John. The road trips started coming back, appearing at night, stalking the recesses of his mind during the day. Except this time it was worse. Much worse.

Towards the end of 1997 he started drinking again. But now his binges were accompanied by volcanic mood swings. He developed a sudden intolerance of everything. A misplaced comment about the washing up; an item on the nine o'clock news; the price of bread. Alexander asked why daddy was so angry all the time. Beverley walked on eggshells. She asked John if the nightmares had returned, but he wouldn't talk about them. 'I became unbearable to live with. I didn't want to live with myself. I don't know how they put up with me.' More than a year after being diagnosed with PTSD, John woke sweating on the floor beside his bed, but instead of climbing back in beside his wife he went downstairs to drink. An hour later he counted out fifty-eight paracetamol and would have taken more but that was all he could find. Again Beverley took him to casualty. 'I got myself in a real downer. Normally after a couple of hours it works itself through but when I've been drinking it works itself too deep. I cannae get up again. I just go rock bottom, dip, dip dip . . . boom.'

They agreed to have a change of scene. It would do them good to leave Glasgow. John was becoming increasingly disillusioned with the city's sectarianism. During Kenny's last visit the twelve-year-old had worn a Celtic shirt but received so much abuse from the locals he had removed it by lunchtime. The bigotry of Northern Ireland had repulsed

John: he couldn't accept the same intolerance happening in his city.

In the summer of 1999 John transferred his Group 4 contract to BAE Systems in Lancashire, sold their house for £42,000 and headed south to Poulton-le-Fylde, close to Beverley's parents and a new beginning. John had convinced himself he could leave his past in Scotland and that somehow his nightmares would disappear on the journey south. Within weeks they resurfaced, worse than ever.

His drinking intensified. He began stopping at the local off-licence on the drive home from work, fortifying himself for the night ahead. At first it was a litre of cheap vodka. Soon, it was the spirits plus six cans of lager. Pictures of the time reveal a cherubic Kenny standing to attention along-side his father, whose face is blotchy and puffed up with alcohol. Kenny was a fitness fanatic and John remembered how he himself was once obsessed with the importance of maintaining prime physicality. As a young man he had de-tested cigarettes, smoking his first fag after returning home from his debut tour of South Armagh, aged twenty-seven. Now his fingers were ochre from rolling forty a day.

The self-medicating failed. John's nightmares became more vivid. His new role at BAE Systems was ostensibly easier than any job he had known, checking visitors' iden-tities as they entered the firm's site at Warton, near Preston, but his nerves were so jumpy that even elementary pro-cesses were too much. 'I couldn't cope with a simple thing like checking ID passes.'

Cars would queue at the site checkpoint and as John ad-vanced to inspect them he couldn't stop thinking of Big Jim approaching the IRA truck. John might have been manning one of the most secure places in Britain but in his mind he was back at Derryard. Blue cars spooked him the most. Instinctively he found himself inspecting their rear left wing for papier mâché. Eventually their colour didn't matter. They were all out to get him.

In 2000 he quit the well-paid job and became a volunteer care-worker for Lancashire Council. He chose home help, spending the days changing catheters, bathing the elderly, pushing the infirm into back gardens so they could feel the sun on their faces. Some may have viewed the move as a retrograde step for a proud military man, but John adored the role. 'I loved looking after such a broad range of courageous people.' In hindsight, John believes he may have deliberately surrounded himself with people who he felt were worse off than himself. 'This was my way of saying, look, if they can cope with their plight then I can cope. I was feeding off their strength to offset my weakness.'

Yet after eighteen months John detected a new phase: survivor guilt. Why had he survived and why not Big Jim? Why had he let Irwin get away, watched impotently as British tanks flattened Iraqis in the desert. He began to feel responsible for them all. In November 2001 he took another overdose, his most potent yet. Three dozen paracetamol supplemented with mirtazapine, an antidepressant prescribed by his GP. The doctor had recommended 30 mg a day. John swallowed 200 mg, washed down with his routine cocktail of vodka and beer. Beverley found him on the bathroom floor and called an ambulance.

John woke up the following morning in Blackpool Victoria Hospital. He remembers feeling an 'awful shame', then frantically tearing the drips off his body and running out of the building. He walked the five miles back to his wife and children in Poulton. He hoped Kenny would never discover that his dad had become a 'suicidal nutjob'. 'I remember being so weak from the drink and the drugs as I walked home sober. I felt such a terrible shame, a selfishness for what had I done. I kept asking: "How can I have stooped so low?" The shame was huge and my self-esteem was nil.'

He lost the job he loved. His employers could not countenance a care worker whose mental condition was considerably worse than that of the people he was supposed to be assisting. He signed on for incapacity benefits, part of the deal being that he attended a treatment centre for ex-servicemen suffering from PTSD run by Combat Stress, a charity specialising in helping traumatised veterans. More than six years after Bonfire Night 1995, John was about to receive treatment. Yet underfunding and a backlog from the Iraq war meant the charity could not cope with the deluge of new cases. John was allowed only two weeks' treatment at the charity's Audley Court centre in Shropshire.

The help had the opposite effect. 'They had opened up a lot of wounds,' said John. Attempts to confront his past merely galvanised suppressed memories. Demons that had lain undisturbed in the backwaters of his mind were prodded into life by the counselling. Soon after arriving home, John's condition scaled another threshold. His nightmare journeys became a circuit with no start or ending. 'Why?' the dead screamed day and night. 'Why didn't you help us?' Beverley would find him mid-afternoon when the boys were at school, alone upstairs, head in his hands. His dulled heart froze. His past engulfed him completely, wiping out the present.

John entered a period of withdrawal during which he could no longer talk to his children. The nights were spent alone, drinking mechanically downstairs while his wife and sons stayed in their bedroom and watched television. Until now, despite everything, John had made an effort with his two boys. Now when they talked to him he struggled to respond. He overheard them asking his wife: 'Why doesn't Dad shave any more? Why doesn't he speak? Why doesn't he take us to the Pleasure Beach any more? Why doesn't he do *anything* any more?'

His eldest, Kenny, was preparing to join the army and John knew there were things he should tell him, but he couldn't. It was easier to say nothing. His looks, his voice seemed to disturb others these days; it was better, he said, to shut himself away. 'Beverley was living in the house with a stranger, even with the kids I didn't respond. I'd completely isolated myself.' He was never aggressive, in fact he was the opposite. In the period before the incident that changed everything, John became so submissive he rarely spoke. 'I began shutting myself down. I was deteriorating, dying from the inside out.' He drank and felt no thrill, no boredom, no delight, no despair. He had no interests and no hopes.

During the six months leading up to April 2002 he tried to kill himself three times. John even coined a term – 'rip and run' – to describe his habit of tearing the drips from his

body and exiting hospital as soon as he regained conscious-
ness. Beverley locked the bathroom cabinets containing his
medication with huge padlocks, leaving his daily dose on
the side. In response John hatched a new plan during the
summer of 2002. He would drink terrific quantities of
vodka until he had reached a ferocious drunken fury. Then
he would call a cab, guiding it down Garstang Road West
into Blackpool, a ten-minute ride. From the taxi drop-off,
he would weave towards the seafront, down Talbot Road,
past the endless takeaways and blaring pubs. He walked
quickly and aggressively, craving eye contact from anyone
sufficiently foolish to stare back. Fucker, bastard, cunt, he
remembers chuntering under his breath, stoking the fury,
letting the hate build. He hated everyone he came across:
the lonesome drinkers, the happy couples, the old and the
young. 'I'd completely lost it by this stage. I didn't want
to live any more. The world was a dark place and I just
wanted to leave it.'

He marched towards Blackpool's clubland, looking for
the hardest nutcases in a town notorious for violence. As
always, he found them guarding the nightclubs around
Market Road. John compared the inevitability of violence
to the emotions experienced before a dangerous patrol: the
flood of adrenalin, the pre-combat acuity. He would march
towards a nightclub bouncer, quickly to retain a modicum
of surprise, then, without breaking stride, throw a right-
handed punch to the nose. 'It didn't matter who it was, any
one of them. I did it knowing fine well another six bouncers
would come along and beat the fucking shit out of me. I

was desperately hoping they would kill me because I didn't want to live.'

On one occasion they pinned him on the pavement and he winces while describing the barrage of kicks to the side of his body, the knuckles pummelling his spleen. Another time, a bouncer punched him so hard in the eye socket he was blinded with blood, but kept on swinging his fists. Once, he felt his nose fold across his face and he thought he had swallowed all his teeth. But each time, much to John's exasperation, the police or paramedics showed up. 'I was taken away to Blackpool Victoria and stitched up. This happened three or four times. They bust my nose, bust my lip, I had cuts to the head, bruising to the body, but nothing was ever broken. I used to joke to myself I was going out in Blackpool, down in a taxi, back in an ambulance. But seriously it was an awful, awful time for my wife.'

That same summer, on 20 July 2002, John was drinking with another former soldier at the Falcon Hotel, the pub around the corner from his neat three-bedroom home at Compley Avenue in Poulton-le-Fylde. The man was in his eighties and in 1942 had served as a teenager in northern France. John remembers clasping his frail hand. 'It is a privilege to meet you, sir, an absolute honour.' John mentioned his grandfather at Neuve Chapelle, his great-uncle buried at Armentières. Together they toasted 'the dead but not forgotten'. John was humbled in the presence of someone who had witnessed the Great War. He remembers talking about Kenny, how he was about to join the army in a few weeks. He described how his son was 'buzzing' with excitement, but also admitted that he was afraid about what Kenny might see.

'I had been drinking before I had gone out, and I slammed my glass down on the bar a bit too hard and the pub stops and this barman goes, "That's enough drink and don't swear at my bar." So I said, "Who the fuck are you talking to?"' The pub fell silent and a crowd began to stare. John says he noticed the veteran's hands, their skin as fragile as rice paper, trembling.

A man stepped forward from a group of drinkers and told John his language was out of order. John said he felt an enormous rage, too mighty to suppress. He leant back as far as his spine allowed and brought his head down upon the man's nose. 'As I stuck my head on him six of them jumped me straight away.' They jammed his body against the bar, walloping the foul-mouthed Jock until it felt indecent. When John finally straightened up, his new friend had gone.

Outside the Falcon the fury returned. He describes sprinting down Hardhorn Way to his home two minutes away. Grateful his wife and children were out, John went to the kitchen and grabbed an eight-inch carving knife. He had always felt grateful that in his fourteen years of service he had never shot or thrown a grenade at anyone. He took no satisfaction in the damage that weapons could inflict. 'For me the military was about discipline and duty. It's a strange thing to say, all things considered, but I've always deplored violence.' But on a summer's Sunday afternoon in Lancashire, John suddenly lost that aversion. 'I'd never used a weapon on anyone in my life but I grabbed that knife and ran as fast as I could back to the pub.' He burst inside, gesturing to his attackers to follow him out.

They came out, but their numbers had swollen. It looked like most of the pub was coming towards him. He held out the knife, but there were too many of them and he dropped the blade as the first hammer-blow connected. Then the kicks came in. 'They booted the fucking living daylights out of me. Again I wanted to be killed.' There, on the forecourt of the neighbourhood's family pub where his kids sometimes ate, John might have died, but the police were quick, a response for which he was profoundly ungrateful. At 8.55 p.m. he was arrested and taken into custody. He was charged with affray, and on 28 October 2002 appeared at Wyre Magistrates' Court to receive a two-year community rehabilitation order and a twelve-month ban from the Falcon. He never saw his veteran friend again.

He woke knowing something dreadful was going to happen. He woke wanting to kill somebody. Often John stirred with a crushing sense of desolation, but this time he felt different; he felt out of control.

He remembers shuffling to the bathroom cursing the Fort Knox security guarding his drugs. As always his reflection disgusted him. He shaved off his hair. For a moment he remembers contemplating whether to put on his military uniform, but there was no point. The man who once wore it was long gone.

It was 23 February 2004, Monday morning, half-term, and Alexander, aged nine, and Andrew, seven, were downstairs messing about. Beverley was preparing breakfast and John tried convincing himself that everything was normal.

He had become accustomed to pretending. But that morning he couldn't maintain the facade. Without a word he sneaked from the house, reaching the doctor's surgery around 11 a.m. He didn't have an appointment, so he explained that this was an emergency. But the surgery was busy. He remembers imploring the receptionist, saying that he was desperate. He said he was scared he might harm someone or himself. When that didn't work he pleaded to be sectioned under the Mental Health Act. For twenty minutes John begged to be taken to a secure psychiatric ward. Take me now, he demanded. Around midday he left the surgery, terrified of what he was about to do.

That afternoon John had an appointment in Blackpool with his solicitor, Allan Cobain of Church Street. During the meeting, according to his wife Beverley who was there too, John became 'very upset' when his worsening mental health was brought up. In the carefully worded statement that she later gave Lancashire Constabulary, she wrote: 'I would describe John at this point as getting "fired up" by the situation.' They arrived home at six o'clock and Beverley said she began preparing tea for the family while John watched television in the lounge. Through the kitchen wall she recalls hearing her husband hollering at the news headlines. George W. Bush was ramping up his campaign for re-election, lauding the war in Iraq. President Bush defending the Iraqi conflict never failed to wind up her husband. Beverley sensed the storm was building. Her police statement continues: 'He seemed to be getting agitated by things that were on the news. John, when he gets worked up goes "off on one" and he gets angry and talks to himself. This behaviour continued throughout our meal and I knew these were warning signs. John was going to go off on one.'

At 6.50 p.m., according to the documents, Beverley went upstairs to bath the children while her husband stayed in the kitchen to wash the dishes. An hour later John shouted upstairs to say he was popping out to get some tobacco. 'Would you like a drink?' he called. Beverley told him no and said that he shouldn't be drinking. 'Stop dictating to me, everyone telling me what to do all the time,' his wife's statement records him shouting back. Beverley then gave him a final warning: if he drank that night she would take the kids and be gone.

John stormed out. Beverley wrote down her feelings, confirming her ultimatum was real. The drink or her: his choice. She left the note in the kitchen for John to read and joined Alexander in bed upstairs to watch TV. Andrew was watching a video in his room. Thirty minutes later John came upstairs with a peace offering for his wife: a vodka and Coke. Beverley refused it. John went downstairs and began drinking, knowing that while it might calm him initially he wouldn't be able to stop and that would make everything worse. Mirtazapine, a strong anti-depressant that combines potently with alcohol, intensified the downward trajectory. Around 7.30 p.m. John realised he was hyperventilating. He considered calling Kenny, but knew his son was probably busy with the demands of his fledgling army career. He decided to keep himself hidden downstairs, away from his family. Occasionally, he heard bouts of giggling upstairs. They seemed happy without him. They would be better off with him dead.

At 11.15 p.m. on their last night together as a family, Beverley heard anguished cries of 'Mummy, Mummy.' She sat up petrified and tiptoed to her younger son's bedroom. Andrew was shivering. She climbed in to comfort him and soon both were asleep. At 1.50 a.m. Beverley woke and went to the nearby loo. It was then she heard an almighty racket downstairs. She went down and found John in the kitchen warming soup on the gas hob.

She saw her ultimatum had been read. John was drunk but oddly calm. He seemed sad, sadder than she had ever seen him. He offered to make a cup of tea, but Beverley refused and returned anxiously to bed. 'I was feeling nervous now because I knew something was going to kick off with John as it usually does when he drinks a lot,' she said in her police statement.

Beverley could not sleep. She lay listening to John stomping around. He had turned the television up so loud the floor was vibrating. Returning to the top of the stairs, she looked down, trying to work out what was going on.

She saw two bottles upright beside the front door. They were full of clear liquid. Paper, twisted like a rope, had been stuffed inside their necks. She could smell petrol. Appalled, Beverley remembered how her husband had once threatened to make a bomb and burn down the Falcon.

'I panicked because I was scared of what John might to do to the house or us.' She crept back to the boys and put Andrew in bed with his brother. She rang 999. Then she lay on the floor with her feet against the bedroom door in case her husband tried to come in.

John had a plan. He was going out in a blaze of glory. He

had gone to the garage and found a two-litre bottle of turpentine, along with two empty plastic bottles that had held Robinson's apple and blackcurrant, the kids' favourite. In the kitchen he poured the turps into the bottles, twisted kitchen roll into a six-inch fuse and shoved it down each neck.

Then he called the police himself, unleashing a string of abuse to provoke the biggest possible response. He wanted SWAT teams, the firearms unit, maybe even some of his old sniper pals to descend on the house. An armed terrorist holding his family hostage. They would take him out, shoot first, ask questions later. Beverley heard him shouting up the stairs: 'They'll be coming soon. Snipers, armed units, bullets flying everywhere. It'll be hell.'

John went out into the quiet suburban street. It was approaching 3 a.m. The night was freezing and he recalls shivering as he stood on the lawn in his socks, T-shirt and loose black trousers. In his palm, he felt the cool liquid of the Molotov cocktail. He fumbled in his pocket for a lighter and lit the wick, igniting the memories of republican riots.

He threw the bomb, watching it explode beyond his drive. It reminded him of Bonfire Night. Then he headed back inside and dialled 999 again. The recording of the call begins: 'Hello, my name is John Meighan of 36 Compley Avenue, Poulton-le-Fylde. I have a knife and I am holding my wife and my two young children at knifepoint. I also have in my possession a petrol bomb and I'm going to blow myself up.'

He put down the receiver and glanced up the dim staircase. Then he checked the lighter was still in his pocket and picked up his remaining bomb.

7

To Kill

Bait Platoon often discussed what it would be like to kill, how they would react when they first saw the enemy coming towards them. They had been trained to shoot as a reflex once they had the enemy identified. On the make-believe battlegrounds of the North York Moors, the flatlands of Surrey and the savannahs of Africa every aspect of killing had been choreographed. There they had shot man-shaped silhouettes standing stiffly in the distance. They hit the figures and, ping, down they went. Identify target. Aim. Fire. Don't worry about a head shot, line up the chest. Gently does it. Two shots. Bam-bam. They fully embraced the doctrines of combat. Them or you. Kill or be killed.

Kenny was conditioned to kill effectively. His tuition was meticulous, practical and dispassionate. There could be no other way. Learning to kill was a skill that required shrewd nurturing until the mechanics of the act eclipsed the deep-seated aversion inside most men to fatally injuring a fellow human.

Despite centuries of bloody conflict, most sociologists agree that man is not by impulse a killer. Fewer than four per cent of men possess a predisposition to kill. This innate resistance to taking human life is quantified in studies revealing that throughout history the majority of warriors have been unable or unwilling to kill the enemy, even when under direct threat themselves. One of the most well-known texts on the subject, by official US army historian Samuel Lyman Atwood Marshall, categorised three-quarters of Second World War soldiers as 'non-firers'. In other words, for every American soldier willing to shoot at the enemy on the battlefield, three were not even prepared to use their weapons.

Perturbed by the shortfall of instinctive killers among their ranks, the US army used Marshall's findings to develop special 'conditioning' techniques aimed at removing the moral dimension of killing during training programmes for the Vietnam war. The results were remarkable. Firing rates among combat troops leapt to ninety-five per cent. The dramatic turnaround remains the most compelling proof that with the right conditioning techniques, men can be indoctrinated to kill.

The techniques were now so advanced that Kenny and the rest of Bait Platoon didn't question whether it was possible to kill casually in battle. They just wanted the chance to find out. Yet the training could not entirely erase one nagging fear: could they perform when it most mattered? Fear of failure stalked them all. And how could they know until the moment itself? The question whether they would freeze tormented them.

Kenny carried the greatest pressure. At point he was most likely to encounter the enemy first. His response mattered most. They had been taught that the initial split second of combat was the most critical: react coolly and you could buy the moments that would save friends' lives. Hesitate and the enemy might as well be shooting fish in a barrel.

It was 5.15 a.m. and dawn was beginning to breathe colour into the desert. Ahead, two hundred metres across the cracked, dusty terrain, was the town of Deh Adan Khan. Intelligence had pinpointed 'DAK' as a significant enemy stronghold. In the still morning it looked utterly tranquil.

Kenny paused, scanning the buildings for movement, waiting for the farmers to emerge. No one came. He crept nearer, his section close behind, halting behind a mud wall on the town's outskirts. The men were in single file, parallel to Kenny just fifteen yards away. They moved jauntily, carefree. It was the opening hour of Operation Silicon, the onset of the largest offensive British forces had launched in Afghanistan for almost a century. Out at the front, Kenny was anxious. He hated it when the enemy disappeared; it meant they could surface where he least expected. He was studying the distant treeline for a tell-tale rustle, a sign of life, when something incongruous caught his eye. It was so unexpected that he recalls performing a cartoon double-take. 'You know when you glance at something and look away then look back. I couldn't believe my eyes.' And then he remembers laughing; it looked so surreal it was funny.

Kenny had been patrolling for weeks and had still to properly see the enemy. Bait Platoon had almost begun to think of their adversaries as sorcerers, able to magically appear and disappear at will, shifting from compound to compound as if the structures were time machines. Yet now there they were, directly ahead, almost within spitting distance. They were walking in front of a towering fortress structure, their shadows bobbing against its brown flank. There were about ten of them, each dressed pretty much the same in black kurtas – long shirts – and turbans, some in grey waistcoats. Their eyes were rimmed with kohl; this close they looked like Goths. But there was no mistaking the fact they were warriors. Most were wrapped in metal chains, ammunition belts that draped off their shoulders. 'They were tooled up to the fucking nines, heavy machine guns, RPGs, not just AKs but PKMs [Russian-made machine guns] over their shoulders, walking past this massive old compound behind them, heading up through a field.'

Kenny studied the lead guy – his rival point man – with a detached thrill, the heart-in-the-mouth rush a child gets when creeping up on a friend. Their point man walked with the same light yet deliberate step he recognised, shoulders slightly stooping as he reached a small incline. On one shoulder a rocket-propelled grenade launcher was balanced nonchalantly, like a plank. Kenny shuddered as it dawned on him where they were headed. Beyond the ridge, B Company were patrolling the green zone. His best mate Chris was over there, oblivious. Kenny steadied himself, reminding himself that the enemy had no idea he existed. He was ambushing an ambush. Kenny brought his rifle up. The enemy had started moving with increased urgency as they reached an open field. He remembers sliding the weapon's safety catch off, how his heart began racing while time stopped. He was conscious of the need to remain cool, to regulate his breathing while swallowing his rising panic. The training came back. Carefully Kenny moved the weapon's muzzle over the lip of the wall, coaxing the tip of the black arrow in his sight onto the opposing point man. Magnified in the lens, he recalls the man's face rushing towards him.

It was a warm, open face, kind and honest. The enemy soldier was young yet had a strong profile, a roman nose. A long tawny beard hung from his chin, its manliness offset by the eyeliner that framed his sockets. Kenny noticed how the man stared anxiously ahead, eyes darting, just as he did when at point. His head nodded slightly as he moved and Kenny marvelled how, for all the circumstances, for all the pressures of point, for all the impending madness that surely lay ahead, he still seemed to be holding himself at ease. Kenny simply held his breath.

He guided the rifle sight fractionally ahead of the man's chest so that he would literally walk into his bullets. The trigger felt odd, foreign against his middle finger, the weapon much heavier than usual. Kenny watched as the young man closed his eyes and drew a deep breath as if drinking the morning calm. Kenny felt the tension of the trigger, its mild resistance, but kept pulling it towards him.

The noise was shocking, a metallic tapping that seemed to fill the desert. His rifle bucked, dust wafted from the wall. 'I dropped the first geezer carrying the RPG on his shoulder, slotted him, three to four rounds into his chest.' The enemy point man jerked sideways, his eyes widening before he lurched away from Kenny and went down. The rest of the section were all up by now. 'We mounted the wall and just mowed the rest of them down, the gunners with UGLs [underslung grenade launchers] and the

GPMGs hammered them. I stopped firing eventually, there was no point.' Even so, the enemy put up a fight. Some even kept it together long enough to squat down on one knee and retort with a few shots. But like condemned men before a firing squad, they would have known it was over from the start.

The man Kenny had killed lay on his back, peering blankly at the brightening sky. His rocket launcher lay beside him, its barrel moistened by the dark puddle leaking from the exit points of the 5.62 mm bullets. His face was benign. He looked around twenty years old. Kenny noticed the dead man's scruffy smock, grubby at close range. His rubber sandals, almost worn through at the sole, still clung to his feet. In truth, the dead point man probably never knew what happened. Kenny's bullets would have passed through him before their sound even reached him.

Almost instantly, from that day, Kenny detected a subtle change in attitude from his senior officers. He had a 'personal kill'. 'I felt that finally I could look my seniors in the eye and they looked back with a little more respect.' But not even his military indoctrination, he would soon realise, could fully extinguish the childhood teachings of what was right and what was wrong.

During the days that followed Kenny thought often about his first kill. At night he could see the body lift off its feet. He peered closer into the young man's clouding eyes and felt a shot of remorse. He did not hate him; in some ways he felt oddly attached to the human he had shot. It had never really occurred to him before, not properly, that the people on the other side were human beings. Before,

Despite suffering acute stomach cramps and being constipated for nine days, Kenny keeps an eye out for encroaching Taliban at the British base in Sangin, September 2007. Earlier the private had pleaded to go out on patrol, when it became apparent Kenny could barely walk upright he was ordered to stay behind.

Back at base after another patrol and Kenny relaxes with the ubiquitous Lambert & Butler. The constant stress of doing point, the exhaustion, the fear of what lies ahead, are clearly evident in his haggard expression.

Kenny scooping rations from a mess tin in the accommodation block at Sangin during June 2007. A combination of endless patrols, poor diet and debilitating heat caused him to lose two stone since April.

Kenny proudly displays his Afghan campaign medal following the battalion's homecoming parade in November 2007. A highly productive tour as point man earned him plaudits among his peers. Yet within four months of the parade, Kenny announced he was quitting the army.

John cradles fourteen-month-old Kenny and his four-year-old sister Zoe, inside the British army's married quarters in Berlin. It is 1987, two years after John's debut tour of Northern Ireland, and mentally and physically he appears indestructible. In the decade that followed, his deterioration was so pronounced he became almost unrecognisable.

Kenny's passing out parade at Catterick Garrison, Yorkshire, August 2003. John, dressed proudly in the Leslie tartan of his old regiment, is trying hard to look happy, but the reality of his life is appalling: 'you can see the illness in my face, the underlying torment.' Within six months of the parade John would commit the crime that would alter his life forever.

The only surviving image of John on patrol in Northern Ireland, taken weeks after Kenny was born, during autumn 1986, at a location somewhere near Craigavon. Despite the grainy image, the fear in his expression is evident.

Wearing the traditional Glengarry cap, John poses in front of Edinburgh castle during August 1990. His first marriage has collapsed and his nerves are starting to shred from rolling tours of Northern Ireland. Days before the photograph, Saddam Hussein invaded Kuwait. Within months John would serve in the Gulf War: his descent into full breakdown would inexorably follow.

The medal collection of soldier 24404628, lance corporal John Meighan, of the 1st Battalion Kings Own Scottish Borderers. Normally the pride of any former soldier, the medals and their attendant memories of camaraderie and derring-do are obliterated by the things John saw in service and his subsequent neglect by the state.

John in the front room of his Colchester flat, January 2010, just weeks after what he hopes will be his final suicide attempt. Less than a month has passed since he gave up alcohol and already the fifty-year-old looks healthier. 'Hopefully that's the last suicide attempt I'll make. I'm not going back there again.'

The memorial to John's friend Big Jim in the grounds of St Mary's church, Wivenhoe, Essex. On the anniversary of the private's death, John makes a lonely pilgrimage to Big Jim's nearby grave. There, he lays flowers in remembrance of the friend he sent in good faith to the checkpoint where he was executed by IRA gunmen.

Coffin bearers carry the body of Guardsman Tony Downes for repatriation to the UK. The soldier, three weeks younger than Kenny, was killed by a roadside bomb while travelling in a British convoy. Kenny helped gather Tony's remains into a body bag while being shot at, an act that would haunt his nightmares for years.

Garland Road in Parkeston, Essex, where Kenny and his family moved after he left the army. Parkeston, an enclave of terraces beside Harwich's international port, suffered during the recession. Its last remaining neighbourhood shop, Garland Stores, closed in October 2009. More than two years later it remains boarded up. Feeling increasingly isolated and unable to find work, Kenny's frustration with civilian life starts to fester.

Shuttered shops on a precinct in Greenstead, a sprawling estate to the east of Colchester town centre. Kenny, a bus driver on route 64, loathed the job of guiding his vehicle through Greenstead. His vehicle ran the risk of attack from packs of youths who would sometimes storm on board to intimidate Kenny and his passengers.

Kenny and Sam's wedding in Harwich, 16 July 2011, four years to the date of their meeting in the nearby Stingray Tavern. That night in the Stingray changed his life; Kenny believes it probably also saved it. 'I couldn't believe my luck . . . I still can't.'

Colchester Zoo, April 2010. Kenny, the ever proud dad, with his son Cayden, a Gaelic word meaning 'spirit of battle'. Kenny admits the prospect of Cayden following the Meighan tradition and joining the army fills him with dread. 'But I can see little signs in him already, that urge.'

they were just the enemy and it was you or them. 'You were trained to kill the enemy, select your target and shoot. But that couldn't stop you thinking about it afterwards.' Kenny kept thinking about the variables that had brought them together. They were both point men. One of them had to die. That's just the way it was.

Over time, troubling thoughts began to plague him. What if the dead man wasn't a warrior? The Ministry of Defence briefed that the Taliban were recruiting farmers for a fistful of dollars to guard their crops. It was plausible that the dead man had agreed to fight to keep his kids and wife in food. Maybe his cornfields had been destroyed by the fighting and, unable to eke out a living from the ground, he had been press-ganged into the war.

Kenny endlessly replayed the sequence of events that had led to his first kill. Could the man have been spared? And who, Kenny wondered, was he? Was he married? Would his wife ever be told how he had been killed? If he had children, would they ever know what happened to their dad? As a boy Kenny had frequently imagined how he would react if his own dad was killed on some operation abroad. Kenny's father had never even hurt anyone, let alone killed, during his eleven tours of warzones. Part of him couldn't wait to tell his dad what had happened, how he'd kept his nerve. But then the guilt would return.

Kenny became absorbed with the possibility that the dead man had been forced to fight against his will. He invented a story that Taliban commanders had turned up in his village, threatened his family and bullied him into carrying a rocket launcher towards the invaders. Reports of the enemy terrorising Helmand's communities were rife. Intelligence indicated that some of those who refused to fight were tortured, their mutilated bodies left dangling from trees like skinned calves in a butcher's window as a warning to others.

Another theory of Kenny's was that the dead man had had no intention of killing. Once he reached the British, he was planning to fire a potshot into the sky and then scarper. Plenty of them did it: 'shoot and scoots', Bait Platoon called them. Maybe the dead man was a born non-firer. Maybe, as Kenny's bullet began its brief journey to his chest, he was asking himself the universal query of the novice soldier: can I kill?

Kenny often considered the man's physicality. His physique seemed more elfin than his own and possibly even younger. He had seen how the land could brutally age the skin with its thin, dry air and ferocious sun. Even so Kenny estimated they were probably the same age. Born in 1986, a child of the mujahideen, the year the Soviets announced their Afghan withdrawal. Undoubtedly he would have been weaned on the heroics of those who crushed the mighty Red Army, but still that didn't make him a fighter.

Over the weeks that followed Kenny's doubts began to subside until they were replaced by a different understanding of events which arrived like an epiphany. He woke knowing what he had done was necessary. He had shot an enemy fighter. More than that, his actions had probably saved the lives of British soldiers. It suddenly seemed obvious. After all, the man he had killed had taken point; he was the soldier guiding the others towards B Company, towards his best mate from Harwich, Chris George, who carried a plastic meerkat as his lucky charm, and whom Kenny considered a brother. It was Chris who, years earlier, had come to stay in Kenny's room when his mother went to live abroad. Kenny shared everything: 'He had no family so he lived around mine with me and my mum. What was mine was his. The only friction was that he supports Arsenal and I support Tottenham.'

Three years later, after Chris had completed his second Afghan tour, the incident cropped up as I talked to the two of them over a pint. Kenny refused to accept that he might have saved his best friend's life. 'Look,' he said firmly, 'you would have done the same, anyone would have. It's not a big fucking deal.' It was only when Kenny went to the gents that Chris leant over and whispered: 'Take no notice of Kenny, he doesn't want to come across as a fucking hero. But if he hadn't spotted them we would have been ambushed. I might not be here. Write that down.' When he returned, Kenny stuck to the conventional military line that he was simply doing his job. Only later did it occur to me that Kenny wanted to avoid glorifying the fact he had killed another human, or even that he was trying to forget he had pulled the trigger. It was not cool to brag about killing someone, he would say months later. 'Even if they are the enemy, it's a professional thing, it's not something you want to make a big deal about.'

Yet that night, three pints later, he eventually conceded that he had had no choice but to shoot. The guy was carrying an RPG. In addition, the Taliban's weaponry was in immaculate condition. Even their AK-47s had their rifle butts intact, unlike many they came across in Helmand. It was his ragged clothing that had worried Kenny. As a child he had imagined fighting an army dressed in matching uniform, not men who looked like farmers.

Kenny also pointed to the enemy's attempt at a fighting withdrawal. 'They kept their head when most soldiers would have panicked,' he said. Only the most disciplined, trained fighters, he stressed, could have attempted that under such firepower. He was a young man who probably had a family, but he was definitely the enemy. Kenny could not afford to think otherwise. He had killed a fellow human, but the wider conflict, he quickly realised, did not change. There was one less man, that's all.

Popular theory suggests that killing becomes easier the more you do it. But Kenny found that the critical factor was closeness. The closer the enemy were, the harder it became. Face to face in the compounds, with his bayonet fixed, was as tough as it got. Some infantrymen envied the helicopter gunners whose guided missiles made killing a clean, no-contact sport. Up there, the enemy were blobs on the screen of a thermal image finder. One click of a switch and the blobs disappeared. Technology eradicated the moral greyness as well as the mess. For Bait Platoon, with every step closer to the enemy the more human they became, and that's when it got complicated. 'They're so close you can see how hard they are breathing, the look in their eyes and you've got to remember that they want to kill you. They were probably thinking the same.'

Kenny discovered that even the most justified of kills is

capable of inducing profound guilt. Killing, he will testify, can never be easy, whatever they teach you.

Kenny's prospects of avoiding being killed, however, had deteriorated. Meeting Sam, he later admitted, had created a distraction that left him vulnerable. Striding ahead at point he found his mind wandering. 'In a way it was a bad thing meeting Sam on R&R, because it could have got me killed simply because I had her on my mind. I'd be on patrol and before we met I was thinking of where's the next cover? Is that a possible ambush point? After R&R I was still thinking about the mission but I was wondering what Sam's doing now. That split second I was not focused on my job could have seen me killed.'

He was point man and a good soldier in a relentless war, and that made more killing inevitable. During the tour Kenny killed three times: that is, confirmed kills from his own weapon. The second came during Operation Ghartse Gar when a Taliban fighter approached through the gloom of a compound and Kenny shot him in the chest. The third was during an audacious attempt by the enemy to over-run the Sangin base. Kenny, high up in Sangar Six, one of the watchtowers guarding the southern flank, shot one of the figures cutting through the alleyways that ran up to the perimeter fence. There were also three unconfirmed kills, unattributable because often in the maelstrom of battle the entire section fights together, aiming at the same targets. 'You could only confirm a kill if you were the only one shooting at the bloke.' Kenny suspected the true total was probably higher. But the nature of the fighting meant that they usually had to keep moving instead of pausing to count bodies. On the occasions they did return, invariably the Taliban had already collected their dead.

None of Kenny's kills affected him as profoundly as the point man. Years later he still seemed haunted by the incident. The reasons, said Kenny, were not only that it was his first kill and that it was so close, but also because he had time to weigh up his shot, to contemplate his actions before firing. 'You replay the process over and over again, thinking, would I have done anything differently?'

Kenny's section accounted for more than thirty of the enemy between them, a 'kill rate' of 3.75 per head. But the men never assessed the war through the prism of a body count; as long as the enemy kept coming they hadn't killed enough.

Another misconception about combat is that some men become addicted to the thrill of killing. Kenny dismissed this as nonsense. For his own part, he reflected deeply about each one, rerunning each incident in detail to determine whether he could have held off or whether the man deserved to die. His analysis always found that he had made a correct decision and for that he was deeply grateful. 'But you'll never ever forget when you killed that man. You never will. You'll just never forget; it's kind of weird. A lot of people say that you cannot afford not to kill, but sometimes you think maybe that man could have surrendered. Maybe if I hesitated for a second or two he would lay down his weapon. But then you realise that if you had hesitated you'd be dead. You've got to follow your training and so that's what I did.'

But it wasn't just the people you killed that stayed with

you. Kenny would learn that memories of those you fought alongside could have an even greater capacity to torment your thoughts.

Almost the moment Kenny arrived in Sangin in 2007, the Taliban had put down a marker, killing three Afghan army soldiers with a bomb in the town centre. But 9 June promised less grief. It was a day designated for logistics and preparation, a day working out how to cope with what might follow.

Kenny was preoccupied with familiarising himself with the district compound's firing points, the enemy's favoured attack positions. But he also knew how the quiet days could turn. As the sun climbed higher, the British forward operating base received an emergency radio call. Audible above a cacophony of screams, rockets and gunfire, an Afghan commander requested urgent back-up. Kenny was told to get his shit together. Something dreadful had happened in the dust tracks north of Sangin.

That morning a convoy of ten armoured vehicles had set off from the base on one of those feel-good missions that brigade headquarters hoped would get the locals onside. The brief was simple: help widen a complex of irrigation ditches in central Helmand. If all went well, they would be back for lunch.

In the rear vehicle, standing behind the machine gun, was a Mancunian, Guardsman Neil Downes, known as Tony. Just twenty, Tony was a legend in the 1st Battalion of the Grenadier Guards. His youthful enthusiasm and un-swerving belief in the campaign's capacity to rehabilitate Helmand had given him mascot-like status among the sceptics and veterans. Soldier 25192572 stood out in other respects, choosing to pass his time off-duty with the Afghan troops. Tony was hoping to grasp the dialects of Pashto and Dari and by all accounts was making reasonable progress, although who knew if the Afghans understood a word of his Mancunian drawl.

Around 9 a.m., as the convoy neared its destination, they heard the jackhammer of machine-gun fire from about two kilometres away. Immediately the Afghan commander in charge amended their itinerary to suss out what was going on. Those on board recalled how their initial good vibes began to ebb during the unplanned detour.

Around 9.30 the procession of armoured cars entered a small kalay with a ramshackle bazaar. Sergeant Bryan De-Vall, travelling in the vehicle in front of Tony Downes, sensed straight away that something was up. Normally one of the busiest bazaars north of Sangin, it was eerily quiet.

The convoy flashed through the village outskirts, one, two, three armoured vehicles. In the final truck Tony, still standing, was scrutinising the terrain for danger. Seven, eight, nine. As the last vehicle entered the kalay, Lance Corporal Edward Redgate recalled hearing a sound like 'a can of fizzy pop being opened followed by a dull boom'. For an instant the road surface appeared to buckle, then it rushed skywards. The shockwave rippled through the metal of Tony's Land Rover WMIK, folding the vehicle's frame towards the sun, its rear end rising as if yanked by an invisible crane. Another soldier in the vehicle, Warrant Officer Wayne Scully, described the moment of impact: 'I remember seeing greyness then being thrown forward. I landed on my front on the ground. I remember seeing the mangled vehicle, the flames and smoke.' Tony had taken the most exposed position and would have known the risks. He caught the explosion's full force and was flung sixty feet across the road, landing in a ditch on the far side.

The deserted bazaar came to life. From positions high to their left, enemy fighters began sending down waves of rocket-propelled grenades and machine-gun fire. It seemed they were going to be overrun, the whole convoy wiped out.

As Kenny's section got nearer, the radio updates had become increasingly urgent. By the time they entered the village, the convoy was a scene of devastation. Smoke billowed from the wreckage of the upturned WMIK. Nearby, Wayne Scully was lying dazed and bleeding after being hurled clear by the blast. Two of the vehicle's other occupants were close by and also looked in a bad way. By Kenny's reckoning that left one unaccounted for.

At first he wasn't sure what it was. Across the road, Kenny saw what looked like a bloodied towel discarded below the Taliban firing positions. Then he noticed its familiar mottled pattern, the shreds of a British army uniform. It was a body, face down in the shallow trench. All around it, the baked earth was rippling with plumes of dust. It took him a moment to compute what was going on and when he realised, he remembers feeling an incredible anger.

'They were fucking shooting at the body. I couldn't handle that. Obviously I was point man and Corporal Brooks looked at me and said: "We're going to retrieve him before they get the satisfaction of pumping him with any more lead.'"

A black plastic body bag was passed to Kenny and they began running towards the corpse. He recalls the air snapping as bullets cascaded down, the noise intensifying with every step. The closer he got to the body, the less human it looked.

The soldier had come apart. A leg was missing, other parts too. Kenny helped haul the body into the bag as the enemy concentrated their fire. He fell on his knees, scooping up the soldier's remains, frantically pawing the dust. Bullets rained down. Where the hell was the leg? The other bits? The enemy fire felt closer. He continued groping the ground for traces of the dead man, running his fingers in the dust as the earth trembled.

'We were trying to pull the dead body into cover, but we were getting shot at. He was in a pretty bad state and we were getting contacted [fired at] while we were putting him in the body bag. At any point I could have been put in the bag with him,' said Kenny. But they could never risk leaving a soldier, even a dead one, in the hands of the enemy. 'We couldn't leave a British soldier on the ground. Imagine what they would have done to the body if they got hold of it? They might have stuck it on the internet.'

Even then, amid the deafening commotion, Kenny was struck by the revelation that a man, when all is stripped down, is largely liquid inside a delicate wrapping. The devastation caused by hidden bombs was, he said, 'absolutely shocking'. He had never properly imagined how they would take apart a body. How the force made flesh stick so fast to the metal of an armoured car that it had to be scraped off with a bayonet. Kenny learnt that humans do not break apart neatly when struck by a hidden bomb. Instead they are broken into something almost indistinguishable as the human form.

The more Kenny discovered about Tony Downes, the more he wished they had met. Both had signed up aged sixteen, almost as soon as they could, and they were nearly the same age. Kenny was twenty days older. Like Kenny, Tony's single childhood ambition had been to join the infantry and, like Kenny, none of his teachers were surprised by his career choice. Tony's art teacher was amused by how often his military aspirations manifested themselves in signature camouflage backdrops.

Not hampered by dyslexia and blessed with a natural aptitude for learning, Tony left north Manchester's Middleton Technology School with sixteen GCSEs. His principal role in Helmand had been to sift through the intelligence reports, deciphering the tribal complexities, the subterfuge and propaganda – who you could trust and what you couldn't – a demanding task Tony handled with panache, the same role Kenny's dad had revelled in.

It was scarcely credible how youthful Tony looked when Kenny later saw his pictures in the papers. In some, he resembles a Boy Scout. They reminded Kenny of when he had first signed up. In one photograph, Tony's fatigues seem to hang off him as if four sizes too big. With both hands he cradles a rifle, its barrel dwarfing his slender arms. In the background, the flatlands of Helmand stretch to the horizon. Like Kenny, Tony was a smiler. Friends said it was as if he considered it a civic duty to lift the spirits of others. A constant theme among the eulogies and tributes was his trademark grin, 'a million-watt smile', said one.

Kenny was consoled by discovering that Tony had also found true love. Kenny identified uncanny parallels in how they had both met The One. Tony had also spied his love across a crowded bar, in his case in Aldershot four months before leaving for Afghanistan. Jane Little was nineteen, almost the same age as Sam. Tony, though, unlike Kenny, had left her a letter, a final farewell to be opened in the event of his death. On a single sheet of A4, in large, neat single-spaced letters, the note began: 'Hey beautiful!!' and went on to joke that, knowing his luck, his 'bloody lottery numbers' would come in now. But the lightness of touch couldn't be sustained. He regretted the pain his death would cause. By the end of the first paragraph he was 'truly sorry' for breaking Jane's heart, the one thing he would have avoided had he been spared.

Primarily the letter was about the need for Jane to move on. She was a teenager and he was gone, for now. They would meet again of course, but in the meantime she had to find happiness with someone new. Tony added: 'Jane I hope you have a wonderful and fulfilling life. Get married, have children etc! I will love you forever and will see you again when you're old and wrinkly!'

In the weeks before he died, Tony had told anyone who would listen about his girl back home. The night before he died they spoke on the phone. He was due home in nineteen days. Instead his body was lowered into the ground at a packed St Mary's Church in Droylsden, Manchester, on the day he was due to see Jane again, 28 June 2007.

Kenny told his dad about Tony. What he had seen. His dad understood only too well. John was twenty-seven when he had witnessed what a roadside bomb did to the body. It was 1985, his first tour in South Armagh, weeks before he would return home and meet Kenny's mother. His unit had been briefed to expect a paramilitary attack on their base, but instead the IRA were lying in wait for a convoy headed north fifteen miles away, carrying £2 million in cash from Dublin to Belfast, escorted by an RUC armoured car. The road began to rise beneath the police vehicle outside the village of Killeen. The remote-controlled bomb tossed it in the air and, as with Tony's vehicle, all four occupants were spat from its mangled shell. Except here there were no survivors.

John remembers gasping at the crater from the thousand-pound bomb as they were helicoptered in, seeing the police officers below searching the tarmac for the remains of their friends, not knowing which bit belonged to whom. He had had no idea that a bomb could actually vaporise a person. 'Parts of the bodies were collected in polythene bags and thrown in the back of a Land Rover. The incident didn't affect me at the time, only later did it start to torment me. I started to think about the way the bags were tossed into the back of the van, it too began to eat me up.' He became worried for his son, now witnessing the same appalling sights a quarter of a century later.

Thirty hours after Tony Downes died, the Ministry of Defence released its account of how the sixtieth British soldier to die in the Afghan campaign was killed: Guardsman

Downes 'died from the injuries he sustained in the explosion', said the press release, as if the soldier had only been badly hurt and somehow failed to recover.

Tony's death affected Kenny profoundly. He had watched the films and listened to his dad, but he learnt that there are some things no one can comprehend until you see them for yourself. Yet it wasn't the first grim sight he had encountered. Weeks earlier Kenny had witnessed how the 30 mm cannons of an Apache helicopter turned a body to mush. He had been carrying a dead Afghan officer when the legs had come away from the body, bones pulped to the consistency of puree. But the damage inflicted by a hidden bomb was of a different order. Tony's death felt different. It was the uniform, the act of putting a British guy twenty days his junior into a plastic bag.

Kenny said that Tony Downes's death was a pivotal point of the war, the event that seared his subconscious more than any other. 'Putting Guardsman Downes in the body bag was the hardest thing I did, even though I never knew him.' Kenny's diminishing sense of youthful immortality took a hit that morning. But Tony's death would present more profound long-term issues for him too. It was harder to be comfortable in his own skin. 'It does have an impact on how you see things. It's the one thing I think about the most,' he said. Years later, when asked which memory of the tour troubled him the most, Kenny didn't miss a beat: 'It was the most scarring definitely, the most real. It was like it hit me right in the face.

'It's still hard to get to grips with the fact I'm putting a British soldier in a body bag. Not an Afghan soldier or a Taliban, but someone like you,' he said, grimacing. 'The worst thing you can see is a dead British soldier.'

Kenny often wondered about the man he never knew. He felt some sort of bond with him. Tony's commitment to the cause, his belief that goodness would prevail, were the things he too had believed in. It was obvious to Kenny that, had the roles been reversed, Tony would have gathered up his remains so they could lie near his loved ones. Anyone in Sangin would have done the same. You always brought back the dead.

Kenny also thought about how Tony's family were coping and how his own parents would have reacted had he died instead. Tony's mum Sheryl quickly transformed her pub, the King's Head in Droylsden, into a shrine. The pub had stood since 1782, the endgame of the US War of Independence, and its stone facade became a celebration of a modern soldier from the latest campaign. Motorists passing on Market Street could not fail to notice the huge brown eyes of a young man staring down. Underneath the photograph, the epitaph: 'Tony: our son. Everyone's Hero.' Townspeople would regularly see his youngest sister, Jodie, on her way to plot D of the local cemetery on Manor Road. She was headed for grave number 218, a journey that took her past Droylsden's war memorial with its twenty-somethings and teenagers from the First World War, boys like David Makin, aged nineteen, whose remains lay in northern France but who was born around the corner on Manchester Road. For decades the town had paid their respects to the sons and brothers it had lost. Jodie was the latest, kneeling by plot 218, confiding in Tony as she always had, as if he could hear every word.

Only later did the uncomfortable truth surrounding Tony Downes's death emerge. Failure to provide adequate equipment meant the twenty-year-old needn't have died. The coroner at Stockport Magistrates' Court heard how the Taliban had planted two hidden bombs in the road leading into the village and watched as the convoy entered. The initial vehicles thundered by, six, seven, eight, but the road stayed flat. On came the final vehicle, Tony standing in the back. Then the ground began to bulge. It emerged at the inquest that the vehicle in front of Tony's was equipped with an electronic countermeasure (ECM) system capable of blocking the bomb's detonation signal. Tony's vehicle had no such protection. It had no chance. Although the Ministry of Defence refuse to reveal the equipment's cost, military contractors say a decent ECM for use in Afghanistan would have cost around £50,000.

Sheryl Downes was adamant the equipment might have saved her son's life. The south Manchester coroner, John Pollard, was similarly so troubled at the shortcomings surrounding Tony's death that in June 2008 he wrote to the ministry calling for an urgent change in army policy. Recording a verdict of unlawful killing, he said: 'It is my view that all vehicles used in this type of operation should be adapted to be able to carry their own ECM equipment. If some vehicles are not so equipped, then it should be clearly understood that the order of march should be arranged to afford protection at all times to those vehicles.' Defence officials maintain that Tony's WMIK was being protected by other vehicles, without addressing why it was travelling exposed at the rear. Since his death £193 million has been spent on upgrading existing vehicles to reduce the threat of roadside bombs.

Kenny had arrived in Afghanistan believing that there were gallant ways to die in war. But Tony didn't die in a *Zulu*-like last stand. He died because no one attached a relatively cheap device to his vehicle before he went to widen some irrigation ditches one morning.

8

Psycho Suite

The boy half-opened his mouth, probing the recesses of his mind for another question. His face reddened as he willed the query to the surface. John was convinced the lad was going to pass out. The boy, saliva bubbling at the corner of his mouth, asked if John was an angel.

'I said: "What?" and he says: "You look like an angel," and I smiled. Then he asks, "How's Zoe?" and I haven't a clue who she is and he explains that she's his girlfriend.'

John told him Zoe was doing fine. The lad, a shade older than Kenny, grinned and John describes watching him skip away down the wing of the secure psychiatric unit. It was the first time they had spoken. Usually the patients never so much as looked at each other. They just scuttled past, locked away in their own minds unless they chanced upon a celestial being with news from the other side.

It was February 2005 and John had been inside the high-security psychiatric wing of Blackpool Victoria Hospital since the turn of the year. He had no idea how much longer they would keep him here, out of sight among the fixed grins and milky eyes.

The wing, a 1960s annexe tucked behind the hospital, was where they sent the extreme cases: the nutjobs, the freaks, the incurables that no one wanted on the street. John, now forty-six, assumed he was probably in for life, consigned by the state as a danger to society. He could hardly blame them. Not after what he had done.

He recalled the night vividly, twelve months earlier, when he had stood on the porch of his family's house with a homemade bomb in his hand. He remembered the front lawn flashing blue under the strobe of the police cars and a uniformed figure approaching. Above, the bedroom light clicked on and he saw the faces of his wife and children pressed against the glass, staring down. The officer stopped and shouted: 'John, what is your intention?'

'Stay away, I don't want to live any more. I'm going to blow myself up,' said John.

The officer gestured towards the bomb, breath condensing in the cold: 'Please John, put it down.' The policeman seemed too casual, too rehearsed, thought John. 'Put it down John. Good man,' the officer said. But John wouldn't fall for that softly-softly training-manual bullshit. Corporal John McCairns Meighan of the King's Own Scottish Borderers had what it took. He squeezed the flask of flammable liquid in his hand.

Sergeant Clive Willacy would have felt apprehensive when the call came. It had been a relatively quiet night on the graveyard shift, but the emergency despatch at 2.45 a.m. on Tuesday 24 February 2004 was so unusual it could only spell trouble. His concerns would have been more than confirmed by the sight of a burning petrol bomb on the drive of 36 Compley Avenue, one of Poulton-le-Fylde's quieter suburbs.

Court documents including detailed witness statements from the officers who attended the scene record what happened next. At 2.55 a.m., the front door swung open to reveal a man Sergeant Willacy recognised immediately. As custody sergeant at Fleetwood's police station, he had come across John Meighan several times. 'He appeared very agitated and gave the impression he had been drinking. He then shut and locked the front door,' reads Willacy's official statement. Police Constable David Banks experienced a similar dread upon recognising John. 'I have had several dealings with Meighan in the past and knew he was quite an unstable man when he had been drinking.'

Two minutes later a downstairs window opened and John screamed that he would release his family, then 'set himself on fire'. A moment later the front door opened and Beverley appeared in her dressing gown, carrying Andrew and holding Alexander's hand. Both kids were wearing pyjamas. An officer escorted them away, past the burning petrol bomb, to a waiting patrol car.

At 3.04 a.m. the order was given to evacuate families from nearby homes. Two minutes later John opened the front door again and let out the family's two small dogs onto the frosted front lawn. 'Please take care of those dogs. One's a puppy, just be good to him,' the police logs record him saying.

The police were now certain John intended to kill himself. Through the glass squares of the front door Sergeant Willacy saw him pick up the bomb and disappear into the house. One officer observed John pacing manically around, while another peered through the kitchen windows to try to see if the gas stove was turned on. In another moment John appeared in the front doorway. 'In his right hand was a bottle with a piece of rag in the neck, he had a lighter in his left hand. I was about eight metres down the drive behind a small rubbish skip,' Sergeant Willacy recorded. He watched as John held the lighter towards the bomb. They stared at each other. John lit the fuse and stood with the bomb fizzing in his hand, the flame sneaking down towards the liquid. PC Ian Tyrell was hiding beside the front door. 'I saw his arm with the lighted petrol bomb swing out and the bomb flying towards Willacy.' There was shouting and a thunderous bang as the device exploded.

Sergeant Willacy survived. The bomb landed in the skip. Yet he was adamant John tried to target him. 'Meighan threw the firebomb, under arm, directly at me. I feared I would be burned.'

Beverley remembers sitting in the patrol car, her two sons shivering under a blanket, when she saw what looked like a firework hurtling from her home. 'I saw a lit petrol bomb come flying out the front door. I don't know who threw it or where it landed, I just saw the flicker of fire as it flew out,' she told the police.

The game was up for John the instant the explosive landed. Within moments the first officers pinned him to the floor, shoving his arms behind his back. He remembers being handcuffed, marched past the smouldering skip that was a sign of how right up until the end John had tried to turn things around. He had promised to build Beverley a new bathroom.

Almost twelve hours later, at 4.28 p.m. on 24 February,

John was summoned from his cell at Fleetwood police station for questioning. Transcripts of the interview conducted by Detective Constable Stuart Dixon go beyond a mere recollection of events, providing an illuminating insight into John's state of mind.

Initially his solicitor, Allan Cobain, attempts to soften the damage, citing his client's history in the armed forces, the PTSD diagnosis, his habit of picking unwinnable fights in order to 'take a beating'. Cobain describes the latter to Dixon as a form of self-harm. But it is only when John is asked why he made the petrol bombs in the first place that the scale of his anguish becomes evident. 'I would say that . . .' There is a pause as he gropes for the right words: 'It's how I think that society's let me down, given what I've done for this country and my queen and I've seen my mates dying. It's too much for me . . . It's too much.'

John breaks down. The transcript notes that he has become 'audibly upset recounting the visions of his experiences'. When he speaks again it is with the voice of someone recollecting an incomprehensible bereavement. He explains that he had become so desperate for help that he figured the only way he could receive urgent medical attention was by committing an outrageous act. The first bomb, he explains, was thrown to 'heighten the sense of urgency'. The second he deliberately threw into a skip.

DC Dixon asks why he told officers that he had a knife and was holding his family captive. John says he made that bit up. 'I did that again for the urgency. To make it more serious than it was.'

'Why did you want the police there?'

John answers immediately. 'I've been to the doctor's, I've been everywhere. I've been trying to get help. I'm not getting help and I thought that if I did something as serious as this then finally I'm gonna get the recognition and the help that I require before, God forbid, I do real damage to someone.'

'So,' says Dixon, 'your aim was to get arrested?'

'Yes, it was a cry for help.' John reiterates that he fabricated the knifepoint hostage situation and that he never had any intention of burning down the family home or hurting anyone.

DC Dixon explains that Willacy believed John deliberately threw the bomb at him. John insists he threw it into the skip so no one would be hurt. Dixon's tone hardens: 'You put yourself in his shoes. He doesn't know you're intending to throw it in the skip. You can appreciate how he would feel.'

'Absolutely!' cries John. 'Of course I can understand it.' He apologises profusely, adding that he never meant to scare anyone because he knows how dreadful fear is.

The interview lasted just twenty-four minutes. By early evening John was charged with 'applying a destructive or explosive substance with intent'. The irony didn't escape John. 'It made me sound like a goddamn terrorist. I'd spent my career fighting terrorism and suddenly I was practically labelled one.' His testimony was later considered sufficient by prosecutors to assemble a case that he threw the petrol bomb with 'intent to burn, maim, disfigure or disable police Sgt Clive Willacy or to do some grievous bodily harm to him'. John was also charged with affray, refused bail and remanded in custody.

Now after twelve months on remand he was in the 'psycho suite' at Blackpool Victoria, waiting to be sentenced. It was going to be hefty. Cobain had warned him to expect up to eight and a half years inside. He would miss his younger kids growing up, eighteen-year-old Kenny's progress in the army.

It had been a month since Kenny rang up with terrifying news. He was being posted to Iraq in six weeks, in April 2005, to Basra province where his battalion would help bolster stability as the rest of the country slid into a quasi-civil war. When his son asked for his advice John felt a fraud. 'But my circumstances didn't put Kenny off. He wanted as much guidance as possible.' Kenny was off to fight for democracy and freedom while John was going down for making bombs in his garage. In two months his son would be wrestling with the brutal ambiguities of battle and here he was, trapped in the funny farm, where the days were always the same.

At the time, Kenny admits, he was bewildered by his dad's disintegration. 'I couldn't really understand it. No one was talking about PTSD, I'd never heard of it to be honest. It was tough because I didn't really know what was happening. I stood by him of course. If you don't stand by your flesh and blood who are you? But back then I didn't know what was going on.'

The psychiatric ward at Blackpool Victoria operated a strict regime. At 8 a.m. John received his first hit of antidepressants, mirtazapine and amitriptyline, sometimes Prozac if he was a little jangly. He never asked if his doses were inordinately generous. It was protocol not to ask too many questions.

Breakfast preceded a long morning of doping about before the in-patients were herded for lunch in the small communal kitchen. They sat at trellis tables with laminate surfaces, like a school canteen, and played with plastic cutlery, snapping the utensils in their grip. The food was routinely wet, dolloped in plastic bowls where it left a greasy slick as it skidded to the bottom. Foodstuff considered capable of damage was reduced to the consistency of porridge so that when thrown it spattered harmlessly. Decrypting what might be lurking within the gloop became John's daily crossword. There were few clues. There was no distinguishable potato, or hard-edged carrots or obvious hunks of meat, although gristle could occasionally be detected. 'It was like the worst hospital food of the Seventies. At least the portions were baby-sized,' he said, and lunch brought respite from the monotony, a prompt for mischief. Some patients would scoop up the goo, using their spoons like miniature medieval catapults to flick dollops across the room. The less ambitious smeared the sludge down their front until their bibs ran full.

A second round of wet food began at 6 p.m. John played Monopoly and Scrabble on his own. He stared at Blackpool's Stanley Park from the locked windows and wished he was free, but the ward was locked and no amount of smooth talking could ever persuade the nurses to let him out, even for a ciggie.

He couldn't do anything without being watched, not

even talk to his family. When Kenny visited before heading off to Iraq, they squatted on plastic chairs in his cell, three paces wide by two, with a nurse in between, monitoring the conversation, making sure nothing passed between them.

Kenny was nervous. He wanted to know what it was like in the desert, the heat and the enemy tactics. John answered as best he could, careful to avoid the Highway of Death, the matchstick bodies piled on the pyres. 'But it was hard to have a proper conversation with a stranger listening. I felt completely dehumanised.'

He spent most of the time in his cell staring at the ceiling. There was no window, no pictures on the wall, no distractions. The cell was pure white – bright nothingness – the one bonus that it was not padded. There was just a sink, a locker and a narrow bed from where he listened to the moans of other patients drifting along the corridor at night. He wondered why he had been unable to process the horrors while others seemed completely unaffected. He accepted that the stresses and poverty of his childhood probably had played a role, but also questioned the influence of the cocktail of vaccines and nerve-gas pills he'd ingested under order before deployment to the Gulf.

In 1997 John would be diagnosed with Gulf War Syndrome, one of an estimated 6,700 British veterans exhibiting a panoply of debilitating symptoms linked to the campaign six years earlier. American researchers have linked rates of ill health among those who served in the Gulf to the combination of chemicals they were ordered to take, the same cocktail given to British soldiers. As evidence mounts that this link may be significant, the US government has steadily increased compensation to American veterans diagnosed as suffering from the condition. The British government, meanwhile, dismisses the syndrome as an 'umbrella' term, arguing that the range of symptoms implicated is too vast to be categorised under a single heading. Research the Ministry of Defence has discounted includes the 2004 findings of the Research Advisory Committee on Gulf War Veterans' Illnesses appointed by the US Congress and, five years later, another congressionally commissioned study which concluded that troops' ill health was caused by nerve-gas pills. John had decided long ago that the British government was looking for anything but evidence. 'They'll use every trick in the book to avoid paying out a penny more than they want.' Two decades on, many of those diagnosed with the syndrome are still battling to receive even a war pension.

John knew all about the ailments affecting fellow Gulf vets, the unexplained bouts of chronic fatigue, the odd rashes and strange marks on the body. When he returned home from the Highway of Death aged thirty-two he noticed the signs within weeks. The hair on the back of his calves vanished overnight. It never grew back. Then came the muscle and joint pains which he initially put down to years of humping heavy loads in the army.

But Gulf War Syndrome, and whether it had exacerbated his mental or physical decline, was a minor worry for John. It was his nightmare road trips that had brought him to the psychiatric ward. Even there they still came for him, the lipless Iraqis, Big Jim, gathering in the ether above his bed. John would will himself to remain calm, waiting for the mirtazapine and amitriptyline to kick in.

The controlled environment allowed little distraction. Respite was sought in the television, its default setting ITV. John's attempts to monitor the unfolding sectarian hostilities in Iraq ahead of Kenny's arrival went largely unfulfilled. His fellow patients cared little for geopolitics, preferring to absorb commercials for consumables they would never buy. There was no one to talk to. Most patients would do anything rather than enter conversation. John had tried, but weeks later he still had no idea where anyone came from or how they came to be here. No one connected one moment to the next. No one knew who they were. Once he asked the boy who had called him an angel whether he had heard anything from Zoe, but the patient stared back as if John was crazy. 'Most couldn't retain anything. I felt like Jack Nicholson in *One Flew Over the Cuckoo's Nest*.'

As the weeks passed, John said he sensed his grip on sanity loosening. The outside world was slipping away. Visitors were rare. Zoe was one of many who never showed. Beverley and the kids came, though, despite the end of their nine-year marriage. In the weeks after the petrol-bomb incident she had issued divorce proceedings. John couldn't blame her, he'd driven her away. 'I don't know how she put up with me for so long,' he said.

John turned to the nurses for company. He had been stripped of all personal possessions and was forbidden to carry a cigarette lighter. But he exploited his material poverty adeptly, asking staff if he could borrow a light before moving swiftly on to the weather, what was going on in the outside world, the latest from southern Iraq. The nurses were good value; they told John he shouldn't be inside. Even his psychiatrist had begun expressing alarm during his routine check-ups. 'He said that being in this place is doing me more harm than good. Rub shoulders with cases like these over a period of time and you tend to emulate them. Abnormal behaviour becomes normalised,' John said.

The ward's mental health specialist was familiar with John's condition, having studied the six independent psychiatric assessments commissioned by the court following his arrest. Some of the finest psychiatrists in the north of England had assessed him, including the Adult Forensic Mental Health Services at Prestwich Hospital and the Mersey Forensic Psychiatry Service. All had broadly reached the same conclusion. He had developed acute PTSD from his combat experiences combined with severe clinical depression. The ward psychiatrist also knew that shortly before arriving there, John had been sent for treatment at the Ty Gwyn residential care home in Llandudno, north Wales, in December 2004.

Ty Gwyn had developed legendary status among mental health experts, the only place in Britain prepared to take ex-military men from the criminal justice system and attempt to help them, the only place prepared to handle the most egregiously disturbed minds. The psychiatric community viewed Ty Gwyn as a safety valve for some of society's most volatile characters, a facility that could deal with veterans so damaged their condition was deemed too challenging for treatment in NHS mental health units.

The consultant psychiatrist who founded Ty Gwyn, Dafydd Alun Jones, considered John to be one of the most extreme cases he had evaluated. Dr Jones identified a perfect storm of causes. An unusually sensitive disposition had been exacerbated by the insecurity of John's childhood and the self-doubt sown by his alcoholic mother. Together, these encouraged introspection and tended to accentuate the impact of the things he saw in service. Another of John's character traits identified by Dr Jones was an unusually developed belief in good versus bad. John was convinced that good would always prevail. Perversely, this value system had worsened his condition. He was incapable of rationalising or accepting that some deaths were futile. A final complicating factor was John's unconditional conviction that the hallowed institutions of queen and country would never let him down.

'He was in a bad way when he arrived, but he responded amazingly well to treatment,' said Dr Jones. 'He was so determined to get better and so grateful to be receiving help. All the staff took to him, they all loved John. He showed signs of getting much better, he was desperate to turn the corner.' And John was turning the corner when the money ran out. After he had spent two weeks at Ty Gwyn the Lancashire primary care trust funding his treatment suddenly pulled the plug. John was forced to leave. The decision made no sense financially; Ty Gwyn charged no more than NHS psychiatric wards. It would have cost £9,600 for John to receive a full course of treatment, the same amount that it cost to detain him inside Blackpool Victoria's psychiatric wing. 'The nurses were distraught, some were in tears because John had come such a long way. He had really bonded with them,' said Dr Jones.

John credits Ty Gwyn for giving him the first hope that he could be saved. But he would never get the chance to return. Three months after treating John, Ty Gwyn announced it was closing. Local health authorities had begun reducing the number of cases they were sending to the facility, despite the NHS admitting it lacked the specialist help to care for traumatised veterans. The decision shattered Dr Jones's lifetime dream of a retreat where those mentally impaired in the line of duty could be helped. 'It was a source of great personal grief. It meant there was no facility where men with these awful problems could be treated.' The decision left more than 1,500 army personnel enduring acute combat PTSD without effective support.

John was far from the first veteran to thank Dr Jones for demonstrating that he wasn't a lost cause. The psychiatrist's dedication was legendary. One veteran had gone to the Severn Bridge determined to jump into the perilous tidal pull of the river below. At 4 a.m. he called Dr Jones from the bridge to leave a message apologising for his actions. But the psychiatrist answered and told him to wait. That night Dr Jones drove across Wales and brought him back to Ty Gwyn, to a place where he might get better. Yet by the end of the year, Ty Gwyn was sold to a private developer for flats.

The judge in charge of John's case had been adamant that John needed counselling, not prison. Andrew Gilbart QC had read the psychiatric assessments and was sure this was a case in which the judiciary could demonstrate its ability to help those who deserved it. He understood the role of the military and believed society had a debt to those who served. He also had strong views on psychiatric recovery, at the time serving on a mental health review of criminals who were detained in hospital for therapy instead of being jailed without support. To Gilbart, John's predicament provided a perfect case study to demonstrate the power of rehabilitation. During the spring of 2004 he wrote to the Lancashire primary care trust recommending that John's treatment be funded under sections 37 and 41 of the Mental Health Act, granting him long-term care while detained in a secure hospital. The health trust, which spent more than £25 million a year on mental health services, flatly rejected the judge's proposal. They would not pay for John's therapy even if that meant he was imprisoned for years without psychiatric help. At one point, health officials claimed they were too busy to attend court and explain their decision.

John was sentenced on 25 February 2005 at Preston Crown Court. In the public gallery were Dr Jones and some of his team, who had journeyed from Wales to offer their support. But there was no Kenny, away on pre-deployment exercises as he prepared to enter war for the first time. This time the director of the primary care trust had turned up. Judge Gilbart asked whether the trust had found the money that would spare John prison and grant him the care required to rebuild his life. The court transcripts of the hearing have been destroyed, but John and Dr Jones both told me how, once again, the trust refused to help. When the judge pressed for a reason, it was explained that they could not afford it. Gilbart countered that the government readily found the money when they sent him to war. John recalled: 'He seemed genuinely irritated and said: "Is it right that I should send a man to prison who served his country with honour and that he should suffer the consequences of that service?"'

Gilbart then explained that since the primary care trust would not pay he had only one option. John describes the judge turning slowly towards him, gesturing to him to stand. John leapt to attention, back straight, jaw out. 'It is with great regret that I send you to prison today for five and a half years with a recommendation to the Home Secretary that you are transferred to hospital as soon as possible.'

Sixty-six months inside. He was taken down.

At least he was on his own, no mean feat in the most overcrowded jail in the land. But he had nothing whatsoever to put in his cell. He had lost everything. There wasn't even the chance of a television in his cell to distract him; they cost fifty pence a week to hire.

Cigarettes were out of the question. John spent the first few weeks scrabbling about in the prison smoking areas picking up dog-ends. Fortunately they were practically ankle-deep. The place was rammed. Preston prison had a capacity of 453 but at the time its dilapidated Victorian wings held 750 criminals. Nine out of ten single cells were shared.

Although John's prison sentence included a judicial request for him to be transferred to hospital for treatment, it soon became evident that that would take time, if it happened at all. He began socialising with other inmates and quickly made a shocking discovery. His own kind were everywhere. One was a sandy-haired sailor who had served in the 1982 Falklands campaign. John remembers he had a mournful air and didn't care for small talk. Rumour suggested he was in for beating up a copper, but John never got the chance to find out. Overnight the sailor was taken from the category B prison and deposited somewhere else in the criminal justice estate.

Sailors had it bad, thought John. Most assumed they just lolled about on the ocean, but he knew the Royal Navy had endured 'horrendous stuff' during the Falklands. Eighteen months after John met the sailor in Preston prison, the Royal Navy hospital at Haslar in Portsmouth was closed. Dating back to 1792, it was the last place dedicated to treating sailors with mental health problems. Now they had nowhere. 'Sailors were better off coming home from the Napoleonic wars two hundred years ago,' said John.

Another Falklands veteran had served in the 2nd Battalion of the Parachute Regiment and when he talked to John it was as if he had never left the windswept summit of Goose Green, the famous battle of May 1982. His story began crouched in the trenches above Falklands Sound, the night's cold freezing his joints. The order came to go over the top and he ran into the dark towards the Argentinian positions. He remembers lobbing a grenade into their trenches, jumping down and meeting a young soldier with lamblike eyes. He jabbed his bayonet into the boy's stomach and the lad stared at him, big glossy eyes that wanted an answer. The battle for Goose Green raged for thirty-six hours but the ex-paratrooper said that another thirty-six years could pass and he would still be staring at the Argentinian with the lamblike eyes.

The prison walls could not stop the boy appearing, nothing could, he said. Goose Green changed everything. He left the Paras two years later and for the last ten years had been in and out of prison for violent offences he refused to talk about. 'You've got PTSD,' John told him, and he recalls the guy laughing. He had never heard of it. 'Get in touch with Combat Stress,' said John. Weeks later the para's former colonel visited John in prison for more information about Combat Stress and whether it could save his old pal. John never discovered whether it had. The ex-para was transferred at the end of the month. 'He badly needed help. I could recognise his trajectory, down and down until he either took his life or someone else's.'

Circumstances meant that keeping in touch with Kenny was problematic. Often John would be left to guess how he was getting on. Counting down the days of Kenny's tour in Iraq became more of a preoccupation than counting down his own sentence. He spent hours wondering if the al-Mahdi militia's reported attempts to turn Basra into a bloodbath had amounted to anything. He prayed that his eighteen-year-old son would not endure his own Goose Green moment or, worse still, follow his father to prison.

The men he met made John sympathetic to the Falklands survivors. They had returned home victorious, cheered from the docksides, but the world moved on while they remained chained to historic events. Those inside Preston prison had received no counselling. They suffered in silence. Starved of help, unable to speak out, Britain's Falklands vets had quietly killed themselves in their hundreds.

Studies suggest that those who serve in combat zones are three times more likely to commit suicide than their civilian peers, but the fate of the Falklands cohort indicates the ratio is far worse for those who feel they cannot publicly admit they have a problem. More men who served in that conflict have killed themselves than died during hostilities. Britain's death toll during the campaign stands at 255, but the South Atlantic Medals Association group say around three hundred veterans – the equivalent of half a battalion of fighting men – have died by their own hand since the Argentinian surrender in June 1982.

The government does not dispute the tally. It cannot because it has no idea. Ministers have never commissioned a study or attempted to keep a tally of what happened to the Falklands veterans, despite warnings from military doctors that thousands were suffering from PTSD. One indicator of the problem's scale is a little-known study by a Parachute Regiment medical officer in 1987 who found that half the Falklands paras he studied exhibited symptoms of the disorder.

In John's eyes the men who took their own lives were as much victims of the war as those killed in action. 'The government prefers to forget those who die away from the battlefield. They see it as another guy who's killed himself because times are hard, nothing to do with their service. If I had succeeded in committing suicide my death would have been recorded as having nothing to do with the military. But it's when you leave the services, long after the event itself, when the ruminating starts. When you're in the services you can cope together, you drink together. It's once you're on your own that the clock starts ticking.'

Inside Britain's prison estate, John was not on his own. A 2009 study by the National Association of Probation Officers discovered 8,500 veterans were inmates, nine per cent of the total prison population. There were almost as many former service personnel in jail as there were troops fighting in Afghanistan. In addition, another twelve thousand ex-servicemen and women were on probation or parole; at any one time more than twenty thousand ex-soldiers, sailors and air force personnel were moving through Britain's criminal justice system. Another group, Veterans in Prison, calculates the number of former members of the armed forces in prison at nine thousand, a proportion comparable to the vast numbers of former military employees within the US penitentiary system.

Attempts to research the problem using official data have been notoriously difficult. Each government department claimed the issue was not their responsibility and so none had quantified the problem. Finally, in early 2010 the Ministry of Defence announced it would clarify the debate once and for all. Its study found that fewer than three thousand inmates were former veterans, under three per cent – a figure conspicuously lower than those of other studies.

Billing theirs as the most comprehensive study of its kind to date, the MoD press release omitted to explain that its calculations were based on incomplete data. It failed to mention that full names and dates of birth were available in only two-thirds of cases, that its researchers were unable to track people by aliases or other name changes, that it took no account of the vast number of reservists and that no checks were even conducted on the huge numbers who had served before the mid-1970s. The MoD explained the discrepancy by claiming that many prisoners pretend to be former soldiers, yet gave no corroborating evidence.

At around the same time an independent audit of three prisons in January 2010 found 10.8 per cent of inmates were veterans. A pilot study at HMP Dartmoor found an even higher proportion, revealing that ex-service personnel constituted seventeen per cent of those kept within its barbed-wire perimeter. But the most shocking data had yet to surface. Six months later a unique pilot study was launched by Kent Police to ascertain the true magnitude of the problem. The officer supervising the research expected to find, at most, thirty veterans a month passing through the force's custody suites. He recorded twenty-two on the first day. Over three months, Kent Police arrested 232 ex-service personnel, seventy-three for violent offences. Almost four in ten were unemployed. Kent Police is one of forty-three forces in England and Wales, suggesting the potential number of veterans arrested each year could run into the tens of thousands.

It was obvious to John why the Lancashire primary care trust had refused to pay for his treatment. There were simply too many cases like his. If they helped him, they risked having to help thousands more. A calculation had been made. They hadn't ignored him after all, John concluded. Right from the start the state had done its sums and decided it wouldn't help. The government could stump up the estimated £150,000 required to keep a soldier in Afghanistan for a tour but the cost of attempting to repair any resultant psychological damage was considered too high. Too much manpower was needed, too much hands-on help, too many resources. It was more straightforward to pay the £46,000 required to keep a person in prison for a year. Let the criminal justice system carry the burden; the penal system can soak them up. Once they were inside, they'd stop asking for counselling and rehab. 'The government must have hoped we'd be forgotten. Rather than rehabilitate, they had decided to lock us up and throw away the key,' said John.

The months passed and more veterans may have moved through the prison, but if so John failed to notice. Partly through routine but mainly through medication, his experience of jail became increasingly obscure. It felt as though his dosage had been upped. Navigating the vast Victorian prison was like wading through treacle, his thoughts in fog. 'They weren't afraid of using the liquid cosh,' said John. The authorities administered such powerful sedatives that he could only climb out of bed at unlocking times, wander in the yard, eat a bit, dribble in front of the TV. Even if he had wanted to start a riot or make a bid for freedom he couldn't. 'I was permanently docile, but that's what they do, ramp it up until you are so blissed out you're no bother to anyone', he said. It was the same for most inside, the majority of inmates dabbling in the steady influx of narcotics. The only difference was that John's pusher was state-sponsored.

Had he been able, John could have got an NVQ in industrial cleaning or sports studies. One prison course was called 'thinking skills', which he couldn't have attempted had his freedom depended on it. Another was called 'life and social skills' and John remembers joking that he could have done with a refresher.

One major item of meaningful news that filtered through the mental miasma came from Kenny. He was alive. It had been a pretty uneventful tour by the sound of things. No decent action, more peacekeeping – he said that he hadn't once fired his rifle in anger. But that was Kenny all over, John thought. If he had plucked a kid from a raging house fire he would have said it was barely alight.

John passed the three-hundred-day milestone inside and although Preston was known for its transient population, the prison authorities kept him there, aware that if he was sent elsewhere he might get lost in the system. And once you were lost in the system you were even less likely to get help.

His release came suddenly. A successful appeal reduced his sentence to three and a half years. When the news arrived John had ten days left to serve. In January 2006 he was declared a free man. The only problem was that he had nowhere to go: no home, no family. Reluctantly he was transferred to Preston's Priory Hospital for the treatment he still desperately required. Even there, the treatment lacked the specialist skills required to improve his extreme psychological condition. No matter: John was held in the Priory for four and a half months, at a cost of £550 a day to the same health authority that had previously refused to help him. The total bill came to £74,250, nearly eight times the amount Dr Jones had needed.

The council found him some digs on Cavendish Road up on Blackpool's North Shore, away from the rock candy and kiss-me-quick headgear. His euphoria was shortlived. The bedsit was appalling. Rain seeped through the window, fostering fresh fungal blooms across the carpet. Damp stained the walls. There was no heating, oven or functioning sink. As the short summer of 2006 drew in, John spent the nights shivering on the sofa in a Woolworths nylon sleeping bag, listening to the all-night bedlam in the flat above. It was a smack den. People came and went at all hours, falling against his flimsy door on their fuddled descent downstairs. 'Each time they banged against the door, I'd sit bolt upright. My nerves were shot.'

For a time he had been happy, walking along the promenade, smelling the salt air, transfixed by the vastness of the horizon. But as months passed, John began to retreat inside himself. A familiar sense of futility returned. He was jobless, homeless, estranged from his family and in possession of a criminal record that made him sound like a terrorist. He had his medication to blur the edges of his existence and benefits to buy drink, but his appetite faded. In the space of three months John shed four stone. Petite at the best of times, he practically shrivelled up. His reflection, he said, reminded him of those shrunken heads in anthropological museums. He was dying.

When Corporal Ian Harvey found John he weighed not much more than seven stone. Harvey and John went back to the beginning. Harvey had been there during the Derryard checkpoint attack in 1989. His section, patrolling nearby, had turned up and managed to force the IRA to retreat from the compound, past the body of Big Jim, and back across the border. Harvey was awarded the Distinguished Conduct Medal for his actions.

Harvey was increasingly worried that John had gone AWOL following his release from prison and, using a council contact, had managed to track down his pal. Harvey, still serving in the King's Own Scottish Borderers, could hardly believe that the frail figure he found lying in the sleeping bag was the same erudite, wisecracking intelligence operative that used to boss him around.

'Get up,' Harvey said. 'Get up! You are better than this. Get your shit together, you're coming with me.' Harvey had a spare flat, also by the sea, 250 miles away on the other side of England, in Clacton-on-Sea in Essex. The heating worked, the walls had no mildew and the nearest crack den was at least a street away. But the greatest draw was to come. 'You'll be near Kenny,' he said.

Harvey adored Kenny like his own son. Like John, he had plenty of photographs of the three of them, some in matching military combats when Kenny was a kid, all standing to attention, mud smeared on their cheeks like storybook Red Indians. 'Come on, let's go and see Kenny', said Harvey.

9

Night March

Kenny usually called home before a high-risk patrol. The men were granted twenty minutes' phone time a week and hoarded them up to use before the operations they considered particularly fraught. The etiquette for calling home was always the same. Keep the tone nice and light so you don't scare your loved ones: Sam, the folks, grandpa. Water down the truth. No outright lies, just enough to take the edge off. The most important rule was never – never, ever – to let on how afraid you were. Some of the men overcompensated: 'Hey mum, been out swimming in the stream, it was lush. Hotter than Spain today. Anyway surf's up, gotta go. Love ya.'

Kenny's section was due out on night patrol, pushing south from Sangin into a place the enemy appeared determined to hold. He felt the urge to call his dad and hear his take on a conflict that was growing uglier each day. But first he had to rehearse his thoughts, fine-tune his presentation of the war. It was critical he kept the balance between asking for guidance and maintaining the illusion that things weren't really so bad. His dad relished offering counsel: Kenny could always expect encouragement from him. He reckoned it stemmed from his dad's eagerness to avoid the mistakes of his own mum, who had belittled her 'soldier boy' instead of supporting him.

Eventually, Kenny had it all mapped out. He would start by asking how the flat in Clacton-on-Sea was shaping up. His dad had moved into Harvey's spare apartment ten months earlier, in October 2006. He was keeping the place immaculate, cleaning it so regularly that Kenny caught the whiff of bleach whenever he had come round during his pre-Afghan training. He was saving £12 a month for a decent new television. John had even started working out, putting weight back on.

Kenny would ask what his dad had been up to, the weather, the football, and of course, ask after his Jack Russell, Rosie. If his dad mentioned Britain's mounting death toll, the flag-draped coffins, the recent research showing that the numbers being seriously injured and killed on the front line were comparable to those of the Second World War, he would blame the media, over-sensationalising as usual. The enemy are good fighters, he would explain, but we're driving them back, Dad, they're on the back foot! But his dad was canny and Kenny feared he'd see through the bluffing. After all, his father had done the same to his parents.

There was a sharp tapping sound, then a slow wobbly hum as if the signal was uncertain. An automated voice told him he had eight minutes of credit remaining for the week. Kenny imagined the plastic brown phone in his dad's living room, behind it the photographs of the two of them with Harvey, grinning in their combat fatigues. The phone was ringing out. Where the hell was he? The beeps faltered, then segued into a continuous drone. Maybe his dad had gone out, maybe it was a hot day and he was wandering around Magic City with Rosie, watching the seagulls from the pier.

In fact, the meticulous care which John had invested in his new home had been spectacularly undone. In the corner of the lounge, lying on its back, was the new television, its screen smashed. The framed photographs of Kenny, Harvey and his dad were torn from the wall, some of them lying broken on the carpet. One picture, the day Kenny and John made a military camp by the River Colne, had almost completely disintegrated, as if a boot heel had stamped repeatedly on the image. The wall was spattered with blood.

Bait Platoon dreaded night patrols. Each one promised something to spook them and this was no different. The mission was to push deep into the green zone near Waterloo, close to the cornfield where Kenny and his section had almost died and which had since attained a mythical, lurid reputation among the men.

Night patrols freaked the senses. Through night-vision gear the world became a shifting sea of green. Dark greens denoted shadows while a dazzling fluorescence flared at every light source. Neon dots studded the sky. It gave the impression that light objects were much closer than they actually were. A moonlit branch would loom close but when Kenny reached to push it away he groped only air.

Most disconcerting was how the night-vision goggles corrupted perspective. The foreground reared up like a ramp while faraway objects retreated. Peripheral vision phased out to a green blur: it was like peering through a moss-lined tunnel. The goggles also flattened the land. Ditches and hollows lost their depth, giving Kenny constant palpitations as he stepped out expecting solid land but found his foot falling as if stepping from a cliff. He distrusted the night-vision equipment. It disarmed his senses, rendering him detached from the land he was supposed to read. If he was going to die surely it would be at night, floundering in the pea-soup fog.

He never told Sam about the night marches. It would be impossible to disguise his concerns. He concentrated on pushing her presence to the back of his mind. Only the clearest minds could negotiate nighttime near Waterloo.

One of the most awkward tasks was negotiating the narrow bridges that crossed the irrigation channels. Twenty minutes in he found a beauty. It was barely six inches wide, a log like a large Cadbury's Flake laid above the black distant depths. Kenny crept across like a tightrope walker, his rifle horizontal to help balance the weight of his pack. He settled down among bushes on the far side to wait for the others.

At first he thought it might be a moonbeam, but the column of light jerked suddenly and Kenny watched as it danced through a distant treeline. The beam moved again, sharply, flashing quickly in his direction. The shaft, so bright it was almost white, sliced sideways through the night, so close it seemed to be right in front of his face.

Kenny knelt down, following the light as it moved through the foliage until it abruptly vanished. A shape appeared to be ambling through the undergrowth close by. The fuzzy form of a human slowly appeared, a streak of light protruding from its hip. Kenny realised it was a torch. From its glow he recognised the familiar outline of an AK-47. Behind the figure was the outline of a large compound, possibly an enemy fortress with Lord knows how many more fighters holed up inside. The figure began heading slowly towards the bridge. Kenny glanced over his shoulder, watching his section move along the log, glowing in the moonlight, lined up like ducks in a fairground shoot.

The sentry approached, slowing down as if sensing trouble. With a surge of panic, Kenny saw the beam of light slice towards the bridge. He lowered his weapon. If he fired, the enemy would come pouring from the compound. In moments, Olly, Hardy, Hicksy – his entire section – would be butchered mid-crossing.

Kenny could never explain what happened next, what impelled him to do what he did. Afterwards he could only say that a 'weird feeling' overcame him. He stood up and began running towards the man with the torch. He remembers the beam sweeping towards him, a blinding flash that, through his goggles, turned the world into a white-out. Kenny dived headfirst into the pool of light. He remembers grabbing hold of the man's neck from behind, then pulling him down, jabbing him in the midriff with his elbow. The man doubled up, his torch tumbling to the floor. They both fell, grappling in the bushes. Then Kenny was on top, the man's pupils rushing towards him. Footsteps came from behind. He turned. It was Private Sam Hicks and suddenly Hicksy was on him too, knee across the man's legs, one hand over his mouth, the other around his throat, pressing down on the squirming body.

Kenny rolled off, leaving Hicks to apprehend the man, and moved towards the compound. The door was ajar and he slipped inside. A strip of light spilled from an entrance at the back. He crept closer, counting the shadows of bodies against the light. They stopped moving, as if they dared not stir or talk. Perhaps they had heard the commotion and were wondering how to react, Kenny thought.

There was a cough and the shadows began to stretch. Someone was approaching the doorway. Kenny hid behind the door as it swung open. A man appeared. Kenny punched him hard in the face and then pulled him by the neck as he rushed into the room. He saw another man in the corner, two AK-47s on the floor beside him. 'I dragged one guy to the floor and put my gun to the side of the other guy's face. He couldn't believe what he was seeing.'

The rest of the section burst in moments later. The suspects were arrested and escorted back to Sangin for interrogation. Kenny never learnt whether they revealed any secrets, but that wasn't the point for him. 'They were Taliban, but we didn't take them out. You don't always have to kill.'

John's hopes of an early night were already gone by the time he heard the noises outside. First the splash of liquid against his front door. It had happened before. Someone was pissing against the entrance to 4 Pallister Road, his new home. The splattering was followed by a thud, as if whoever stood outside was so drunk they had collapsed headfirst against the doorway. 'By that stage I was getting to my wits' end. The whole town seemed to be on the swally,' said John. An hour earlier he had been woken by fighting outside the late-night kebab joint, the Buffalo Cafe, behind his bedroom. It was August bank holiday, Clacton-on-Sea-style. The resort was mayhem as closing time neared.

There was another bang on his door, louder this time. A rapid hammering noise followed, growing in intensity until it was incessant. John felt sick with anxiety. The frenzied knocking sound took him back to Crossmaglen. Outside the paramilitaries had come to drag him away. The next thing he remembers is losing his temper and yanking open his first-floor window.

Three figures stood beside his entrance, one fat, two thin. He bellowed at them to 'stop fucking pissing on my door' and that they had 'no fucking manners'. John recalls the smell of booze drifting up. Their insolence, their lack of apology, infuriated him. He screamed at them again, that he 'fought for your fucking country' and the least he expected was some fucking respect.

It had the opposite effect. It seemed to ignite something frenzied, hateful, in the men below. John thought he heard something like 'fucking army bastard'. He definitely heard them shouting: 'Let's see how fucking hard you are.'

The fat man began manically kicking the door, occasionally stepping back to throw his considerable weight at it. John could see its flimsy panels bending inwards. The others joined in, taking turns to run up and hurl themselves at the door. John had only just realised they were actually trying to break in when there was a crack as the fat man's boot burst through the wood and the sound of splintering as he fell into the hallway. He opened the door from the inside and the others came on in. There was a pause, then heavy footsteps, closer and closer as they climbed the staircase.

John shut the lounge door, shaking as he had done on Bonfire Night twelve years earlier. Maybe, he remembers thinking, maybe they could talk this through. There had been a bit of a misunderstanding. Perhaps they could chat over a cup of tea.

The footsteps stopped as the intruders reached the landing, its floorboards creaking as they moved closer, past his Gulf War wallchart, his medals. Eleven tours. They hesitated outside the lounge. John heard them panting, shifting their weight from one foot to the other. There was a burst of hard sudden laughter. John heard them whispering about what they would do to the cunt.

He remembers sitting on the sofa, trying to appear as passive as possible but conscious that he had started to tremble violently. The door swung open and the men burst inside. The larger one first, probably in his mid-thirties, followed by his pair of scrawny younger sidekicks. They towered over him, blocking out the light, the fumes of alcohol overpowering. Even among the crazies in Blackpool Victoria, John said he had never seen such demented expressions. He tried to remonstrate, explaining that he wanted no bother, that he'd fix the door. One of the skinny lads kicked his television screen, shaking his boot free from the hollowed box as it tumbled off its stand. The big one asked him if he still thought he was a fucking hard man. John thinks they might have called him a 'fucking soldier boy', the same insult his mother once used.

They threw the photographs of Kenny off the wall and

stamped on them. They moved to the CD rack, destroying his collection of war documentaries and old classics, the Cary Grants, the Charlton Hestons. The fat man hoisted the rack above his head and brought it down on John's skull.

It felt like the back of his head broke open. Instinctively he curled into a ball on the couch. One of them, which one he has no idea, grabbed a table lamp and started thwacking his body. He tried holding his arms aloft to soften the blows but the ornament was too heavy. His attackers grew more intent, they no longer spoke, concentrating on the assault.

He woke on the sofa, drenched in blood. Around 2 a.m. he called 999 and was taken to Colchester General Hospital, just down from the ward where Kenny was born. They gave him four stitches for the head wound where the CD rack had sliced through his scalp, and glued his broken elbow together.

The police never caught the men, never even checked his flat for DNA, according to John. He reckoned his attackers were out-of-towners, probably up from London for the bank holiday.

John was typically sanguine about the attack, principally relieved that it was Kenny's mother's turn to look after Rosie the dog that weekend. 'They would have booted the fuck out of her, smashed her off the wall. It could have been worse – they could have had knives. Barmpots, the three of them. They could have easily killed me.' There was a time when John had actively tried to get killed by strangers, but not any more, not with his new life in Essex. Things had started to seem a little brighter of late.

Kenny heard about the attack the following day. John, appreciating it was his turn to convince a loved one not to worry, tried to sound phlegmatic. Thank goodness, he thought, that Kenny couldn't see the back of his scalp, the neat row of blood-encrusted stitches, the mottled bruising that ran down his shoulders, his arm in a sling.

The news made Kenny fume about the lowlife of England, the 'headcases' who poisoned the towns he knew. The irony did not elude him. 'I was over there to protect Britain from terrorists and my dad is attacked by idiots in his front room. I'd send the bastards who did it to Afghanistan, see how long they'd survive.' It made him miss all his loved ones even more. The tour ended in six weeks and he hoped nothing awful would happen to Sam in the meantime. Lately Kenny had started to imagine seeing her during daytime patrols, coyly standing by the trail waiting for him. Sometimes he almost winked at her. At other times he pretended that she was gliding by his side.

But it was up in the air, in the Chinooks, that he imagined Sam most vividly. Amid the roar of the rotors and rattling metal, relieved temporarily from the pressures of point, it was safe to think about her. The soldiers sat in facing rows, some looking terrified, fingers fiddling with their chinstraps. But Kenny loved the choppers and the inevitable appearance of Sam. Above the flat fields and smooth desert, he could see elements of her that he struggled to recollect on the ground: her smile, her slim wrists. He reminded himself how pretty she was.

When the Chinook began its descent, Sam disappeared. The men's faces opposite hardened as the chopper dropped. Kenny vowed to write more letters: he'd brief Denning when they got back to base, that's what he would do: But such plans could wait: dust was pouring into the helicopter, they were almost down. Above the din was shouting, the collective clicking of rifle safety catches being flicked off. Then a heavy jolt and the men began scurrying towards the sandstorm outside, past the searing heat of the engines, wondering what was waiting for them.

10

Blue-Eyed Wolves

The longer the war went on, the stranger it became. The patrols grew more surreal, the firefights steadily more ferocious. Kenny would not see the enemy properly for weeks on end. Over time the suspicion grew that they were locked in combat against a spectral force, apparitions who would shoot from distant compounds and dissolve into the land.

Yet they knew they were out there; the men listened to them squawking down the Icomm system. The enemy sounded crazed. Some of the stuff they talked about was pure madness: references to mysterious rockets that they rode, fire-breathing dragons in the sky and midget men who inhabited the recesses of the green zone. Once they listened to the enemy watching a remote-controlled surveillance plane; they concluded it must be piloted by a hamster because it was too small to fit a human. They heard of plots to assassinate Tony Blair and claims to be holding the US president hostage in a village near Sangin. Frequent references were made to 'blue-eyed wolves', which Bait Platoon interpreted as meaning them.

Most of the enemy were cunning fighters and capable of making several sophisticated flanking manoeuvres in a single skirmish, but others sounded smacked out and

Kenny reckoned they probably were. Colleagues corroborated each other's accounts of wild figures hanging in the treelines before battle. During seat-of-your pants exchanges Kenny swore he saw enemy fighters cackling like witches, belly-deep guffawing as if combat was the best trip around. Once they found syringes and spoons, the paraphernalia of a junkie's bedsit, in a Taliban hideout.

Bait Platoon usually talked about regular things like women and football. But as the war rumbled on, talk turned to the future. They discussed what they'd do when they got out. Kenny talked about the woman waiting for him, how much they had to do together. They had all heard of men who were killed days before they were due to fly back or who arrived home without legs because their final patrol took an unlucky turn. But it seemed to Kenny that the closer they got to leaving Helmand, the more men allowed their loved ones in. He noticed Hardy and Denning in particular spending more time writing letters, queuing for the phone. He detected a new pensiveness in the movements of the older men, the fathers.

In between the talk of football and women, the soldiers adopted a ritual, late at night after a meal from Menu B, of swapping tales of the gunfights that bound them closer. They had plenty of material. Brigade command estimated every frontline soldier in the battalion had been involved in at least forty violent clashes. As a whole the battalion had been in 350 close-range firefights, throwing more than five hundred hand grenades and shooting more than a million bullets. Every member of Bait Platoon had accumulated a rich repertoire of war stories. They would start by sharing the things they had learnt in Afghanistan. They knew that a man could go on living with part of his skull missing. How a scrap of hot shrapnel can slice a leg clean in two. What a roadside bomb does to a human. The smell of the dead; how some bodies kept their blood while others couldn't wait to let it all go. They knew a man could drag himself to safety with his legs blown off, recalling how one afternoon an Afghan army officer had crawled on his stumps. They had seen men with their eyes missing, their jaws missing, their faces gone. Sometimes they would laugh about the day when a bullet bounced off Badger's chest and whether it had actually enhanced his sex appeal. They developed their own vocabulary to describe what they had seen. Men killed were zapped, waxed, slotted, smashed and wasted. They described heavy contacts, crackpot contacts, fuck-me-I-nearly-died contacts. And they discussed how gunfire sounded. Kenny's favourite was 'duff', others went 'kerpow' like in old movies.

Each had felt a fear they never knew existed. Pre-combat anxiety bordered on the unbearable, the period when they knew it was inevitable but had no choice other than to wait for the trees to start firing. Many of the men, Kenny included, admitted feeling acute nausea in those moments, a heaving sense of foreboding like the start of your worst exam multiplied by a million. Yet they kept it together. None of them revealed their dread. A panicked glance, they knew, would transfer among the men like a rash. In the vacuum of peace before a firefight they learnt to look each other in the eye, their insides a mess.

But there was one thing they never talked about. They

never talked about winning. They never talked about whether the war was being won or even if it was winnable. It was too big a question to comprehend. Privately, some conceded they were unsure what the war was about. Was it actually about stopping the flow of heroin into Essex or preventing suicide bombers in Colchester? Was it a titanic clash of ideologies, of civilisations, or an audacious land grab? Emancipation or occupation?

They realised their place in the war and accepted the bigger questions would be left to others, that it was silly to delve too deep when there was fighting to be done. The moral basis of the war mattered little to Bait Platoon. It was not their problem.

Yet as the war rumbled on, Kenny became doubtful. Parliament debated the need to reduce the amount of heroin entering the UK, but all around the fields swayed with red poppy buds. Opium production in Helmand reached record levels during his tour. Eradicating the enemy would make Britain safer, they said, but Kenny saw that their presence galvanised their opponents. The longer they were in Helmand, the more fighters poured into the province. The enemy's knowhow evolved, forever adopting fresh guerrilla tactics that forced a constant reappraisal of British strategy. By early autumn, an assignment that had initially seemed daunting but exotic had descended into a wearying stalemate. But the men could never afford to dwell on the war's worth or wonder if their blood would drain into the dry dirt for an ill-defined foreign escapade. That, they knew, was the mainline route to madness. Within weeks of arriving, even the most idealistic members of

Bait Platoon had ceased talking about the wider picture. The enemy was upon them.

Yet among the senior officers the conversation regularly turned to the same question: 'Do you think it is winnable?' The obstacles, they agreed, were stacked high. Progress, by comparison, seemed stunted. Few of those who asked seemed sure of success. Some sensed it was possible, others calculated at what cost, but they all knew more young men from Britain would die. The nagging dread that they might die in vain was palpable even then. Back in Whitehall the defence briefings of the time ducked the question, choosing largely to focus upon the simple, heartening word 'progress'. There was lots of it apparently. Progress in the reconstruction of schools, progress in the provision of fresh irrigation ditches, progress in the advancement of local governance. The establishment of several women's groups in Lashkar Gah was considered particularly progressive. Things were never easy but that was the *nature* of progress.

Closer analysis exposed a darker reality that summer. Below the surface was a growing sense of confusion. The Foreign Office and the Department for International Development talked about reconstruction, stressing how Britain had been invited to 'rebuild and develop a country'. The Prime Minister stuck rigidly to the theme of preventing Helmand 'exporting terrorism to Britain's streets'. The MoD reported various tactical successes but was increasingly preoccupied with issuing statements that began: 'It is with sadness that the Ministry of Defence must confirm the death of a soldier from . . .'

And what of the enemy? No one even seemed sure how

many were out there. Briefings in London twelve months earlier had placed the number of Taliban as low as a thousand. Yet Kenny's battalion had alone killed that number, the nature of certifying 'kills' suggesting their real tally was considerably greater. By any calculation, the enemy should all be dead. Instead they were becoming more deadly.

As the summer wore on, the patrols kept going out. Each time, Kenny would shed a little more weight, lose another part of the fresh-faced youth who had arrived in Afghanistan. The other side grew wilier. Kenny knew he was watched from the moment he left base. Once they cleared a compound near Tank Graveyard only for the enemy to plant fresh mines almost straight away. An unfortunate guardsman stood upon one of the devices an hour later. Kenny saw his leg lying on the other side of the courtyard. As he knelt to apply the tourniquet, the man leant forward and began punching Kenny repeatedly in the side of the head. 'He was in so much agony, he'd lost his mind. He was screaming like a fucking madman as he hit me.' A medic arrived, grabbing the guardsman in a headlock as Kenny tried to staunch the flow of blood from his ruptured thigh.

For a brief period Sangin did seem to calm. The bazaar was up and running and for a moment, deep in the summer of 2007, even the soldiers could truly see progress. Plans to build a new school were approved, traders began appearing along Route 611 and growing queues of locals assembled where the British troops handed out medical supplies. Strategists had talked lustily of the 'ink-blotter effect', the establishment of small patches of security that would gradually bleed into one another. One day, no one quite knew when, the people of Helmand would wake up within a protective bubble of peace.

But Sangin's inkspot never bled into its hostile surroundings. The front line remained formless, shifting. A 360-degree battlefield. The war turned nastier. Casualties mounted. The death of Captain David Hicks in early August struck Bait Platoon particularly hard. For the previous three weeks Hicks had been issuing daily requests for a medical officer to be sent from Sangin to Inkerman, the exposed outpost just to the north. But no doctor had arrived when the twenty-six-year-old was struck in the chest by shrapnel from an enemy rocket targeting the tiny base. Hicks refused morphine so he could continue leading his men but, without help, he quickly succumbed to his injuries. The following day a medic arrived in Inkerman.

Later that month news reached Kenny of another dreadful incident, at dusk on the battlefields further north near Kajaki. A group of Royal Anglian soldiers led by teenage point man Robert Foster from Harlow, Essex, had come under astonishingly aggressive attack while moving through an abandoned village. Amid the gathering gloom, they made frantic calls for a US bomber to help them escape. Minutes later an F15 fighter jet roared into sight, swooping low over so-called Essex Ridge towards the nearby enemy. Those present recall a thunderous explosion and a complex of buildings being flattened by a five-hundred-pound bomb. Their joy was shortlived. Given the wrong co-ordinates, the aircraft had obliterated the wrong target. Beneath the debris were British bodies. In the ensuing panic their numbed colleagues dug out the bodies of Privates Aaron McClure, aged nineteen, from Ipswich and John Thrumble, twenty-one, from Maldon, Essex, before retreating under intense enemy fire. Only back at base did they realise their point man was also missing. In darkness, the unit marched three kilometres back to the ruins. They found blond-haired Foster beneath a metre of rubble. The nineteen-year-old had suffocated in a tomb of debris. Another point man was dead.

The incident stunned Kenny, who had passed his driving test with Thrumble, and shocked the entire battalion. But few dared ask what it was all for. The question simply hung awkwardly in the back of their minds. Zapped, slotted, waxed, smashed and wasted. As the tour progressed the latter term seemed the most apt. And plenty got wounded. Twelve, twenty-four, thirty-six, forty-eight. More than fifty were sent home, like Badger, with battle injuries. Disease and the heat compounded the toll. D&V gripped entire outposts, sending a relay of soldiers scuttling back and forth to the wooden platforms above the large metal drums that quickly filled with their watery faeces. There, crouching amid the flies and vulnerable to sniper fire, they feared becoming the first soldier in Helmand to be shot having a crap. Kenny would imagine the thud of the bullet, his body lolling backwards into the vat of shit below.

The rate of attrition began to perturb senior command. So overstretched were those who remained free from shrapnel, bullets, diarrhoea, poisoning and heatstroke that the virtue of maintaining their health placed them in greater danger. Bait Platoon arrived in Afghanistan with thirty-two men. By the tour's end it numbered just sixteen, according to Kenny. 'It was down to illness, broken legs, gunshot wounds, explosions, compassionate reasons, but a lot of illness. One bloke's spleen blew up because of the bad water and shit food he was eating.'

Kenny was one of the few who did not succumb, the company's longest-serving point man that summer. 'I was the only point man never changed, constant stress, not one minute on patrol could you put your thumb up your arse.' Denning too kept standing, except when falling over during firefights. Those who still could followed Denning anywhere without hesitation. The twenty-four-year-old cared deeply about his men. Occasionally he would be seen in the middle of the night, standing guard when he should have been asleep. If one of his men felt too exhausted or ill he would order them to bed, volunteering to endure their stupefying hours of sentry duty. '"Ken," he'd say, "you're hanging. Get some rest, I'm taking over."'

Towards the end, as the finishing line approached, the men became fixated with time. Time left. What time it was back home. Thirteen hundred hours and Kenny said he would think of Sam finishing work. Fourteen hundred hours: Sam would have left the gym. Sixteen hundred hours: Sam was at the Stingray with friends, missing him. He hoped.

They were doing time, passing time, hoping to avoid dying before their time. Between bouts of fighting they were killing time. Eventually most of Bait Platoon began crossing off the days. Makeshift calendars appeared where the posters of models in bikinis once hung.

It didn't matter whether it was a Monday or Friday, it

was all about numbers. Five days, six hours to go. Four days, three hours. Time itself adopted surreal qualities. A single moment in a firefight could be seared upon the subconscious with such ferocity it might stay lodged forever. Yet if any of Bait Platoon asked Kenny what had happened during three hours of guard duty, he could only shrug.

When darkness fell and the chat about women, football and war was exhausted, talk would again turn to the time left. The final countdown was the worst. Then the counting really got daft. The men tallied whatever they could to make sense of the tour: the number of times Denning fell over, how often Kenny mentioned Sam, the frequency with which Hardy lamented West Ham's strike force. They calculated their near misses, the times they nearly died. Kenny reckoned that was about a dozen. But most of all it was about counting the hours.

The soldiers stopped off in Cyprus for their 'decompression period', a quick debrief, a twenty-four-hour pseudo-psychological pitstop before flying home. They were told to keep an eye on each other, watch out for pals who changed. The signs, the officers said, were obvious. Watch out for friends who sank inside themselves and re-emerged irate and confrontational. War can change people, they were told. It can make you angry and sad. Watch out for the black moods, the recurrent nightmares. Some of the distressing things they had seen might re-emerge and haunt them. But the soldiers just wanted to get home, back to their loved ones, back to normality.

Sam was waiting for him. She was even more gorgeous than his dreams had suggested and their courtship blossomed. Liberated from the war, they got on better than before. Ten weeks after arriving home, on Boxing Day 2007, Kenny proposed. Sam said yes.

It was a period when Kenny's life felt perfect. Everyone was so proud – his father, mother, Sam – and among the battalion's hierarchy he'd come of age. Senior ranks now bought him drinks instead of blanking him; his opinions were suddenly valued. Among the regiment Kenny was considered some soldier, a natural. The future of the British army, ran the consensus. There was talk of promotion. His commanders had already mentioned lance corporal, and then, who knows? His one dream had been to serve his country. Now Kenny's career was about to fly.

But then in January 2008 Sam fell pregnant. Kenny quit the army.

11

Cannon Fodder

It was a Monday morning, midwinter. Colchester's Castle Park lay bleak and empty, the nearby shops ticking over as normal. An unusually biting breeze whipped through the High Street, but otherwise the town seemed pretty much the same.

It was 23 February 2009, Kenny's first day out of the army. He remembers feeling peculiar, liberated but also missing his previous life. Six years in the military and now he was free to do whatever he fancied.

To Kenny the prospect of being a battlefield father was out of the question. He had always vowed never to start a family in the army. Afghanistan was arduous enough with just Sam on his mind. He remembered the strain on the fathers' faces, the long-distance phone calls with infants who could barely talk. 'Honestly I don't know how the men with children handled it.'

He also wanted Sam to avoid army digs, the claustro-phobia of barracks life, the gossip and camp politics. The conditions at the Royal Anglian barracks at Pirbright had been a constant cause of disquiet among Bait Platoon. Kenny had been back from Afghanistan one week when a scathing report on army accommodation by the Commons

Defence Select Committee singled out Pirbright's quarters as 'disgraceful'. The report made headlines mainly with comments given by men from Kenny's battalion, who informed MPs that the rudimentary frontline sleeping arrangements in Helmand were 'more comfortable' than the billets provided for them in the Home Counties. 'They were rough. You could actually hear the wind whistling through barracks when it was windy,' said Kenny.

There was no chance Sam was becoming an army wife. Kenny had first-hand experience of the pressures of infantry life upon young parents, the strain caused by his dad's perpetual rolling tours of Northern Ireland. Kenny's father had adored his mother, but the stresses of raising a child when there was a war to be fought had proved too much. His parents managed little more than a thousand days together. John was twenty-nine when his first marriage collapsed in December 1989. Kenny was barely three.

He didn't want to return home frazzled and preoccupied to realise he had drifted too far from his wife. Becoming the best father and husband possible would be his new ambition. 'That is how I decided how I would measure myself,' said Kenny.

Sam gave birth to their son on 17 October 2008 in Colchester General, a few beds from where Kenny was born, and twelve days after the outgoing commander of British forces in Afghanistan warned that the war against the Taliban could not be won. Like his dad, Cayden came into the world smiling. Kenny chose his son's name. It was a Gaelic word, a warrior term. It meant 'spirit of battle'.

On that first day of civilian life, Kenny stopped at the

war memorial to pay his respects then headed west along the High Street. He remembers a jolt of adrenalin, an instinct to find cover, when across the road he saw a six-foot-tall combat soldier guarding a doorway. Impassively monitoring the pockets of passing shoppers, the marine clutched an MI6 assault rifle. His unflinching gaze locked onto Kenny's. Beyond the lifesize cardboard cut-out marine, inside the doorway, Kenny saw a row of leather armchairs. Sat there were several teenagers. They too held guns. For a moment he watched them wildly zapping the enemy. They were wasting too much ammo, Kenny thought, going for the head shot. But it was their money, £4.60 an hour to play at being a good soldier.

Sam Tolmie, who ran Colchester's Xtreme Gaming, England's first dedicated Xbox 360 gaming centre, said the 'shooters' were the most fashionable genre among the many youngsters who frequented the store. Particularly popular were *Battlefield 2: Modern Combat* and *Call of Duty: Modern Warfare 2*, which kicked off with a US army ranger nuking insurgents in Afghanistan.

Kenny moved on, passing W. H. Shephard, funeral director, directly opposite. Dominating the horizon loomed the Roman-style gatehouse of the Mercury Theatre. The High Street was wide and straight; a sniper up there could pick off pedestrians at will. Kenny's impulse was to move through the street as if it was an urban battleground, studying shoppers for sudden movements, noting possible choke points, the most likely killing zone. 'It's instinctive, your training never leaves you, even when you're shopping.' He noted the rat-runs off the strip, the points where he could safely return fire, but whoever had the gatehouse controlled the street. On he marched, past the Roxi bar, the Liquid nightclub – noticing its BOGOF promotion, £1.60 a drink before midnight, was still going – and past the town hall before stopping outside the Jobcentre Plus.

The centre's entire left-hand window display was dominated by army recruitment adverts, display shelves creaked under stacked copies of *Army Life* magazine. Adverts for the Royal Anglian Regiment, the Royal Corps of Signals and the 37th Signal Regiment hung alongside, and in front was a glossy photograph of an infantryman screaming in battle, his face partly obscured by a pall of smoke. It looked exciting, a decent way to make money. Visitors to Colchester, Kenny remembers thinking, could be forgiven for thinking that the army was the only employer around.

Next door was estate agent William H. Brown and Kenny stopped to inspect some nice-looking three-bedroom pads in Dovercourt in Harwich. But the numbers, he recalls, were way too steep. Westwards, closer to the gatehouse and near Yates's Wine Lodge which he had boycotted ever since the time the manager refused to serve him, although their official line was that they were happy to serve soldiers in uniform. There the road forked right to North Hill, and just down the slope was the Army Careers Information Office where he had showed up almost seven years previously. A large poster advertising pay scales hung in the bay window. A junior could expect £250 a week, a private £327.21. Kenny said he couldn't resist glancing up to the ranks he would have reached if promoted. Lance corporal commanded a £24,074 salary and that suddenly seemed enormous. Beside the column of numbers was a picture of local lad David Beckham. A quote from the England footballer accompanied his ubiquitous grin and slowly Kenny pieced together his accompanying statement: 'If I hadn't played for my country, I'd have fought for it.'

But could Beckham have handled it? Kenny wasn't convinced: 'Football's demanding at the top level but soldiering requires so many skills, an incredible fitness as well as intelligence.' Beckham could whip in a mean cross and was handy in a deadball situation, but could he kill? Could he outrun the Taliban? He wasn't even that quick, said Kenny.

Further down North Hill were the offices of the *Daily Gazette*, the local paper covering north Essex. When in Afghanistan Kenny, like most of Bait Platoon, had fantasised about how they would be remembered by the media. They swapped outlandish narratives of how their deeds would be immortalised. Riotous accounts of the cornfield fight, the scrap near Now Zad, the section who wiped out an enemy battalion singlehanded.

Kenny had been home from Helmand less than two months when he starred in a *Gazette* article. The account was not quite what he had envisioned. It was no eulogy to bravery, no breathless account of a point man in action. Instead he was accused of murder.

Three weeks before Christmas 2007 Kenny had returned to Harwich School as a favour to his old head teacher, Nigel Mountford. His brief was to offer pupils a first-hand narrative of military life. Regimental command thought it was a splendid idea; Kenny with his easy charm and boyish good looks would doubtless be the perfect poster boy for the young soldiers of tomorrow.

But the newspaper report on 6 December was significantly less effusive. Beneath the headline 'Soldier's talk to school slammed', Kenny was condemned for representing an institution that 'runs around murdering people'. The article quoted John Tipple, a local lawyer and branch secretary of the Harwich Respect Party, who dismissed his return to the classroom as a 'recruitment exercise by the tools of a government who go round murdering people in an illegal war'. Tipple went on: 'These soldiers are simply the government's cannon fodder.' He warned that if he did not receive a satisfactory explanation for Kenny's visit, he would take further action: 'we will leaflet the school and encourage the young pupils to question the war-mongers.' Head teacher Mountford did respond, explaining it was his duty to inform youngsters of career options. Kenny was simply one among many representatives from business and other employers including the police.

But Tipple had articulated the concerns of many who condemn Britain's recruitment of 'child soldiers' – the Ministry of Defence's targeting of sixteen-year-olds, often those from the poorest backgrounds. The practice is banned across the rest of Europe as unethical. Despite an ongoing campaign, the UK has the lowest deployment and recruitment age on the continent, remaining the only European country that routinely sends under-eighteens into armed conflict, a stance criticised by the United Nations.

The MoD shrugged off the likes of John Tipple, reiterating its right to deploy under-eighteens where there is a 'genuine military need' and when it is 'not practicable to withdraw such persons before deployment'. If anything, it has become more honest about exposing its younger recruits to danger, giving sixteen- and seventeen-year-olds basic counter-IED skills as part of their training at the Army Foundation College in Harrogate.

Of the first 320 British soldiers killed in Afghanistan nearly ten per cent were teenagers, including Kenny's fellow point men Chris Gray and Robert Foster. In the obituary published in his local newspaper Chris 'Grayman' Gray was celebrated as a superlative soldier, a young man with a big heart and a generous, trustworthy personality. Even the defence secretary stepped forward to offer his gratitude for Gray's 'exceptional' contribution. Robert 'Fozzy' Foster was likewise memorialised as a man of 'seemingly limitless reserves of courage and strength of character way beyond his years'. Colleagues queued up to pay tribute to his dependability while his family recalled a 'most wonderful son'.

Kenny agreed with everything said about Grayman and Fozzy. He only wished he hadn't been described as murderous 'cannon fodder', a feckless puppet in an illegal conflict.

When John had left the army, he had stopped at the camp gates and cried. 'I looked back with a tear in my eye and I said there goes fifteen years of my life. I felt the loneliest man in the world, back in a world I didn't know or understand.'

Camp life though had started to bore Kenny, the drills and dawn starts. 'When you first leave the army you're quite excited really. You haven't got to get up at six o'clock in the morning, none of that bullshit.' After Afghanistan being back in England was quite a comedown, but simple things like going for a drink could seem oddly difficult, a test of nerve. He would find himself outside a pub weighing up its location, the layout of the surrounding streets, the entrance and exit routes. 'When I walk up to a pub I convince myself it's gonna be dodgy, but I'm careful not to go to a place where I'm alienated. I look for good firing positions, good exits so I can withdraw easy or find cover easy. Good exit points, good entry points. If I go into a pub and sense someone's going to have a pop at me then I have to ask if I am going to be able to do a fighting withdrawal. Am I going to be able to get in and out quick enough?'

Once inside he had to swiftly weigh up the clientele, identify potential troublemakers. Some were harmless, merely irritating, like the 'fucking materialists' as Kenny called them, the couples who sipped expensive wines, their feet obscured by glittery designer bags whose names he wouldn't know. Kenny said he sometimes heard them discussing what they had bought and what else they wanted. He said their shallow prissy lives 'annoyed the fuck' out of him before he remembered he was one of them. A civilian. 'You hear people going on about their new shoes, how much they spent on a new pair of jeans as if it was the most important issue in the world. That shallowness, designer goods, buying things as if it's something to be proud of; all that pisses me off.'

His dad had felt the same, recounting the Friday night after his unit returned home from the Gulf, when they all headed into Edinburgh. 'I remember standing at the bar and there's some guys with their wives talking about how they need to get new carpets fitted and the conversation goes on and on and my brain is back on the Iraqi Highway of Death and I'm thinking: "Your fucking new carpets are nothing compared to what I have seen," and you feel like grabbing them and telling them what fucking bad things in life are all about. But you can't say that because they can't comprehend what you have seen.'

Then there were the solitary daytime drinkers. Kenny said he sometimes contemplated joining them for a quiet pint and telling them about Afghanistan. But what if they didn't understand? Or didn't believe him? Kenny admitted he was nervous about facing people who might not understand what he had seen.

But the people who got under his skin the most were the students. It was weird, Kenny said, how they could bang on for hours about stuff they had never done, regurgitating hypotheses and theories as if they were their own, and yet he had fought in a war and couldn't talk about it. There were a lot of students in Colchester, around twelve thousand out of a population of a hundred thousand, mainly from the town's university. Many of the shops and bars in town offered special deals for students. Even Yates's had got in on the act, hosting 'Colchester's busiest student night. Drinks from only £1.50.' Kenny felt the town cared more for its students than its service personnel. 'Shops and pubs were all doing student discounts and I couldn't get served in a bar.' Most of the students were probably against the war, Kenny recognised that. He knew groups were going around town handing out leaflets against the 'occupation' of Afghanistan. Anti-war banners had begun flapping from the University of Essex accommodation blocks that towered above the south-east side of town. One reportedly read: 'Bombing for peace is like fucking for virginity.'

The anti-war movement in Colchester was gaining traction around the same time Kenny left the infantry and even in October 2007, the month he returned from Helmand, the MoD had been forced to cease recruiting on the town's university campus, such was the level of opposition. But it wasn't just students who were opposed to the Afghan conflict. Hundreds of townspeople had signed up to the Stop the War movement in Colchester. Campaigners described an 'endemic anti-war feeling' in England's earliest recorded town. Mark Bergfeld, an Essex graduate around the same age as Kenny and a prominent figure of the anti-war movement, described how residents would sidle up and hastily scribble an indecipherable signature on a petition. 'They didn't want to be seen giving their name but wanted to register their dissatisfaction. The war polarised the town. Some passers-by would scream at us, call us communists or hippies, but there was a lot of support in Colchester.' He estimated sixty per cent of the garrison town was against the Afghan war.

The most startling aspect, said Bergfeld, was the volume of military families who supported a withdrawal. 'We had a lot of children of army officers and squaddies supporting us, then as the war went on it was military families themselves.' When the armed forces minister visited Colchester during this period it was the families of soldiers who demanded their sons were brought home. On one occasion anti-war campaigners held a demonstration as a number of squaddies arrived at Colchester's train station. 'They seemed very receptive, very open to listening to us. They seemed almost submissive, shy. It was like they were learning things for the first time,' said Bergfeld, whose predecessors founded Colchester's anti-war faction ahead of the invasion of Iraq in 2003. One of the first events they organised, several months after Kenny had signed up, was a 'die-in' at the university during which undergraduates lay down covered in fake blood to a soundtrack of air-raid sirens.

The movement's support peaked six years later. 'The rapidly rising death toll in Afghanistan during 2009 created a mood of bitterness you could clearly feel in Colchester,' said Bergfeld. In December that year the death of the hundredth British soldier in Helmand in 2009 prompted a series of candlelit vigils beside the war memorial next to Castle Park.

But the students got bored or moved on. The following year the Coalition government came to power: domestic cuts soon preoccupied protesters' energies. The anti-war demonstrations dried up, the media moved on. Soldiers kept on dying, but any concerted outpouring of anger quickly receded from national view.

Kenny shared the misgivings over the mounting casualty rate, but was unsure if the students in the anti-war movement were best qualified to pass judgement. 'They haven't been out there, they don't understand what's going on.' Each British death was another reason to make sure the war was won, he said, not an excuse to cut and run.

He felt much older than the students and suspected they viewed men like him as dumb peasant warriors. He wished he could explain to them that lots of intelligent men, characters like Guardsman Tony Downes, joined the infantry because they wanted to make the world a better place. 'They've never done what we did, they probably couldn't. They haven't earned the right to feel superior.' While Kenny was generally reticent about what he thought of the students who protested against the war, he did reflect upon the fact that at the age of twenty-two – the average age of British soldiers killed in Afghanistan – he had probably experienced the most eventful episode of his life while they were still waiting for their life to start. Their closest experience to war would be downing 'jager-bombs' or playing dead in their university halls. Soon they would move on from Colchester, their youthful optimism intact, to opportunity and wealth while he was left to do the best he could. 'That's the way it is, I suppose,' he shrugged: 'I tried being the best I could be, everyone should strive to be that.'

On the streets of Colchester there were other groups of young men that irked him. The heroin addicts, whose hollow eyes reminded him of the lads after Operation Ghartse Gar. Kenny hated the skagheads and he said they were everywhere. Not for nothing was Colchester known as a 'brown town'. Recently his dad had told him about a BBC investigation that had found a heroin hit in Colchester cost less than a pint. 'Madness,' John had said: 'The day putting that shit in your veins is less than a drink.' Across Europe a gram was fetching between £25 and £40. In Colchester in 2009 it was said to be a quarter of that price, up to ten times cheaper than when Kenny was born.

Kenny noticed the junkies everywhere, running round town in packs, pestering people for spare pennies. Reports of young people being offered free hits were rife. Once you had the taste you were hooked and once you were hooked you weren't going anywhere. Open Road, the drugs charity on North Hill, along from the army recruitment centre, said more than a fifth of drug users it knew were injecting heroin. It came in through Harwich or the other Essex ports, more or less mainlined in from the fields around Sangin. When Kenny was stationed there, the UN had confirmed a record opium harvest in southern Afghanistan, a rise of forty-nine per cent from the previous year. The bobbing red faces of the poppies were everywhere, he said. 'At times you were completely surrounded.' Back in Harwich, a stream steady of locals were being arrested. Police at the town's docks had recently found a stash buried in flowerboxes. Two sisters from the town had been convicted the year earlier of trying to smuggle heroin worth £5 million through the port.

That first day out of the army, Kenny remembers picking up the shopping for Sam, wondering what to buy Cayden – something fun but educational, because his fiancée was determined to give their son the best future possible. It was never too young to start learning, she said. Walking the streets of Colchester, the war felt more surreal than ever. From now on he would be reliant on television updates and occasional messages from Bait Platoon: Denning, Slater, Hardy and the rest. On Civvy Street it was like nothing had ever happened. Afghanistan resembled a dream, said Kenny, speaking at a time before the nightmares began.

Maybe, he once admitted, things would have been different if he'd got a medal. Not the Afghan tour medal, because everyone got that, even the 'flooseys' – the support staff – sat on their arses watching Sky Sports in the air-conditioned tents of Camp Bastion got that, even those involved in the benign peacekeeping tours in Kabul during 2001. The MoD had refused to award Helmand's frontline soldiers any special honour to recognise the ferocity of their fighting. It was a stance that had infuriated Kenny's officers, to the point that one had pulled me aside in Sangin to vent his fury and express his hope that the news story I was writing would change things. The following day news came through that David Hicks had been mortally wounded at Inkerman. The same officer rushed over and hissed: 'That's another fucking reason why you should write it.'

Kenny tried to be philosophical, saying that throughout history some of the best soldiers had never been decorated and some of the worst had. Yet on Civvy Street a medal assumed a new importance; it was something tangible, something Kenny could one day have showed his son. Some of his colleagues told John that Kenny should have been mentioned in dispatches. 'All his friends said he deserved as much. Kenny would never admit it to anyone but the fact he was overlooked I think hurt him,' said John. But honours were arbitrary, he added, as much about politics and timing, who you were with at the time and where. 'A bit like life really.'

12

Isolation

There were no vacancies for a point man. Sure, there were jobs out there: account managers, multimodal execs, web developers, telesales. But Kenny didn't have a clue what they entailed.

He had no academic credentials or IT skills. He had never visited an office, uploaded or created a spreadsheet. Institutionalised from the age of sixteen, he was wholly naive about the basics of finding a job and constructing a career. He had only ever had one job interview and that was for the army. He'd never had to assemble a CV and was at a loss for what to say. His skill set focused upon closing and killing the enemy; his ambitions had evolved from avoiding death to ensuring Cayden had a long-term father.

At Harwich's Jobcentre on the High Street, nothing stood out. Eventually he saw a vacancy that didn't demand an inventory of qualifications he'd never heard of: a telephone interviewer for an unnamed company. It paid £5.93 an hour, thirteen pence above the minimum wage. He enquired but it had already gone. There was a £16,000 position as a leisure duty manager, and another opening that looked promising except that it required 'a real head for figures and good keyboard skills'. Most specified at least two years' experience of things he had never done. He applied for six positions that he thought he might stand a chance of getting. He never got an interview. In fact, no one replied; they wouldn't even return his calls.

There were no jobs for a former soldier with dyslexia in recession-hit Essex. He considered picking fruit along with the seasonal workers in a few weeks' time or training as a painter and decorator. He looked into becoming a plumber. He was only twenty-two but life's pool of opportunity seemed to have already evaporated. It felt to Kenny that he belonged to another era. In an age of globalised hi-tech communication he was marginalised, his learning disability both prompting and aggravating his technophobia. Kenny had never Skyped, blogged or tweeted and cared little for email exchanges. He avoided texting unless it was absolutely essential. Sam managed the administrative side of things: applying for jobs online, emailing about possible openings.

Kenny had no desire to own an iPhone or disseminate his every third thought. He preferred objects, people; things that were real. In the worldwide information explosion, Kenny was obsolete.

The recession weighed on the coastal margins of Essex, suffocating Harwich until entire neighbourhoods seemed to expire. The place began to resemble a ghost town, not quite Now Zad, but somewhere that people seemed keen to leave. Derelict shops were boarded up, pound stores proliferated among them. At the time almost sixty per cent of Harwich's retail premises were empty, according to research by Experian. Only Walkden in Greater Manchester and Gateshead in Tyneside suffered more shop closures in 2009. Unemployment soared by almost seventy per cent on the Tendring peninsula where Harwich lay, clinging to its easternmost tip. Its status as an economic backwater was confirmed by the government's Index of Multiple Deprivation 2010. In a league table of 32,482 local authority wards, an area bordering Clacton-on-Sea finished bottom of the national poverty table in terms of income, employment, disability, crime and living standards.

Kenny realised that he was looking for work at a time when most of the unemployed were turning to the armed forces, one of the region's few recession-proof industries. During the twelve months from April 2009 demand for initial training was so huge they even began turning youngsters away. Kenny often saw the young recruits who'd made it, jogging through the Harwich streets in their new kit, fresh-faced and eager. He mourned the period when he had carried similar hopes and was excited about the future. He felt the same watching the army's latest television advert: 'Who do you want to be?' it asked. Kenny had no idea any more.

All he had ever wanted to be was a soldier. His dreams had stopped there. Even now, he saw a simple soldier living off the land. He had no idea how he would spend the rest of his life. 'I will never be as good at anything as I was at soldiering. I haven't got the love for anything else. I could play professional football and I wouldn't love it as much. If God gave me the choice to be Beckham or a soldier, a professional footballer or a professional infantryman, I know what I would choose every time. Football? What the fuck is it? It's a beautiful game but it doesn't make you somebody. You get people like Beckham who are naturally good at football, but I felt naturally good at being a soldier.'

The army didn't let Kenny down, quite the opposite. His regiment had begged him to stay and offered him several tempting promotions. Major Dominic Biddick pledged to 'up-scale' him through the ranks, even recommending him for the special forces unit of 1 Para. When he turned that down, a position on the close protection team shadowing the defence secretary was mooted. But the father-to-be knew that if he wavered he'd never go. Kenny was leaving the extended family of the infantry. He had one of his own now.

When his superiors recognised his mind was made up, they offered him a role with the army recruiting team in Colchester so he could remain near Cayden. But Kenny knew he ought to leave the military as a young man with time to build a new career. But out here, no one wanted him. He felt washed up. He kept thinking of the 1982 film *Rambo: First Blood*, in which an ex-Vietnam veteran played by Sylvester Stallone returns home to an indifferent, often hostile country. In a key scene, Stallone's character wonders how it had come to this. 'Back there I could fly a gunship, I could drive a tank, I was in charge of million-dollar equipment. Back here I can't even hold a job parking cars.'

Almost three decades later in Essex, *Rambo* acquired a relevance Kenny could never have conceived. He didn't want a tickertape welcome or any special favours, just a 'fair crack of the whip'. 'One minute I was trusted with the most expensive, dangerous equipment out there, and then you come back to find another job and people look at you as if you're stupid, they wouldn't trust you with a spud gun. People constantly belittling you, you know?' Kenny seemed physically pained by people's willingness to dismiss him as just another soldier who'd quit the army. Once, during this period, we discussed why no one seemed persuaded by his achievements. It must be getting him down, I said. He smiled and said: 'Can you imagine?' There was no point answering. Kenny went outside for a fag.

He never gave up trying to find a job. Week after week he plugged away, accepting the wearying ritual of applications, rejections, unanswered messages and unreturned calls as if it was just part of the process, a bit like basic army training is designed to weed out those who can't hack it. In the spring of 2009, a position came up that Kenny had a good vibe about. It was assisting engineering works on the London underground when the network shut down. It would be hard graft, scrabbling about in the damp rat-warren of tunnels while the city slept. Kenny didn't get the job. He didn't even get an interview.

In desperation, he began looking for private security jobs, leftfield postings like cruising the pirate channels off Somalia or guarding the oilfields of Nigeria. He missed having a gun, not out of any bloodlust, but because he was used to working with a weapon. The money sounded good and his qualifications might actually mean something. Again, though, the search was futile.

An old military contact, Colonel Richard Kemp, a

former commander of British forces in Afghanistan who had become the head of security at London's Canary Wharf, stepped in to help after learning of his predicament. Kenny was tasked with attempting to evade the financial centre's 'ring of steel', smuggling suspect packages into the capital's new node of commerce. If he couldn't succeed, the place must be watertight, Kemp concluded. Kenny spent several afternoons wearing fake suicide vests or carrying pretend bombs as he attempted to infiltrate one of Britain's most sophisticated security cordons. Once employed to kill terrorists, he was making ends meet as a bogus extremist.

Although Kenny knew there were others in his position, he felt isolated. Twenty-four thousand, he had been told, left the armed forces every year. What happened to them? No one seemed to know, not even his dad. John claimed the reason there was no data documenting how many ex-forces men and women were long-term unemployed was a deliberate government ploy. His views appeared to be substantiated when the MoD refused the Royal British Legion's repeated requests for details of soldiers leaving the forces. The government claimed its hands were tied by the Data Protection Act. The Legion said that was merely an 'excuse' to not do more and that providing the information would prevent hundreds of veterans falling into a life of addiction and crime. 'It suits the government to keep it hushed. You leave the army and you disappear, that way the government loses responsibility,' said John.

There were, however, clues to the scale of the problem. The Legion calculated that joblessness among ex-services personnel was twice the national average. Recruitment agencies estimated that at any one time there were fifty-thousand unemployed ex-forces members, half the size of the British army. But even these figures were skewed because the MoD designated anyone applying for a tax code, even for a day's bar work, as employed. It also stopped recording how many veterans were unemployed after the first six months. Instead it was assumed most became so desperate they accepted any dead-end role to avoid the dole. Commandos became supermarket checkout workers, former snipers took to cleaning cars.

Kenny found pitching himself to strangers difficult. It was hard telling employers about his service. He remembered leading the platoon, his feel for the land, how the valley went silent before a showdown, how friends look in the moments after a gunfight, but he couldn't articulate such experiences on demand. Some employers had never heard of a point man. Some asked about Sangin; one asked where it was. 'The ignorance of some people, what can you say?' said Kenny. But it wasn't their fault they never gave him a job – they just wanted 'proven experience in a high-energy business environment' and 'good keyboard skills'.

Kenny managed to put aside some savings from his stints as a make-believe suicide bomber and in April 2009 the family moved into 23 Garland Road, Harwich. Cayden was six months old. The new family home was in a maze of redbrick terracing in the Parkeston district of town, next door to the family-run Skippers chippy. Parkeston was a small enclave of housing squashed between the bleak docks of the port terminal and Ramsey Creek which separated it from Harwich, itself adrift from the remainder of Britain.

Trapped on its hinterland, estranged and unwanted by the mysterious controllers of civilian life, Kenny experienced a deeper sense of abandonment.

But the young family were eager to make a fresh start. Their current hardship was just a blip, they kept telling each other: things would pick up. Keep looking long enough and something was bound to turn up. Money was tight, but Kenny found the sudden increase in free time the toughest aspect of his new existence. It encouraged his thoughts to meander back to the war, particularly as darkness fell. Back to Tony Downes. They began with a staccato sequence of images: flashes of gunfire, blood, Tony facedown in the ditch, his fingers groping the dust, scrabbling deeper in the dirt. He must be here somewhere.

Then a woman would squeal, shrieking his name over and over. 'Kenny! Kenny! Are you all right?' Kenny would awake, soaked in sweat. Sam would place her hand on his forehead, smoothing the skin.

At first the nightmares were sporadic, but during the summer of 2009 Kenny's nocturnal restlessness started to become routine. It began to be normal, he said, to change the bedclothes twice a night. 'I was sweating so much it was like I'd pissed the bed. Sam, who was really supportive, would wake me up because I was screaming and I'd come round, absolutely soaked, wondering where the hell I am,' Kenny told me, blinking rapidly, jerking his head from side to side to mimic the symptoms of bewilderment.

But the days were generally good. They had peace and quiet, each other. The days with Sam and Cayden, buying bibs and doing normal things, even looking for a job to care for them all, were fine. Normal things, but they never seemed humdrum.

Outside Parkeston, the land felt increasingly alien and hostile. The local television news, *Anglia Tonight*, had recently shown footage of the homecoming parade of Kenny's old sister battalion, the 2nd Battalion of the Royal Anglian Regiment. Under ashen skies the march starts in upbeat fashion, the crowds in Luton applauding as the brass band rumbles louder. The bonhomie is abruptly punctured by a barrage of expletives and a section of the crowd begins jostling. Well-wishers scream. The cameras home in on a cluster of placards: 'The Butchers of Basra' and 'Anglian soldiers: Cowards, Killers.' Another said: 'Anglian soldiers: sent to die for £17,000' and Kenny remembers thinking that it suddenly seemed an awful lot of money. Above the parping of the band, shouts of 'Terrorists' and 'Baby-killers' are audible as the soldiers returning from Iraq march past the protesters. Police dogs bark, the crowd's screaming becomes louder. An elderly couple cover their faces as a wedge of young men surge towards the placards. Chants of 'No surrender to the Taliban' can be heard and then it all kicks off as police try to separate the sparring parties. The footage mystified Kenny. He couldn't comprehend how the protest had even been allowed to happen. His dad was right: the country was going to the dogs.

A few things were happening that did not seem right to Kenny. There were reports of forces personnel being instructed not to wear their uniform in public for fear of causing upset, of more landlords refusing to serve soldiers. Rumours had even begun circulating that the Fox Inn in Bisley, near the Royal Anglians' Surrey barracks, had stopped pulling pints for lads fresh off the plane from Afghanistan.

And then there were the young British soldiers fighting young British jihadists in the dust of Helmand. Bait Platoon had heard for themselves the lilt of Brummie accents on the Icomm system. They couldn't believe it at first: they had assumed the enemy must have been putting it on, but then other units began reporting hearing English voices among the Taliban ranks. Yorkshire and West Midlands accents appeared to be the most common. In the month that Kenny left the army, intelligence documents confirmed that rising numbers of Britons were heading to Helmand to target UK troops. Senior military sources described the emergence of a 'surreal mini-civil war' throughout the river valley.

Kenny, like most former soldiers, avoided being drawn on the politics behind the war but it was true – wasn't it? – that they were trying to stop Afghanistan becoming a base for international terrorism and to arrest the heroin flow into Britain's 'brown towns'? 'We were there, we were told, to make Britain safer,' he said firmly. It was a statement he repeated frequently, albeit with less conviction over time. Occasionally, though, the mask dropped. When I returned from a whistlestop trip to Helmand with the then prime minister Gordon Brown in August 2009, Kenny asked if I had grilled Brown about the escalating mortality rate. 'Did you ask him why good men were dying? Why so many good men are dying out there? Did you ask him *why*?' He sounded indignant, anxious. I said no and he looked away.

The young family lived an austere life. Kenny's treat was an occasional pint in the Captain Fryatt, a backstreet boozer two minutes away among Parkeston's terraces. There he chatted to veterans of various conflicts, men who would frequently toast the character after whom the pub was named, another of Harwich's proud wartime sons.

Captain Charles Fryatt had attempted to ram a German U-boat in 1915 as it surfaced to torpedo his merchant vessel off Harwich. Overnight he became an Essex hero, an icon of British resistance, but the Germans would soon exact revenge for his eccentricities, capturing the mariner while he was sailing from Holland to Harwich the following year. Despite being a civilian, the forty-four-year-old father was executed on 27 July 1916 by firing squad. After the war his body was exhumed and brought back to Harwich, but Harwich, like much of the land, was not the same place where heroes had been so publicly acclaimed. And in the deep recession of 2009 it was changing more quickly than ever.

In November that year, the Captain Fryatt called its final last orders. There was no ceremony, just the usual smattering of old veterans from various campaigns gathered by the bar for a last hurrah. Within weeks the grocer opposite had closed down, the neighbourhood's only convenience store. Parkeston's isolation was complete.

His dad's quality of life reminded Kenny there might be worse to come. John had led men into battle, but now he eked out a living on the poverty line. The government's definition of poverty stood at £115 a week after housing costs for someone with no dependents. John received benefits and a war pension worth £117 a week. Rent gobbled up half of this straight away and much of the remainder went on essentials: water, gas, electricity, phone rental, television licence and the upkeep of his home. A fiver was put aside for Rosie's food. 'She'll not suffer,' he said. According to research by the Joseph Rowntree Foundation a single person needed £158 a week for an acceptable standard of living, a figure that did not include housing costs.

John estimated he had around £25 a week for clothes and food. He made contact with Kenny by text message because he couldn't afford a proper conversation. He survived on self-made ration packs as if on a permanent military manoeuvre. A 47p loaf of white bread could deliver a week's worth of breakfasts, even if he preferred wholemeal. Four-packs of baked beans, 29p a tin, accompanied frozen meat pies for lunch and dinner. But he always got branded tea bags: hell would freeze over before he skimped on a decent brew.

His annual treat was travelling to Blackpool each summer to pick up his sons, Alexander and Andrew. They adored their dad, accepting that he had been simply unwell before the firebomb incident, and they loved Essex, the three of them reliving the fishing and camping trips he'd once enjoyed with Kenny. Beverley, who also understood John's behaviour had been caused by illness, joked that he lived on 'toast and beans' for three months in order to pay the train fare to Blackpool, an observation not far wide of the mark.

In mid-2009 John's finances became even more desperate. Government officials decided it was time he underwent a fresh medical assessment to ascertain whether he should continue receiving Incapacity Benefit. The issue would be decided by a twenty-minute interview in Ipswich with a nurse on contract to the Department of Work and Pensions. It was a simple process. The nurse would ask John a series of questions and award points based on his answers. If he accrued ten points his mental health would be considered sufficiently impaired for him to remain sectioned under the Mental Health Act and continue receiving support. John scored seven. The diagnosis was instant: he had made a miraculous recovery from PTSD and was fit to work. There was no reference to the six independent psychiatric evaluations that had chronicled his complex, acute condition.

John didn't mind being told to get a job. He was desperate to work again, but the decision saw his disability allowance cut by two-thirds to £18 a week and he would not be entitled to Jobseeker's Allowance or any of the benefits traditionally used to lever people back into employment. When he asked why, officials at the DWP explained that his war pension took him £13 over the limit. 'I told them that I was even worse off than before and I was struggling to make ends meet, but they said there was nothing they could do.'

The fifty-year-old began visiting the local jobcentre, competing with the unseen hordes and his son for the same scarce opportunities. A former point man who had no IT skills and an ex-corporal with a criminal record. One had severe dyslexia, the other acute post-traumatic stress disorder. John's conviction for making petrol bombs was particularly unattractive to potential employers. No one looked beyond the word 'explosives'. He couldn't blame them. He'd have probably done the same. 'I just wished I could explain the context, that I never meant any harm, that it was all a cry for help.'

Kenny's flashbacks were starting to intensify. 'Sometimes a dead person would start talking to you, looking you right in the eye, or you'd see something bad that didn't happen but your minds tells you it did. They were pretty vivid, but normally they would be about things I'd been involved in, bodies in British uniforms, Guardsman Downes. He kept appearing.'

His nightmares had yet to follow a pattern, but one he described began with him standing in a cornfield, talking to Tony. The sun is behind his face, spreading light like a halo, his boyish eyes still bright. In his dream Tony looks fine, skinnier than his pictures, but otherwise all right. Kenny studies the maize. When he looks up Tony has gone. It is suddenly dark and in the murk, amid the bunched stalks of the cornfield, something stirs. He sees a bag, moving as if a creature is trapped inside. A hand punches through its plastic membrane and Tony's head emerges, peering up at Kenny. But it is bleached like an over-exposed photograph. His face is featureless. He has no face. 'Then I'd wake up. Sometimes my screams were so loud they'd wake me. The bed would be soaked in sweat, I'd be confused where I was.'

The nightmares seemed to become more vivid over time. That was the problem: time. There was too much of it. Distanced from the regimented strictures of the military, Kenny's mind fumbled through formless days. During this period, he said that he began to feel guilty for having survived. In other nightmares he saw Bait Platoon marching through the flat desert as corpses. Other figures join the hobbling column: Chris Gray, the dead Afghan army soldier, the enemy, the men he killed. His first kill, the Taliban point man, also started to feature more prominently in his dreams. 'You can't forget the man you killed. I kept thinking of him, shit like that.'

In between Kenny's job searches, the dead came more often. During the afternoon sometimes, flashing through his mind as he wandered through the skeletal High Street. His visions made him feel brittle, he said, compounding his frustration at unemployment. He wondered why no one would take a chance on him. He was loyal and hard-working, even if he couldn't use a keyboard. The brittleness grew.

By this stage, it was obvious to me that Kenny was changing. He seemed tense and uptight, a far cry from the composed soldier I'd met in Sangin two years earlier. There was a new defensive aspect to his character. And he was angry. His wrath found innumerable targets: druggies, doleites, slackers, US 'cowboy' soldiers, peaceniks, scallies, big business, bankers and BMW drivers. Even some of the old lags who drank in the Captain Fryatt were disparaged; Kenny felt they patronised him even though he had seen more real fighting than they had seen on TV. His body language too had changed, the hands-in-his-pockets lope replaced with a skittishness that reminded me of his father. He had started glancing over his shoulder every other minute, weighing up who was following us, assessing anyone who entered the pub.

His greatest contempt was for civilians, a species he

could never understand and who would never understand him. Sometimes I felt that Kenny only confided in me because I had been there, to Helmand. I had seen him in his element, not sitting in some crummy Essex pub, chosen because it served the cheapest daytime lager in town. 'You're one of us,' he once said and I was certain he meant it. Society was split in two: them and us.

The nature of war tends to draw its survivors closer. In those months after leaving the army Kenny sought sanctuary with his dad, bonding over competing accounts of their combat roles. Privately they admitted things they never would to civilians, how they missed the rush of a gunfight. They marvelled at their time in the infantry, the way it gave them a sense of self. 'Give me a soldier who doesn't miss it? In forty years I'll still miss it. You might be in the pub watching football with civvies, but in your heart you'd rather be training with the lads on Salisbury Plain. It's why you get ninety-year-old blokes sitting in the pub with their medals on fifty years after they last served. It's who they are,' said Kenny.

For the first time in his life he said he began to properly understand his dad. He began to realise the force that had almost broken him, the emptiness that followed his separation from an institution that had defined his identity. Away from the infantry Kenny began to appreciate how the past, its highs and lows, had the power to overshadow the present and future.

For John, Kenny's decision to leave the army offered an opportunity to share his suffering in a manner that had never seemed possible. It also made him grateful that, unlike his son, he had never had to kill. 'You've taken the life of a human being, albeit guided by the arm of the law. Unless you're a psychopath you've got to be affected in some way,' said John.

During this period, Kenny said he began to understand for the first time what his dad had meant when he told him: 'Be the best, be better than me.' For years he had assumed his father was laying down a gauntlet, a Meighan challenge. It was nothing of the kind. 'There was always a pressure of meeting the mark of my dad. I was constantly trying to be one step above him otherwise in my mind I had failed. I suddenly realised what he was saying by being the best. It wasn't a case of being a better soldier, it was a case of being better at how I handled things. He was saying: "Don't turn out like me."'

John had also noticed changes to the happy-go-lucky boy he knew. The pair would exchange cross words more frequently, more easily, a dispute over an offside goal sufficient to ignite a blazing row. John detected a new spitefulness in Kenny's voice, a sour undercurrent that he had never heard before. The father recognised the signs with a terrible foreboding. He knew how the sudden prickliness coagulated into bottomless black moods. He knew where the journey ended.

Towards the end of July 2009, John became convinced something awful was going to happen to his son. When I spoke to him in his small flat in Clacton, its door reinforced with three steel struts in case his attackers returned, he seemed more anxious than usual. 'I'm worried about Kenny,' he said, rolling another cigarette: 'The smallest things are starting to get under his skin. He gets upset more easily than he used to.'

John was convinced he had to act quickly. Later that week he invited Kenny over to his place and encouraged his son to talk about his nightmares. It was important to purge the memories before they hardened. They talked, but Kenny later admitted that he found it too difficult to describe the visions that haunted him. Explaining bad dreams, he said, only seemed to make them more real.

'Look what happened to me,' John said. 'I became lost because I never talked about things. I bottled them up until they burst. I'm a warning what can happen if you don't rationalise the things you've come across.' Even so, Kenny remained convinced it was just a bad phase. Once he'd ridden it out, things would be OK.

13

Route 64

He was deep in enemy territory when they stormed his five-ton vehicle, rushing on board, gesturing violently at him. One leant forward, his face bent with fury, and jabbed a finger at Kenny's crisp uniform. Another hissed a torrent of invective. A third recommended he should back well off. He had been ambushed in broad daylight. They had struck while he was distracted, as he slowed to pick up a bunch of elderly locals. Now he was in trouble. No back-up and, from experience, Kenny knew more attackers would be waiting. He glanced in the rearview mirror and saw them goading him. They were waiting for him to make the first move.

'Right lads, come on,' Kenny shouted, concentrating on keeping his voice authoritative but steady.

'Fuck off wanker,' one spat back. 'What you gonna do 'bout it?'

Kenny weighed up his options then turned the ignition key. The single-decker bus juddered to a halt. 'We're not moving until you get a ticket,' he said.

The youths stared back, standing their ground beside the seats reserved for the old and infirm. 'Fuck off mate, drive on,' they barked, all dressed in grey sweatpants, pumped-up white trainers and windcheaters.

The few passengers, the odd mother and pensioner, stared hard out of the windows. Kenny thought about leaving the driver's cabin, but that was frowned upon in the company regulations. The youths edged forward. 'What you gonna fucking do about it?' they asked, their heads tilted back, feet wide apart. Kenny knew characters like these fed on fear, but he was a past master at suppressing anxiety. He stared straight at them. The standoff was moving towards an undetermined outcome.

There was a banging on the bus doors. Kenny turned. Another two teenagers were slapping the Perspex furiously, screaming to be allowed on board. Now Kenny had no choice. He breathed deeply and called the depot to explain that another bus was being attacked on Colchester's Greenstead Estate. As he did, the three youths swaggered towards him and tossed their shrapnel into the coin tray. Kenny had already figured that they had the correct change. They always carried the ninety pence for a single. On Greenstead they refused to pay not because they were broke, but to incite confrontation.

Kenny's bus had pulled alongside the ninth stop on route 64, which bisected the sprawling streets of Greenstead, an enclosed warren of cul-de-sacs, rat-runs and cut-offs that lay on the eastern fringes of the town. Two years ago he was a war hero. Now he was a bus driver for FirstGroup, 'transforming travel' for the good folk of north Essex. He was paid £9.50 an hour, thirty-five hours a week, leaving the family little room for indulgence after rent, council tax and bills. Two months earlier, in June 2009, he had been selected out of thirty applicants, a surprisingly tepid level of interest for a job in Essex at the height of the economic downturn.

His bosses had raised their eyebrows when they discovered he had fought the Taliban in Helmand, but had been impressed with his eagerness, evident intelligence and obvious talent for working under pressure. He would be well equipped to handle the particular challenges of route 64. The previous summer a local cab firm, Town Cars, had stopped sending taxis there after dark since one of its drivers had been attacked by hoodies on the estate's approaches. Bus drivers remained to ferry Greenstead's populace, but some were getting weary. The attrition rate of drivers on route 64 was discussed among the staff in a company that prided itself on the longevity of its employees.

It tickled Kenny that he had become a bus driver. During the war the soldiers had asked each other what they would do if they were not in the army and Kenny had joked that he would drive a bus. His only basis for this was a training exercise near Catterick Garrison in North Yorkshire in January 2002. It was pissing down and as Kenny set off, humping his kit in the driving rain, he turned and saw their coach driver, in the warmth, tearing back the foil of his packed lunch. You had to be careful what you wished for.

Route 64 ran from the windblown city-centre bus depot along Barracks Road and past Military Road which led five kilometres south to Britain's last functioning armed forces jail. On a bad day Kenny imagined himself locked up in Colchester's Military Corrective Training Centre. At least there, he would be close to a mindset he knew, a system he understood.

The approach to Greenstead provoked dread among some of the FirstGroup drivers. There was only one route in and out, through a labyrinth of avenues that mostly ran nowhere, usually bending round to where they began. Kenny reckoned an invading force would struggle to emerge from a foray into Greenstead. He viewed the estate as a mile-wide maze of sniper alleys and rubbish-strewn dead ends where troopers would be isolated and picked off.

He had started his shift with a final check in the rearview mirror. The short back and sides of his military days had been retained and his driver's uniform was scrupulously ironed and pressed with a crease down the front. His Stead & Simpson lace-ups, touched up with a fresh coat of black polish, gleamed as they rested on the pedals. Neat enough, Kenny hoped, that if his old sergeant major happened to catch a ride on route 64 he would whistle his approval.

Despite the blue sky, Kenny entered Greenstead with a heavy heart. His pulse quickened as he drove into the wide avenue of Avon Way which marked the estate's western boundary. Boxlike homes with closed curtains and reinforced doors lined the route. Many of the gardens looked like fly-tips, interrupted occasionally by manicured lawns framed with hanging baskets and women who risked cautious greetings. You never knew what to expect in Greenstead; some days you could meet the most pleasant of folk, other times you were greeted with a hate you could smell.

The local toughs congregated at the bus stops, manning them like checkpoints. They spat abuse and forced passers-by to cross the road or trudge, defeated, to the next stop. They wore more or less the same: McKenzie windcheaters or hooded tops with loose sweatpants and either Reebok Classics or Nike Air Max. Their colours were usually grey, black, brown: camouflage against the monochrome estate they terrorised. They ruled by fear and patrolled in packs. As the weeks had passed, Kenny had formed the view that Greenstead was under enemy jurisdiction, controlled by an unruly, amorphous sect who, much like the Taliban, terrorised their own and punished the weak. He fumed at their surliness, the way they deliberately barged into other passengers and brandished out-of-date tickets with disdain.

After the Avon Way stop he would push further into the estate and past Laing Road where months earlier youths had set fire to parked cars. Next up was the worst spot in Greenstead, the Hunwick shopping arcade, which backed onto the squat flats of Charles Pell Road where the previous year a fifty-year-old man was fatally stabbed in the groin and dumped in an empty flat. Two young thugs had tortured him for several hours to get his cashcard PIN before killing him. They tried eleven times to get money out of the cash machine, the same hole in the wall where twenty-six-year-old Westley Oakes-Odger was stabbed one sunny Monday afternoon. A man tried to push in the queue and Westley said that queues were there for a reason. He was still waiting for his money when a car pulled up and two men got out. It looked like a punch on the CCTV footage, but Westley was stabbed in the neck. He died on the pavement outside the One Stop grocery store.

Beneath a bank of CCTV cameras and a row of spikes

and heavy-duty shutters, there were just three shops open as Kenny drove past, a betting outlet, a chippy and the One Stop. That day the youths appeared to be obeying the 'no loitering' signs. Six and a half minutes behind schedule, he pushed north along Hawthorn Avenue, past the martial arts club and the launderette and up to the Signpost Resource Centre, the local jobcentre. A small group of men loitered outside, sucking cigarettes and glancing furtively towards him. The crowds outside the centre had grown over the summer. During June, 550 estate residents visited Signpost seeking employment, two hundred more than the previous monthly record. Colchester, like the rest of Britain, was enduring the bleak reality of the recession. But it was in places like Greenstead where its effects seemed most profound.

The young men felt it worst. Not many of them could hold down a job and, outwardly, few seemed that bothered. Some might wander into town and scout the High Street for casual work at JD Sports or Gamestation. Some might get really fed up and join the army, but in Kenny's mind they were enrolling for the wrong reasons. It was absurd, he thought, that a teenager could end up in Helmand's cornfields because they were bored in Greenstead or because JDs had ceased taking casuals. You went to war because it was your turn to make a difference. You went to Afghanistan because it was your duty. But most importantly to Kenny, service was an appreciation of what had gone before, the sacrifice and courage of those who had fallen. 'A lot of youths, my generation, have forgotten what Britain is all about. The military history, the stiff upper lip.

They forgot that we're British and that we'll take the fight to you. The Taliban outnumbered us in Helmand, but that didn't matter at all. We are British and history says we're gonna mix it and you join up to make sure you carry that on.'

But the truth is that most of the boys who signed up alongside Kenny did so because there was nothing else to do. In his year at Harwich School Kenny estimated a quarter of the boys in his class applied or considered joining the armed forces. Others secured jobs or apprenticeships, fewer still drifted into higher education and the rest mooched around the Essex seaport doing drugs, getting lairy, storming buses for kicks. Kenny said: 'Around here it's simple: you either go in the army or you join the gangs. Or you leave, but where do you go?'

North again, past Conifer Close where the previous year fifteen youths cornered Jon Payne and his teenage son Toby, who had intervened after they saw the group bullying some younger kids. Within moments it was apparent to both they would be punished, but neither could have guessed quite how cruelly. A samurai sword was brandished and slammed down on the back of Toby's head as he called the police for help. The two-foot blade sliced through to his skull. He survived, but the youths had smelt blood. It was their estate. For the next four months they hounded the Payne family, smashing their windows, making threats and rendering the mother an agoraphobic wreck unable to open the front door. Eventually the Paynes packed up and left.

Such incidents meant that many people gave up on

Greenstead. Few believed that conditions could be changed. Kenny had recently heard that the *Evening Gazette* had run a feature about two monks and a nun who wanted to move onto the estate in order to propagate the virtues of poverty, obedience and chastity. Brothers Philip Bartholomew and Martin John and Sister Chris had advertised in the local press during August 2009 for local families to put them up. No one responded. 'Typical,' thought Kenny. 'A dose of proper discipline would work wonders around there.'

On Kenny went, round and round route 64, eight times a day, five days a week. Greeting strangers, getting grief. Sometimes it wasn't the hoodies, or 'rats' as Kenny started calling them. Mothers fought on his bus, absent fathers too. 'Sometimes you'd get whole families fighting each other on board, in front of their kids. You see it all the time, every day, all day.' Unclaimed luggage was another problem. FirstGroup preached the necessity of vigilance to its bus drivers: the company's eyes and ears against a terrorist strike. 'Public transport was considered a soft target, particularly in a military town. Anyone who left a bag on board would create a major security alert. But I suppose, in a way, I was still fighting terrorism.'

Occasionally, he navigated the estate pretending he was in control of a FV510 Warrior armoured vehicle. Eyes peeled for danger, he scanned the rat-runs and side-streets. His operational objective was to transport local dignitaries unscathed and away from the threat of ambush. Sometimes his mind would contemplate the miles walked in distant cornfields, the patrol where his shirt rotted beneath his body armour, the times he couldn't swallow through fear. He grew to understand that only men like him could comprehend the terror of Helmand. The hostility of Greenstead, the cowardice of its young men, made him boil inside. He felt used.

Lunch was usually a hasty pitstop for a sandwich and a Lambert & Butler back at the depot. His new colleagues were different. During the lulls in fighting, Kenny and his platoon had chatted about trivial stuff, football, what was on the box back home. Hardy was obsessed with the Hammers and their lack of decent strikers, Slater fretted about soap-opera plotlines that had been and gone. In the confines of the bus depot, his new colleagues would talk about the same things, but it was different. They talked as if football really did matter more than life and death or the whims of busty soap stars actually counted for something. One lunchtime, the talk turned to the estrangement of Jordan and Peter Andre. Kenny had never seen his new colleagues so animated. One driver almost threatened to storm out in defence of Andre.

'They can whinge about the most pathetic things,' Kenny said, 'a little bit of heat, how they've been in the cab and only had one bottle of water, and they'll bitch at each other like women. In the army if a bloke's got a problem he'll go up and tell them but in Civvy Street it's all behind each other's back. One minute they're bitching behind their backs and then they'll go up to the same person they've been talking about like they are their best mate.

'Civvy Street, it's a dog-eat-dog world. No one's out to really help you out, you've got to look after yourself, there's no team-building, there's no buddy system. I found that very hard. If you have a problem you can't just go and speak to somebody. The only people I can call are my army friends, or Dad if I have a real problem. It's hard.

'You're sitting in the canteen at work and it'll come up that a British soldier's been killed in Afghanistan and all you hear is people bitching about crazy stuff and you'll be like "Hang on, someone's died . . .".'

Occasionally the subject of the war surfaced during lunch breaks. Kenny's colleagues, more out of duty than genuine curiosity, he sensed, would ask in which regiment he had served and whether he had ever killed anyone. Kenny would offer blandishments like how 'mental' it was and how it was so hot you couldn't hold your weapon if you left it in the sun for two minutes. Once, they were sitting chatting and one of the more experienced drivers had said it must be a right laugh shooting all those fuckers. Kenny had nodded. Some bits were good fun, but not those bits.

Usually the drivers weren't bothered. One day, after hearing about the *Mirror*'s latest report from Sangin, Kenny was itching to talk about the land he remembered, the friendships and the time he was almost recognised for his bravery. He mumbled something about the time Badger was right behind him and got shot, but none of them looked up. If they had he might have gone on to tell them about Operation Ghartse Gar, the battle of Now Zad or the day he saw a figure moving towards him in a cornfield. Kenny had always known it would be different on Civvy Street. But two years previously, when he had returned home during a fortnight's break and met Sam, things hadn't seemed so alien. Maybe he was the one who had changed in the meantime.

Route 64 leaves Greenstead via the Bromley Road before tracking down the Harwich Road across the River Culver and into East Street, back in the direction of the Military Corrective Training Centre. Outside its gates, crowds were gathering, at first just a hardy few, but their numbers were starting to swell. They chanted 'Stop the war' and waved placards condemning the Afghan campaign as immoral, urging 'Jobs not bombs', 'Warfare not welfare'. The peace protesters called the soldiers patsies. Their most recent cause célèbre was a young Royal Logistic Corps private from Yorkshire called Joe Glenton who was sentenced to Colchester's military jail after going absent without leave in the summer of 2007, just as his unit was preparing to return to Helmand at the moment when Kenny's battle group had made it home.

Glenton, like Kenny, had joined the army buoyed by a 'wave of enthusiasm'. A doctor who later assessed him described his eagerness as bordering on naivety. When he landed in Afghanistan in 2006 Glenton was thrilled: he had never even been on a plane before. But his zeal quickly waned. Glenton saw civilians maimed by a rocket but couldn't help because he was forbidden to leave Kandahar air base. Once he stacked the coffins of fourteen British servicemen whose plane crashed because of faulty equipment.

The pile of coffins, the 'pointless waste of their life', made Glenton think. But the tipping point for him was still to come. He was tasked with helping to organise ammunition supplies for British forces. Midway through the tour, his team realised they needed to order more: the troops had exhausted their entire stockpile of ammo. Yet Glenton saw no proof of progress. Overnight, the war seemed futile. On leave in England he began drinking heavily, his nights interrupted by screaming fits.

He was told to return to Afghanistan but refused, saying the war was wrong. So he fled to Australia, coming back eighteen months later to campaign against the conflict. Glenton, now twenty-six, became the darling of the Stop the War movement, delivering a letter to the Prime Minister and addressing peace protesters in Trafalgar Square.

The army placed him in Colchester's Military Corrective Training Centre after he was charged in the summer of 2009 with going absent without leave. Outside, his supporters gathered. His lawyer was John Tipple of Harwich solicitors Linn and Associates, who branded Kenny a 'murderer' in the *Daily Gazette* when he visited his old school. During Glenton's court martial in Colchester in the summer of 2009, prosecutors said his decision to abscond could have left his unit undermanned. Judge advocate Emma Peters said: 'There are many soldiers in the army today who have extremely unpleasant experiences, who watch friends die or suffer appalling injuries, but they have to return and do their duty.' Psychologists and Glenton's wife Clare argued that the soldier had developed PTSD, describing in detail how he woke up shrieking at night and jumped at loud noises. Glenton was jailed for nine months.

Kenny understood the judge advocate's arguments. He knew men who had refused R&R or returned early to the front line because of a sense of responsibility to those they had left. Some died when they weren't even meant to be there. But Kenny also appreciated why Joe Glenton had run away. He was, after all, starting to feel the weight of his own memories. Glenton had questioned why people were dying, and as Kenny's dad had discovered, when you couldn't answer that question, it was hard to come back.

Cayden was the nucleus around which Kenny's life began to revolve. Sam was a brilliant mother, instinctive and alert to their son's needs. Often they would play together on the lounge floor and when they did, Kenny was glad he had left the infantry. He missed the army, but he adored his son and Sam more. Yet one night, cooing over Cayden, he felt the familiar dark stir of his imagination.

His ten-month-old son had started to blubber as babies do and maybe that was what reminded Kenny of the tiny girl he had met two years earlier in southern Afghanistan. She was a toddler, not much older than his son, and when she sobbed her whole body shook. Kenny knew straight away that something was wrong by her blank, confused stare. Beneath her torn rags, the child's insides were spilling out. A shard of shrapnel had sliced through her right side, the weeping tear impossibly vast on the small body.

It was 5 August 2007, a hot Sunday morning, and an Afghan family had turned up outside the base in Sangin. The father, his face puffed with grief, cradled the battered bodies of his two surviving daughters. Another three lay dead beneath the rubble of their home, flattened by a bomb dropped from an unseen US plane. Kenny had heard its dull crump just after 10 a.m., momentarily wondering what the explosion meant. Now he knew. The father fell to his knees and screamed at the empty sky.

Denning carried the girl with the shrapnel tear into the base. She was mumbling. By the time he reached the command centre the lower half of his uniform was black with blood. For thirty minutes medics tried to save the child's life, her blood edging across the floor of the makeshift canteen where the men ate their B rations. Outside, Bait Platoon sat on the steps listening to the children crying and the wailing of their father.

Forty minutes later a Chinook helicopter touched down and the men stretchered the two girls on, the hunched figure of their father behind. As he boarded the helicopter a small crumpled envelope containing six hundred dollars was handed to him by a British officer, compensation for the destruction of a family home and three dead daughters. The chopper left in a swirl of dust and the men watched it recede. Denning, normally so composed, snapped at a private who uttered a banal comment. Kenny helped wash away the blood in time for tea.

They were never sure whether the children made it. Nor did anyone know why the bomb fell, what intelligence had prompted the decision, what the pilots had seen. The incident went unrecorded by the authorities. In London and Washington no government statement was issued, nor was there any mention of a military investigation. It was as if nothing ever happened; even while it was happening, it wasn't happening. And this was far from being the war's first innocent civilian death. Many others came to the gates at Sangin. One afternoon a father arrived pushing a wheelbarrow. Curled inside was the bloodied body of a boy.

'Rumours were going around that we were sorcerors or something. Our medics were so good they could patch up dying children,' said Kenny. But the boy in the wheelbarrow was dead. His body had already started to stiffen with rigor mortis. Kenny and a medic tried to explain that there was nothing they could do, but the boy's father wouldn't listen. Eventually interpreters had to explain that it was too late to save the child. 'He wanted us to bring his son back to life, he really believed we could do it.' The father refused to go, standing outside the gates, beside the wheelbarrow, until nightfall.

Sometimes it was the enemy who were at fault, sometimes it was unclear. The identity of the culprit didn't seem to matter, said Kenny, to any of those who arrived at the gates wearing the blood of their children. Nonetheless, dead civilians became central to the war's propaganda campaign, each side using the fatalities to win back support from the local population.

Kenny could not forget the woman and her two infants whom he had nearly killed during the battle in the cornfield near Waterloo. Again he credited his 'sixth sense' for not following the order to clear the compound with grenades. 'I got this feeling to hold off otherwise I'd have fragged them, killed her and her children. Killing the enemy was bad enough, but I wouldn't have been able to live with myself if I had killed an innocent person and children. You've taken their life away, how do you explain what happened?' When he talked about the mother he would have killed had he obeyed orders, Kenny would rub his forehead as if imagining that he had in fact lobbed a grenade into her bedroom. Once, over a full English breakfast at a pub near Colchester, he pushed his plate away and said: 'I think about her a lot. I wouldn't have been able to handle it had I killed her. You can talk about the casualties of war, the odds of war, the fact you don't know what's around the corner, but that doesn't change the fact you killed a family, nothing can.'

But Kenny knew that civilians were being killed all the time in the war. He heard the updates, the bulletins chronicling the missiles that hit the wrong targets, the bombs dropped on homes where the enemy had been but had since departed, leaving only a dead family among the debris. Officially 629 civilians were killed by coalition forces in 2007, against seven hundred by the Taliban. But Kenny learnt that the numbers rose sharply the following year, reaching a total of 2,118. The Taliban's increased use of homemade bombs along with a growing reliance on Nato air strikes made the war more deadly the longer it continued. In 2010 civilian casualties grew by a third in the first half of the year. By then, more than seven thousand innocent people had been killed in Afghanistan since 2006, according to the UN. The figure is widely considered a conservative tally. Leaked military documents confirm hundreds of civilians have also died in unreported incidents, alongside evidence of systemic attempts by the US to cover up civilian casualties. 'People aren't stupid. You need to get their trust, you can't win by lying,' Kenny said.

As the civilian death toll rose during the summer of

Kenny's tour, pressure mounted for changes to the rules of engagement. Two days before the Sunday morning when the Afghan father brought his two bloodied daughters to the Sangin base, Nato issued instructions to troops fighting in Helmand to alter the way they fought in order to curb innocent casualties. Until then the British had been able to shoot without being fired on or without comprehensively identifying whether the enemy were carrying firearms. From then on, they could only shoot if they definitely saw a weapon. Some of the younger soldiers were furious because it made their situation more dangerous. Kenny said it was the right call. Good soldiering was about restraint. It was about killing the right people.

The enemy were typically quick to respond, learning to stash guns in hollow tree trunks and farmers' wheelbarrows instead of carrying them. But more damagingly, the Taliban became adept at disseminating stories of collateral damage, torture and rape by foreign troops. Mobile-phone footage claiming to show the crumpled bodies of Afghan civilians following a coalition air strike frequently surfaced online. British press officers were furious; there is nothing quite as damaging as the truth.

Round and round Kenny went, looping the loop on route 64. By night his mind ran a different circuit. It wasn't just the children. Guardsman Tony Downes was a fixture, his young face flickering above images of his obliterated body. Then the first man Kenny had killed walked towards him, his youthful features magnified through the rifle sight. 'My nightmares started to repeat each other, you'd get bodies in the same position, lying face down or whatever. You'd know what was coming next.'

Away from the bus route and his nightmares, Kenny was making good progress as a husband and father. He had managed to store up some savings and in July 2009 they moved to a new home on the posh side of Harwich. Finances, though, were still pretty tight. He was on £16,500 a year – £1,375 a month for the family before tax, and rent alone was £490 a month – but their new place was spacious with a large garden where they could hold barbecues and Cayden could play. The family could keep growing. For a start they got a black Staffordshire puppy called Tia, after the drink Tia Maria according to Kenny, although it was never clear if he was joking. Cayden adored the new arrival and the pair were soon inseparable. Kenny, for whom loyalty was perhaps the greatest virtue, could spend hours watching them. 'Thick as thieves,' he would say, watching the toddler and the puppy on the back lawn. It was a period of harmony: the family bonding through the rituals of domestic life and private competitions like whose plant would outlast the rest. Would it be Sam's spider plant or Kenny's baby bonsai tree? There was a comfort in nurturing what you had.

The morning news had carried bulletins of the second stage of Operation Panther's Claw, the offensive to clear the enemy from the towns of north-central Helmand. Two more British soldiers had been killed, bringing July's tally to twenty-two.

Kenny's bus was approaching the upward ascent to Greenstead when his insides began to tighten. This time it was not the estate's young men who caused his stomach to flip, but a middle-aged lady. Her eyes were puffy and bloodshot, the look of someone who had been up all night crying. She glanced at him and Kenny sensed enormous grief. He had no evidence to support the idea, but he couldn't help wondering if her boy had been one of those who had died on Operation Panther's Claw.

He wanted to say something but thought it rude to pry. Instead he moved the bus forward. He imagined a simple shrine in the living room behind the net curtains. Photographs of a teenage son, pictures of his passing-out parade, the day he joined.

Kenny said he felt strange as he drove past the small houses that day. He found himself wrestling a powerful sense that he should still be out there. 'Some days it hits home that you'll never do anything like that again, but other lads are still putting their life on the line.' By the time he arrived at the next stop he was anxious. Some hoodies came on, refusing to pay, daring him to react. There were just three other passengers on board, an old man, a young mum and a lady with eyes that looked like they had been rubbed raw.

The attack came later that week. As he pulled up Avon Way, three or four youths on scooters, in formation, began to close alongside his bus. They were shouting and gesturing at him. Kenny accelerated, but still the scooters came in closer. There was a loud bang on the side of the bus, the clatter of smashing glass. In his side mirror he watched the 'rats' lobbing beer bottles at the vehicle. Kenny willed the bus faster, trying to outrun his pursuers as they wound uphill through the estate. But the scooters approached for another attack, this time coming right up alongside the driver's cabin, giving Kenny the wanker sign. 'It was like a scene from *Mad Max*, the way they chased the bus like bandits.' On he pushed, towards the estate's exit, ignoring the bus stops until, suddenly, the scooters peeled away. 'As soon as they started to get out of their comfort zone, they just turned around. They were protecting their estate.'

The experience infuriated Kenny. Something terrible was in the making. He could feel it. His dad had expected it, telling him: 'Calm down Kenny, you can't react. You'll lose your job.' Kenny found he had to concentrate hard to subvert the military training that encouraged its disciples rarely to back down in a confrontation. Different rules applied out here, his dad said. You've got to remember that or you've no chance.

But they both sensed he was going to snap. Kenny's resentment towards the 'rats' of Greenstead had become too intense. He hated how they thought they were hard but knew nothing of real violence or true suffering. They had no empathy, no loyalty. He despised how they stuck together out of cowardice rather than camaraderie. 'They wouldn't die for each other, or risk their lives to help an injured mate or carry their kit for twelve miles without thinking about it. When you meet them on their own they're nothing. They need to be taught some respect. If I had my way I'd round up all the crackheads and the yobs and parachute them into Helmand with a nine-millimetre. Think you're hard now?'

Kenny managed to calm himself, but knew that it was

temporary. The next time he was going to do something bad. He had to get off the buses.

14

Rage

It was the local madhouse where the sailors came ashore to let off steam. Wedged among the old port's warren of streets and bounded by water on three sides, the Billy had been the place where Harwich's reputations were made, vendettas resolved and fresh ones sown for more than 250 years. The rest of the town knew it was closing time at the Billy by the sound of breaking glass.

The police also knew it pretty well, venturing within its low-ceilinged cobalt walls more than fifty times in the past four years. The reasons were various – underage drinking, licensing misdemeanours, drugs – but often it was violence. One typical spat at an eighteenth birthday party ended with two locals following one man home and savaging him with an axe in his own lounge. The trial heard that one of the perpetrators, from the year below Kenny at school, had recently strangled a swan at a nearby boating lake and hurled the limp bird at a passing motorist. On both occasions his defence centred upon the fact that he was drunk. He was a Billy regular: of course he was. The Billy: 'Harwich's No1 fun pub, the place 2B', where the affiliates of the port's roughest fringes had gathered since 1756.

Saturday night, 11 July 2009, and things hadn't changed

much. They may have got worse. The men who had fought in Afghanistan were now a key part of its incendiary mix. 'It was some concoction. A lot of angry men went down the Billy,' Kenny said. He was pretty wired that night himself. The previous day was the bloodiest of the war for British troops. Eight had died in Helmand in twenty-four hours, almost as many as Kenny's battalion had lost in six months. Five died on the same patrol close to his old base in Sangin.

The patrol had been negotiating Pharmacy Road, a narrow thoroughfare in the east of the town that was riddled with so many booby traps it had been renamed IED Alley. Kenny remembered the road well. Pharmacy was hemmed in on both sides by towering baked mud walls that smothered those inside. He recalled the overwhelming claustrophobia, the slits carved in the lofty ramparts, shooting holes where invisible snipers could lurch. There was no high ground, no way of knowing who or what skulked on the other side. Once on Pharmacy, there was nowhere to go but straight ahead. The worst thing was the baked loose dirt of the road itself. Bomb-disposal experts had once found thirty-one booby traps in a single sweep. It was six hundred metres long and each step was potentially your last. Pharmacy Road spooked even the most fearless soldiers.

Shortly after dawn on 10 July, 9 Platoon the Rifles found themselves on Pharmacy Road moving towards the patrol base at Wishtan, effectively separated from Sangin by the buried devices that laced the ground between. A landmine went off, killing one soldier. Moments later another erupted, killing three of the riflemen and fatally wounding another. Two others ran to help and detonated a secondary device. One casualty was a point man. Three of them were eighteen years old.

The war was getting worse. Kenny could see that even from Essex. In Harwich it was hard to get a sense of progress, the vacuum of knowledge making it seem they had died for nothing, at least nothing palpable. More than 230 British soldiers were dead and Kenny wondered whether any of their deaths had made a difference. At least they were there; at least they were trying to a make a difference.

He asked Sam if it was OK to go out for a drink. As soon as he left his family, Kenny realised he should have stayed at home. The place, the people, the pubs only wound him up tighter. Groups of lads were hammering slammers and ogling girls. The girls in turn were eyeing up the boys by the bar. It didn't seem right to Kenny, how they were cackling at the bar as if nothing mattered. The lads were all prime fighting age, necking sugary, blueberry-coloured loopy-juice as if it was the coolest thing they had ever done. Kenny could think only of Pharmacy Road. All over Helmand, at that very moment, in ditches and dusty corridors, his successors were dying as their non-combatant contemporaries blew their brains on blue WKD.

That night he only wanted to talk about the war. He was dour company and the drink did nothing for him. He drank steadily, solemnly, feeling the wire tighten within. In the Billy he met another figure in need of a late drink, a young Royal Anglian soldier heading to Afghanistan in twelve weeks' time. Kenny bought him a lager. Hollering above the unremitting beats of house DJ Double J with his acid-house smiley icon, they discussed the dead, the enemy's preferred ambush techniques, the IEDs. The teenage Anglian said he was shitting himself. He wanted to learn from a veteran and Kenny remembers feeling honoured to oblige.

The Billy began to fill up. They moved to a quiet corner. Double J cranked it higher and the crowd thickened, wedging the two against the far wall so there was nowhere to move. Revellers jostled them, spilling drinks. There were no apologies, no manners. 'They wouldn't say sorry for anything, that lot,' Kenny said. He recalls a growing sense of fury uncoiling inside. Men had died, eight in the previous day, and he remembers thinking: what had the Billyites done in the previous twenty-four hours? 'I suppose I felt a bit raw, everyone pissed up, no one giving a fuck.'

It was the wrong moment for anybody to tell Kenny that the war was a waste of time.

Kenny recognised him as one of the local layabouts. He had dated the guy's niece years ago and never cared for him then. He was about ten years older, but as far as Kenny was concerned had achieved less than most ten-year-olds. Unemployed, a life on benefits, never leaving Harwich. A Billy regular. He had overheard Kenny and the young soldier talking about Afghanistan and decided to share the firm theories he had developed on the war. It was a 'load of shit'.

Kenny told the guy to sod off, he wasn't in the mood. But he kept standing there, saying they should pull out the troops tomorrow because no one had conquered Afghanistan and it was fucking pointless. Kenny, his body tensing like a coil, said that the British were doing a bloody amazing job, that guys were being killed trying to protect the likes of him and he should show more fucking respect. But the bloke laughed.

'I don't give a fuck about the troops dying.'

Kenny just went for him.

It had happened before, a few weeks earlier. Kenny was sitting at a bar, nursing a quiet pint when a group of 'scallies' entered. 'They stood in the middle shouting their heads off. Other people trying to have a normal conversation could hardly hear themselves speak.' The group gathered around a well-built bloke and for half an hour the pub was forced to listen to him whinging about his twenty-first birthday preparations. 'On and on he went, going on about where they should have it, who would turn up, who wouldn't, that sort of bullshit.'

Kenny said he felt the rage begin to bubble. The birthday boy droned on, dominating the pub. 'People, especially younger people, are too spoilt these days. They don't understand what discomfort means. My generation has never been uncomfortable in their whole life, they don't appreciate what they have.'

He remembered his own twenty-first birthday. His section had just passed the water fountain near Sangin's bazaar when he found the plastic bag with a bomb inside, gift-wrapped with eight wire ribbons. His twenty-first was the day he might have lost his arms and legs.

'But the Hanover is bollocks, no fit birds, full of old farts playing darts . . .'

Kenny put down his drink and went over. The birthday boy was huge by comparison, but there was no risk assessment or calm appraisal of facts. Kenny grabbed him by the jacket and in one movement rolled him over the bar. 'I said: "There are lads around here who never saw their twenty-first birthday," the fat bastard.' He didn't look at the others, he said, knowing they wouldn't make a move. Then he downed his pint and left.

'It's like an instant temper. Snap,' Kenny said, clicking his fingers: 'I get instant adrenalin and anger like my dad's. One minute I'm as calm as fuck and the next moment something pisses you off. You grit your teeth. Snap. Boom. I was never like that before. It grows inside you.'

The only escape was to drink. Like his father should have been persuaded off liquor by his mother, Kenny had his dad's drinking as a warning. 'To be honest the only way you can actually chill the nerves out is having a beer,' he reasoned. It was a far from unique approach among soldiers. Government-funded research at the time found up to twenty-three thousand of those in the armed forces – around one in seven – were drinking 'hazardous and harmful' levels of alcohol. Those who had served on the front line were twenty-two per cent more likely to suffer serious drinking problems than other troops.

But Kenny had to be careful. A drink too far and the effect swung the other way. It was like his body remained hardwired for Helmand, permanently ready to respond to an omnipresent risk. But the constant state of alert required to carry a man through the war wasn't required back home. In everyday life, hypervigilance was a hindrance. There was no need for trigger-point clarity in Essex. Drink soothed the nerves, it took him down a notch. The problem was that he tended to drink a lot.

He kept in touch with the rest of Bait Platoon, the peers who best understood him. In their company, Kenny felt like he belonged. They might not see each other for months, but like all friends who'd shared formative times they plugged straight back into a connection, a time when they were bonded in the dust.

They discussed how the war was getting dirtier with the increased use of IEDs, and how their tour seemed to belong to a more innocent age when the enemy liked to stand and fight. They discussed those who called them 'baby-killers', the perceived hostility binding the men tighter. They talked about going back out, finishing the job. And the nightmares. No one had admitted he needed help and no one had been diagnosed with PTSD, but they all described morbid dreams. Kenny still remembered their screams at night in the barracks after they returned from the war. 'You live in a room of eight men and you see them having nightmares, shouting out through the night. To be honest it worried me. I didn't want my friends to come out like my dad.'

Some had stayed on in the army. Nick Denning had put on hold his dreams of becoming a television anchorman, risen through the ranks to captain and begun instructing new recruits at the Infantry Training Centre in Catterick – although he privately admitted he'd rather be back in Helmand leading Bait Platoon behind enemy lines. Badger had made a full recovery, eagerly showing the knot of gnarled scar tissue above his wrist to anybody who would look.

He had accrued more scars in the meantime. One night out drinking he had been started on by a civvy who had pulled out a knife and gored Badger in the leg, leaving a mark that looked like a pale snake had been welded to his thigh. Shot by the Taliban, stabbed by one of his own countrymen. Badger considered calling his snake a war wound, reasoning that two scars would double his pulling chances. There was little evidence either had enhanced his appeal. No matter: Badger stayed on in the infantry, hoping to add more scars to his collection.

Hardy was going to get hitched, one of the war's worst-kept secrets to those who had heard him talk about Charlene and how he missed her scratching his back. They had finally saved enough for a deposit on a home. Hardy was being groomed for great things and about to sit his officer-training entry exams. In fact, those who had chosen to stay in all seemed to be doing pretty well. Slater was becoming a lance corporal. But Sam Hicks, who had said he could remain in the army another twenty years and nothing would beat the night Kenny sat on a Taliban sentry near Waterloo, had suddenly decided to leave. Now he was a supervisor at a security firm.

During the regiment's subsequent tour of Afghanistan Hicksy had volunteered to become a medic. One incident affected him so grievously it effectively forced the twenty-one-year-old to abandon his military career. A friend had stepped on a pressure-plate mine north of Sangin and lost both legs. Hicksy followed his training and tied a compress tourniquet to each stump, but the soldier continued to lose blood. He added supplementary bandages, applied extra pressure, but still the blood came. Even when the Taliban began firing, he stayed there, trying to stem the flow. His friend was already dead when the medevac helicopter arrived. He could not have done more, no one could, but Hicksy was inconsolable. 'It only takes one thing, one patrol to change you,' said Kenny. 'Being a medic he saw a lot of people fragged. When he got back he had a lot of flashbacks. He's had a rough time.'

'Olly' Olivero had also had enough, departing the military and joining an electronics company designing apps for mobile phones. But those who stayed on never tired of trying to persuade Kenny to rejoin. When the Royal Anglians were due back in Afghanistan in 2009, several begged him to reconsider. They wanted their point man back. 'Just one more tour for old times' sake.' But Kenny wouldn't put his family through the war.

Yet while Kenny had guided his friends across some of the most inhospitable lands in the world, the daily incursion through Greenstead was doing his head in. He began to question his capacity to endure another confrontation. His instinct was to carry the fight to the young men of the estate, but doing so would risk his job and ultimately his family would suffer.

His bosses were sympathetic when he explained his position. They had seen former soldiers struggle on route 64 before. In October 2009 Kenny stopped driving the buses and began working in Colchester's FirstGroup depot. The role was essentially maintenance, cleaning the buses for the next journey, preparing them for the next dawn patrol. The shifts were laborious and antisocial, starting at 4.40

p.m. when the first bus came back and finishing after midnight. 'You've gone from being one of the proudest persons around to mopping sick out of a bus or cleaning toilets at the bus station. That plays on your mind a bit.' But Kenny gradually identified its virtues, solid honest graft that allowed more time with Sam and Cayden during the day. And it kept him off the drink.

Kenny was starting to experience a desperate urge to talk. He had mentioned snippets about the war to Sam, but didn't want to burden her or worry her about the things he had seen, the things he was seeing. Similarly, he was wary of adding to his dad's stresses. Kenny took to confiding in strangers.

It was an odd habit. Once on the train back from London, he spent the ninety-minute journey talking non-stop about Ghartse Gar, Inkerman, Waterloo, to a chap whose name he never knew. How the stories started Kenny had no idea; often he wasn't sure if the listener had even asked. But afterwards he always felt elated. For a brief moment the shackles seemed to loosen. Yet Kenny would fret later that the recipient might have thought he was a fantasist. 'Because I'm baby-faced, people look at me and go, "Fucking hell, *you* fought in a war, you fought in *two* wars?" I suppose it was a kind of therapy, talking to complete strangers.'

But the therapy was not enough. John continued to see his son deteriorate. The initial crankiness, the upswellings of anger were shaping into something more significant. 'I started to see little character changes in Kenny, little personality changes. He was such a relaxed kid and I remember beginning to see those changes. I said: "Fucking stop it, stop going down that road. I lost everything going down that road."'

One night it came to a head between father and son, shortly after the Billy fracas. Kenny had finished one of his final shifts on route 64 and had popped around to his dad's for a chat and a drink. The row began over nothing, neither could even recall how it started, only that things quickly got testy. In an instant they were fighting. As they went down John knew beyond doubt his son was changing.

Later Kenny was convinced his dad had started the argument deliberately, twisting the release valve of his temper in case it flared elsewhere. John said he was probably right. He never thought Kenny would become angry with Sam or Cayden, but he was worried about the rest of the civilian population. Sam, though, was increasingly anxious. She knew Kenny's father suffered from PTSD post-combat and had taken a keen interest in researching the symptoms. Now she found herself scouring the internet for indicators to her fiancé's mental wellbeing. Sam was quickly convinced Kenny required professional intervention before it was too late.

The fight with Kenny deeply troubled John. More than ever he feared that his eldest son would turn out like him. He wondered how close Kenny was to experiencing his own meltdown. Experts said it took an average of fourteen years before the full symptoms of PTSD materialised. John's breakdown had been relatively prompt: nine years. Kenny was only two years in and the signs were growing. He needed help.

If anyone could make a difference it was Steve Pettitt, the east of England's welfare officer for Combat Stress, the charity dedicated to helping military PTSD sufferers. The retired RAF squadron leader had left the armed forces three years earlier, when he was in his mid-forties. Now he travelled the region visiting those who had sustained psychological damage from service, the vast majority of them from their experiences in Northern Ireland. Some responded well, but others could not stop asking: 'What if?' One of those was a veteran of the war in Bosnia who had caught a Serbian rebel about to rape a girl. The British soldier pressed his rifle against the rebel's temple but was unable to shoot because of the United Nations' rules of engagement. The Serb simply smiled and walked off. Two days later, on a routine patrol, the British soldier passed the farmhouse where he had seen the girl. He saw her in the window, strung up in the shape of a crucifix. She was naked and had been set on fire. Her fate, his inability to help, had consumed him ever since, according to Pettitt.

John once told me about an old friend, Big Irish Pete, who fought in the Kosovo campaign. He was among British peacekeepers who arrived hours too late to prevent a massacre of farmers in the fields south of Priština. 'He's completely fucked now,' said John. 'Mass killings are happening, but you can't do anything about it – now that's fucked up.'

John had been seeing a lot of Steve Pettitt since arriving in Essex, although of late it had been getting harder to catch him. Combat Stress's caseload was rising rapidly. Young men who had served in Iraq and Afghanistan were starting to fill the charity's books. When John moved down to Essex in 2006 Pettitt had 240 patients, and this number had increased by more than a quarter since then. Two new people were coming forward every week asking for help, the organisation recording more than a hundred fresh cases a year in the east of England alone. Some of those were Second World War veterans. Pettitt's oldest client was ninety-two, his youngest nineteen.

The trend was mirrored nationally. From three thousand cases in 2006, the number was now approaching five thousand. Across the UK, Combat Stress was receiving 1,400 new referrals a year, a thirty-three per cent increase. The charity could barely cope. Pettitt told John the trend was only going to become more pronounced. 'There's more to come. We're only seeing the tip of the iceberg in terms of psychological problems.'

In an attempt to manage, the charity had launched an appeal, 'The Enemy Within', to raise £30 million for a national network. The appeal chairman, Chai Patel, suggested up to fifty thousand veterans had some sort of mental health problem relating to their time in Iraq and Afghanistan. Patel warned there were too few resources for a problem that was misunderstood by so many. Ominous signs were also emerging that the government was not interested in attending to the after-effects of war. To considerable fanfare the Ministry of Defence had announced plans for a screening programme to aid early diagnosis of PTSD in combat troops, only to promptly ditch the plans. Cognitive injuries were not taken as seriously as physical wounds. A soldier suffering long-term mental problems could expect a tenth of the amount of compensation received by one who had been blinded.

During the autumn of 2009, John rang Pettitt to tell him about Kenny. The caseworker immediately recognised the symptoms as the early stages of PTSD. It was crucial to catch the illness early, Pettitt said. Young veterans usually needed a 'short sharp shock' treatment to quash their demons. 'The sooner we get the younger guys in, the better. If you're not careful it can creep up and get you by the bollocks. Sooner we get them the better, otherwise they don't know how to move out of it.' It was reassuring that Kenny had secured a job, but the fact that he was a bus driver aroused Pettitt's curiosity. Other former soldiers who had driven buses had been known to take their passengers on sudden unscheduled diversions. When asked, most explained that they had spotted an ambush ahead.

Sometimes the help available was not enough. During a conversation I had with Pettitt in the summer of 2010, he seemed at a loss after losing two clients out of the blue. One was a former RAF servicewoman who had started a university course and had ambitious hopes for the future but who took an overdose one evening. 'There was absolutely no hint of anxiety when I saw last her,' Pettitt said. The other was an ex-army guy who seemed to be improving by the day but then suddenly began to suffer profuse rectal bleeding one afternoon. Medics had seen nothing like it, the sheer rate of blood loss. His wife took him to hospital where in the space of three hours doctors pumped twenty-two litres of blood into him. It was no use, the flow couldn't be halted. The man's life literally drained away.

The diagnosis seemed to be an astonishingly acute form of irritable bowel syndrome, itself linked to emotional upheaval or stress. 'It's often the most unexpected cases,' said Pettitt.

On his rounds the caseworker had met a number of young Afghan veterans, observing how the conflict was inducing its own peculiar symptoms. Afghanistan, he said, was peculiarly adept at provoking tremendous guilt and remorse among those who survived. Why him, not me?

John, however, was experiencing a good patch. He hadn't landed a job, but one afternoon out shopping he'd met a woman he described as 'terrific'. Karen, who worked in the local police's domestic violence unit, says she was bowled over by a man of rare sensitivity and perception. John couldn't believe his luck.

Up at dawn, time to get on the old kit, pin on the medals and head down to the smoke. John and Kenny were going down Whitehall, to the Cenotaph, joining the other vets on Remembrance Sunday 2009. Side by side, father and son stood to attention, just like the old days, bowing their heads as the bugler sounded, listening to the battle hymns of history.

Afterwards they went for a pint, giddy with pride. Strangers bought them drinks and shook their hands, thanking them for what they had done. Just doing our duty, the Meighans said. It was the best of days.

Only when the train rumbled back to Essex through the eastern sprawl of the city, the grateful crowds slipping further away, did John's mood begin to dip. Kenny raced back to his family while John went back to his past. For an hour he sat on the sofa, dapper in his crisp uniform, fingering the medals clasped above his heart.

He fancied a nightcap and nipped across the street to Tresco's convenience store for a cut-price litre of vodka. Even before he began he knew it was a bad idea. It had been an emotional day. His head was full of people who were absent. People like Big Jim, his face frozen in time as if nothing had happened since the intelligence briefing at 10.10 a.m., 13 December 1989. He had been dead twenty years, almost longer than Kenny had been alive.

That night, as the vodka took hold, John felt it was time to do the decent thing and join Jim. He'd left it long enough, too long for the gesture to mean much but the least he could do was apologise in person for what had happened. He felt like a feckless bastard. Everything he touched had turned to shite. He had lost so many things, the hunger and ambitions of his early childhood, the countless hopes. He convinced himself that only death would grant him peace.

He kept nailing the vodka, knowing how the drink sucked him under and that after a day when he was encouraged to remember, he was sinking fast. But he was powerless to resist. He thought about calling Kenny, but his son had his own troubles and his own family. As he sank deeper, he ceased thinking of the people he loved. Logic disappeared. There was no reflecting on the hurt his death would cause those who adored him. In the moments before he tried to kill himself none of that registered. He had lost all connection to reality.

It was time to let go. He was still taking powerful doses

of mirtazapine, the antidepressant from the Seroxat family that helped soften the spectacle of his road journeys. His initial dosage was 30 mg, but over the years it had doubled. With the last of the vodka, he downed his remaining stash followed by a dash of carbamazepine, administered to control electrical activity in the brain. It was John's largest overdose ever.

Kenny said goodnight to Cayden and went to bed early. It had been a great day, though his dad had seemed a touch emotional towards the end. He had considered calling, but thought he might be overreacting. His dad was on the mend. In fact recently the tables had been turned: Kenny was the one they should be watching, said John. Maybe he would hook up with Steve Pettitt as soon as possible, Kenny thought; at least that'd ease his dad's worries. Anyway he had a few questions of his own. Recently he'd noticed his nightmares were becoming ever more structured, following an identical sequence like Powerpoint slides. The marching corpses, the man he killed, and then Tony, in the cornfield, trapped in the bag.

He wanted to ask Pettitt if that was normal. He thought he should also mention how he sometimes experienced an immense guilt that he was alive and others were dead, a grieving sense of injustice that went deeper and deeper and made him angry. And was it normal to see the dead as if they belonged in the real world?

Kenny held his dad's hand. It was limp and cold. John looked rotten, stretched on the hospital bed, his face pallid and clammy. When he spoke it was softly and slowly. He apologised to Kenny and then to Karen, who until then had not realised the full extent of his torment.

John was enduring the shame and self-hatred as the memories of nine previous suicide attempts returned. Afterwards he could not believe what he had done. It was at that point, gripped by remorse and compassion for the people he loved, that he fully appreciated how dangerously ill he was. But that suicide attempt in November 2009 was never intended to succeed, he admitted later. As John felt his faculties starting to fail, the delirium kicking in, he had dialled 999. 'It was another cry for help. I want so desperately to get better.'

Three weeks later I visited John, unaware that he had tried to kill himself. Only in passing, during our second cup of tea, did he mention the overdose. Throughout the process of writing the book I had always feared he might make another suicide attempt, but it still came as a shock.

'My coping mechanisms are not quite as robust as the next person's. It doesn't take a lot for me to start falling and then I just drop like a ton of bricks,' he sighed as if he couldn't believe it himself. The suggestion of extra counselling was met with a weary shrug. John said he had exhausted every avenue. Everywhere was either too busy or didn't offer the necessary treatment, he said. 'I'll keep taking my medication and make sure I keep my mind occupied.'

In retrospect it was obvious where the problem lay. His suicide attempts only occurred after excessive alcohol binges. His drinking, he admitted, had started to spiral out of control again. But I already knew that. A month earlier,

I had rung John at 2 p.m. on a Wednesday to say that Dr Jones from Ty Gwyn was asking after him. 'Who's this?' he slurred loudly instead of his customary polite greeting. He managed an apology, but kept pouring vodka throughout the call. His mood deteriorated. 'Do you think I'm a bad man?' he kept asking. No, I said, but he wouldn't listen. His outlook continued to darken.

'I feel so much shame for the things I have done, so embarrassed that I went to prison, my criminal record,' he started saying over and over. By 2:45 the vodka had begun to suppress his senses. He could barely speak. By then he'd resorted to calling himself 'a fucking piece of useless shit'. Afraid he was becoming suicidal, I pleaded with him to call Kenny but he hung up. That night he didn't answer his phone. We spoke the next day and both apologised: John for getting pissed when it did him no good and me for not making sure he wasn't dead that night.

The nurses kept him under observation in Colchester General for three days. Upon his release, John vowed to make some changes. For a start he was leaving Clacton-on-Sea. He had to escape the late-night kebab houses, the taxi-rank squabbles, the lunatics who pissed on his door. His nerves were shot. Most nights he wondered if his three assailants would return to finish the job. But the final straw was the distress that his other sons, Alexander and Andrew, had endured during their last stay. 'They couldn't sleep because of the noise and I'm jumping out of bed like a bag of spanners.'

For Kenny's sake, for Karen's sake, for all his children's sakes, he pledged to make yet another fresh start. At the start of December, he moved down the A34 to Colchester, with financial help from the Royal British Legion and the Soldiers, Sailors, Airmen and Families Association. Tacked onto the town's southernmost periphery, the top-floor apartment overlooked the local military firing range and the distant pop of cannon often provided the soundtrack to his afternoon brew. Despite the frequent reminders of combat, John said it was the best place he'd had since Compley Avenue five years earlier.

There was another positive development. The community mental health team introduced him to Colchester's Miletree Workshop which taught veterans with mental illnesses to build bespoke furniture through joinery and carpentry lessons four days a week. John was a natural, creating enviable hatstands, shelves and tables with dovetail joints that he gave to Karen or installed in his new flat. Soon his craftsmanship was of a standard good enough to sell. The rediscovery of purpose elated him. Most mornings he could be found outside the workshop, waiting for it to open. His mum used to ridicule him as a boy who 'cannae even hammer a nail in the wall'. Now he was showing her what he could do; now he was bouncing back.

Twelve days before Christmas John did not show up at the Miletree Workshop. Instead he left the flat in his one and only suit, carrying a poppy cross that he'd made earlier. He caught the number 62 from Colchester bus station where Kenny would be arriving later for work and, in driving rain, skirted the southern suburbs. Past the military prison where deserter Joe Glenton was awaiting sentence, across the River Colne, down St Andrews Avenue, past the

University of Essex and along Brightlingsea Road. Another five minutes and the 62 made a sharp right along the avenue, downhill into the village of Wivenhoe. It was an intensely emotional journey for John. He referred to the trip as his 'private pilgrimage', one of the few things he didn't like discussing in detail. 'It's something I do on my own, in private, it's a very personal mark of respect to someone I served alongside.'

He climbed off the bus at Belle Vue Road, crossed the street and went straight ahead, through the plain steel gate. He remembers the rain turning heavier, the clouds battering fast across the sky, the graveyard deserted as usual. A thin gravel trail cut through the tombs and John followed the path, steps crunching in the quiet. He stopped by the grave and noticed flowers in the fading light. His wife and son must have left them. Daniel must be twenty-two now. John wondered what he was doing, whether he had followed in his father's footsteps. And Shirley. He hoped she had found happiness again. It had been a long time.

He knelt down and planted the poppy cross in the damp soil by the headstone. Then suddenly he jerked upright and saluted his old friend. 'Pte James Houston. King's Own Scottish Borderers. Killed Northern Ireland 13.12.89.'

When he returned home John said he resisted the urge to drink, knowing where the binge would end. Christmas was coming and there would be plenty of time for that. He was looking forward to Christmas. He'd save himself.

True to his word, he held back until an hour before the queen emerged on Christmas Day. He was over at Karen's, turkey and all the trimmings. She seemed thrilled with the hand-carved crafts he'd made. Gifts exchanged, it was time for a snifter. By the time darkness fell, John had polished off a bottle of vodka. Come on, it was Christmas, everybody over-indulged, he said. Karen replied that he'd drunk enough, but John wasn't finished. He drank another bottle. 'I couldn't stop.' He couldn't even remember what the row was about. But Karen threw him out.

He staggered home and carried on drinking. He was due at Kenny's on Boxing Day for a belated festive lunch and had been looking forward to it for weeks: Kenny, Sam and Cayden, a full spread, gifts under the tree. But when Kenny rang that morning, his dad was so sloshed he could barely communicate. 'He wasn't impressed.' Kenny, his most loyal fan, told him not to bother coming over.

So he drank some more. He drank the next day too, another bottle of vodka, and drank for the rest of the year. New Year's Eve came and went with Big Ben on the box like all the other lonely people, fireworks zipping over the Thames like tracers, the crowd goofily cheering in another year of hope and promise.

He made no resolutions, other than determining to start this year in the manner in which the last had ended. 'A litre a day keeps the family away,' he muttered to himself. The booze gave him no highs, it merely deadened him until he had no feelings. He stopped answering the phone or the door. 'I got up and drank, drank the whole day, had a nightcap, got up and did the same. Day after day.' He drank out of self-pity, he admitted, because he had told himself that he was destined for loneliness. He became adamant that he'd lost the ability to live contentedly with others. Only the visions of his road journeys stayed loyal.

He drank with the television muted and the radio off, Rosie watching. He stockpiled cheap drink to avoid leaving the house, his keys redundant on the wooden table he had carved when things felt better. Kenny's military dogtags hung off the keys, a keepsake from his son to protect his dad. Blood group: B positive. Army number: 25162300. KJM. Kenny John Meighan. Atheist. John said he smiled when he first saw that. Once he had asked Kenny why he had categorised himself as a non-believer despite being christened in the Church of England. Kenny had grinned: 'That was before I went out to Afghanistan.'

He drank for eleven days solid. He can't remember how many litres of vodka he drank, how many roll-ups he smoked or how little food he ate, only that it was too much, too many and too little.

On 6 January 2010 he woke up and wanted things to be different. 'Poor me I was, poor me. Then I woke up nearly a week into the year and realised I needed fucking help. I knew I had to change.'

John promised himself it was all over, the drink, the suicide bids, Big Jim, the dead Iraqis. It was time to start looking ahead. Shortly after breakfast he made the call he hoped would begin dismantling the juggernaut of his memories. He rang Alcoholics Anonymous and remembers precisely what he said: 'I cannot drink safely. I am a binge drinker. When I take my first drink I have no control, I have an overwhelming compulsion to drink a litre of vodka. I am powerless. Every time I drink it is getting worse and worse. I want to start again. Please help me.'

15

Toy Soldiers

Hardy died on 16 March 2010. He had been dropped off by helicopter in uncharted territory twenty-one kilometres north of Musa Qala, the high-altitude moonscape that felt like the roof of the world to the young men from Essex. Intelligence had suggested the area was safe, as safe as anywhere could be, and that it posed a low IED threat.

Recently promoted to lance corporal, Scott Hardy was leading the way alongside twenty-one-year-old Private James Grigg when they paused behind an earth embankment to check co-ordinates. A nearby section described hearing a thumping explosion. Moments later Hardy's voice drifted from the radio and warned those following to hold their position. 'Contact IED wait,' he said. The rumble of another bomb boomed across the desert plain.

The first medics to the scene found Grigg on his back, wreathed in blood. He had lost both his legs. Witnesses said the cricket-mad soldier appeared chilled out, almost serene. Grigg even winked at the approaching soldiers. But Hardy was gone. He never had a hope. Like Tony almost three years earlier, the IED had obliterated him. Grigg wouldn't make it either, ceasing to breathe before he could hear the throb of the medevac helicopter.

Bait Platoon convened two months later, this time to toast Hardy's memory when the battalion returned from the front line to Surrey. It was 6 May, the night of the General Election. The rest of the population was queuing outside voting booths, but Kenny had no interest in politics. A change in government would not bring back Hardy.

The men gathered also raised a glass to Charlene, whose stoicism made Kenny realise why Hardy had loved her so much. During his funeral, at the chapel of rest, the twenty-four-year-old solicitor had whispered goodbye and softly scratched his coffin, the same way she used to rub Hardy's back.

The turning point came a few weeks later for Kenny. He overheard a young civvy standing outside the Royal in Harwich yakking on about the war, its pointlessness, the usual mantra. At first he experienced the customary surge of fury, but then something unexpected happened. His anger melted away. Kenny had carried on listening. The guy wanted the troops out of Afghanistan but admitted that he hadn't a clue what the war was about. The acknowledgement prompted an epiphany.

'I saw that I needed to appreciate that many people don't really understand Afghanistan and I had to get to grips with that fact. Of course they are not going to care like I do. There's no point in me explaining it to them or getting wound up because they have a different view.' That summer evening outside the Royal, Kenny said he realised that it wasn't their fault that they didn't grasp the meaning of the war. Nobody was to blame. You cannot force people to understand things they couldn't know, said Kenny. His drinking steadied. There were to be no more dust-ups, no sudden flashes of temper, no Billy reprise. 'What's the point in me going out there and kicking off? The only person who's going to get a bad rep is me by getting checked in and out of prison, done for disorderly, fines here and there, eventually community service. I'm the one who's going to lose out. The selfishness of my generation is just the way it is. I can't do anything about it.'

It was obvious, he said, now that he thought about it. It also occurred to Kenny that he had fought for freedom so people could express themselves. 'I had been to Iraq and Afghanistan fighting for democracy, I have to remember that.' People were entitled to their own opinion. That included the pacifists, the students, the politicians, the public who thought the war was worthless. 'A lot of people come up to me and say: "We should never have been in Afghanistan, what are we doing fighting and dying out there?" And then you've got to explain that it's not just fighting the Taliban, it's fighting the world's terrorists for their sake too. The world's terrorists are going to Afghanistan to train, they have to train somewhere. But there are some people who will never want to understand a justification for the war. It can feel like you're just wasting your breath, it gets frustrating, but you learn to see the bigger picture.'

The laidback boy returned. John noticed it almost overnight. His son seemed less spiky, able to laugh more readily, like he used to. John's attempts to kick the drink had triggered an immediate rapprochement between father and son, and both subsequently agreed they had never felt so close. 'Kenny's doing really well. He knows he can talk to me and hopefully he's caught it in the early stages,' said John. Steve Pettitt was certain they'd got to Kenny in time, knowing it could have been very different. 'Kenny could have been one of those servicemen who come out and have too much time on their hands, too much anger in their heads.'

The chief factor was Cayden. When Pettitt met Kenny he was impressed by how the former point man balanced his work demands with looking after his son. In many ways, said Pettitt, Cayden was looking after his dad. 'He seems to thrive on the responsibility of caring for his little boy.' Pettitt felt good about Kenny's future, his ability to cope.

Kenny said he was starting to see beyond the fog of the war, his feelings of guilt softening, his mood swings flatlining to the cool Kenny of old. Even on 25 June 2010 when defence officials announced they were withdrawing UK forces from Sangin to be replaced by US marines, Kenny was relaxed when a year earlier he would most likely have been incandescent. He just sat there, sipping a pint in the Royal, watching the Sky News tickertape confirm the planned withdrawal, occasionally pointing out a dusty track or compound he thought he recognised. 'To think we had that place under control at one point. The bazaar is nowhere near what it was like then.' He turned away from the montage of coffins and British troops crouched under gunfire: 'Things do change, don't they?'

On the day Kenny and I first met, Sangin was being promoted as Helmand's great success story. Schools were being built, the bazaar was booming. Neither of us could have envisaged that three years on, British troops would simply pull out on a technicality and that Sangin would have become the most lethal place in the river valley. Of 353 British troops killed at the time of writing, 106 had died in the town or, like Tony Downes, in its lethal hinterland.

Part of Kenny's change in outlook was a fresh cynicism towards war itself. The lusty rhetoric of taking the fight to the Taliban had gone. Instead he seemed suspicious of conflicts whose motives were unclear. He could only support fighting on humanitarian grounds. 'If it was clear that there were children suffering, women getting raped, mines being planted and people forced to walk over them, then I'd love to go and sort it out. You join the army to do some good, to take out the bad boys, the child-killers, the rapists. You have to fight for something you believe in.'

Similarly, his once unswerving belief in the army had dimmed. Three years earlier, when asked if he would encourage others to join, Kenny almost shook with fervour. 'Definitely,' he cried: 'The British army is the best job in the world.' Now his answer was qualified. 'If you're from a dead-end town and you've got nothing going for you then it'll give you a decent foundation for the rest of your life. But not the infantry. Join the Royal Engineers, get a trade.'

The war would never leave him, Kenny knew that, but through the later stages of 2010 he seemed to develop a system to prevent his memories getting in the way. He began to treasure rather than fear his recollections. Bait Platoon, Denning, Slater, Olly and Hardy: they were among the best people, he said, you could ever meet.

He was Kenny John Meighan, aged twenty-three, an age he once considered unreachable and for that he felt blessed.

Plus, civvy life wasn't so bad if you knuckled down to work and kept your nose clean. The recession had taught him to be grateful just to have a job and FirstGroup treated him well. Even the workers were sound, just different from the colleagues he had known before.

It was on a journey to work that his nightmares about Tony Downes were exorcised. As he entered the outskirts of Colchester in October 2010, the words of the dead guardsman drifted from Kenny's car radio. Tony's final letter to his girlfriend Jane and his family had been adapted into a song by the Soldiers, a band of serving troops. 'I'm up here in Heaven, you're free to start again . . .' The reappearance of his final words seemed to liberate Tony in Kenny's mind, somehow eclipsing the brutal reality of his death. 'It was weird, thinking I'd carried him in a bag, and now hearing it on the radio, it sort of made him different, human again.' He could never forget Tony, but the trauma of the incident seemed to subside. His other nightmares too became less lurid, less routine.

Kenny felt *he* was free to start again. There was a lot to live for. He and Sam set a wedding date: 16 July 2011, the fourth anniversary of the night they met in the Stingray. 'Sometimes I don't know what she sees in me, she's so intelligent, so perfect,' he often said. Kenny was being completely straight. He truly believed he had met the best woman on the planet. 'I'm entering a new chapter in my life. I'm trying to aspire to be a good dad and a good husband. Hopefully I'm doing a good job, but I'll only find out when Cayden grows up.'

Kenny enjoyed dedicating himself to the living. Watching

Cayden grow made Kenny realise that a person's calling is to care for others: to love, not to kill. Like most fathers, he had a sense of primal wonder at his son's development. Cayden's thirst for knowledge, his curiosity, his first steps, the first 'Daddy' made him surge with a pride he hadn't felt since he was point man for Bait Platoon of the 1st Battalion of the Royal Anglian Regiment. It was important to cherish new life, to not reject the future.

The year had also been positive for John, a steady improvement originating from his sessions at Alcoholics Anonymous. For the first time since his mental collapse on Bonfire Night fifteen years earlier, John found the clarity to focus on the present. Much of his spare time was spent perfecting wooden ornaments, walking Rosie with Karen – who had eventually forgiven his vodka binge – and regaining the level of fitness that had once defined him. Off the drink, his suicidal tendencies disappeared as his lucidity returned alongside a new-found energy. In a single week in July, he redecorated Karen's flat, made two coffee tables, weeded the apartment's flowerbeds and painted its walls. He even went to court and without legal representation persuaded the magistrate to rescind his driving ban, imposed after a failed breathalyser test in 2002. Kenny, Sam, Karen, Rosie, Alexander, Andrew and his terrific new grandson Cayden: there was much to live for.

Alcoholics Anonymous not only relieved his introspection but, almost a decade after his last paid job, took him into employment. The sessions introduced him to a reformed alcoholic who ran a sandwich business in Colchester. She only employed recovering drunks and John, with his rediscovered vigour and way with people, seemed a canny acquisition. His shifts began at 5 a.m. and at first John couldn't sleep because he was so excited to be getting up and going to work. Steve Pettitt could not believe the turn-around he saw in John. He said that full-time employment often represented the final piece in the jigsaw for those on the road to recovery: John was a textbook example.

John fizzed with energy, not the skittish nervousness of the old days but a new vitality. He talked more slowly and calmly and with greater authority. His words were unfail-ingly upbeat. It struck me that usually we had talked about the past, but now, for the first time, he wanted to embrace the future. 'I've got everything a man could ever want, I'm looking ahead, I feel excited. And I'll tell you something else. I've never felt happier, honestly. Never.'

When we had first met, in his old flat in Clacton-on-Sea, I remembered being struck by John's impressive recall, his easy intelligence, but above all by his immense sadness. On several occasions he choked back the tears and later, when we headed down to the promenade for a pint, his mood sank further. He rang several hours after I'd left for Lon-don, explaining that he'd carried on drinking and was on the vodka. He kept repeating that he wanted to help people avoid what had happened to him. He also apologised for blowing some cash that I'd given him for his time, although it transpired he'd put it in an envelope and posted it to Combat Stress.

That night I asked him whether it was a wise idea to carry on with the book project if it reopened old wounds, but John was determined: 'I have to stop someone going through this shit.' He almost shouted, 'If I can encourage a single person to come forward and get help then it'll be worth it. There are so many still to come forward. It was a taboo topic when I left the army. I'd do anything to change that. Save one person from the fucking shite I've gone through and it'll be worth it.' He did, though, make one request: that his struggles should not overshadow the achievements of his son. 'We're both ordinary men, we don't pretend to be anything else, but Kenny makes me proud.'

John seemed a different man now. His mind had recalibrated from the past to the present. Memories of the events which had dominated so much of his life had begun to recede. Until recently he had yearned to go back to the days before Big Jim and the dead, lipless Iraqis, back to the glimmerings of his youth and childhood aspirations. That was, he said, before he realised he could build a future. There was no going back, John vowed. He was going to live a life of gratitude from now on, a life in peace.

At the start of October 2010 he felt sufficiently emboldened, encouraged by Karen, to commence a four-year Open University course on the rise and decline of the British Empire. His primary motive was understanding the Meighans' place in history, learning the context of his forefathers' service, the Battle of the Boyne and on through Northern Ireland's struggle to the peace process. He wanted to study the history of Iraq and of Afghanistan from the nineteenth-century massacre of Britain's forces outside Kabul through to Kenny's tour. Each generation of Meighans had fought their own war and John reasoned more were bound to follow. 'My family had played a part in the building of the empire and a part handing the empire back. It was important I could evaluate their contribution. I taught myself to read and write, I might as well use it.'

History was critical in evaluating the cycle of conflict, he said. A new generation of men was already growing up, preparing their own campaigns. His and Kenny's battles would slowly fade into the past until they, its survivors, were mere symbols of a previous era's folly. 'But history, apart from a few examples like the fight against Nazi Germany, shows that war usually doesn't achieve anything,' said John. Yet it was inevitable that humans would always wage wars against one another and people would not stop conceiving superior ways to exterminate. But it annoyed John that despite the advances in medical science, the fact that it was easier than ever to keep a man alive after he had lost his legs and arms, they still couldn't repair him, not fully. 'They're happy to stitch a man back together, keep him breathing, and that's a good thing, but what about all those poor fuckers whose wounds are invisible?'

Nothing would ever change, he concluded. Crossmaglen and Sangin would become mere footnotes of a bloody past. The names might vary, but the details often stayed the same: the same weapons, the same tactics, the same impulses. The first weapon fired against Kenny in Afghanistan was a DShK machine gun, followed by an AK-47: the same guns the IRA had used on the morning they killed Big Jim eleven years earlier. Kenny had experienced the same hatred and fear among Helmand's locals as his father had in South Armagh. The Taliban and the paramilitaries both scared people with their threats of punishment, they both tapped into the same fear and both used the tactics of 'shoot and scoot' across the border, into Eire or Pakistan.

The combined age of Big Jim, Chris Gray and Tony Downes totalled sixty-two, less than the average lifespan. The young, as in most wars, still tended to die first. But it was important to stop thinking in terms of good and bad deaths, honourable or futile, because that made you go fucking crazy, said John. 'All you can do is remember, never forget. You owe them that, but it's difficult letting go.'

The fact that Big Jim, Chris Gray and Tony Downes were all privates was not surprising to the Meighans. History had already proved that the lowest ranks were the most likely to die. 'People are the army. The lower ranks, their attitude, their bravery, they're the ones who make the military, the ones most at risk,' said Kenny. He and John agreed that like the wars of the past, the wars of the future will be fought by privates, as they always have been, waged by the kids from the council estates, the sons of soldiers, bricklayers and cab drivers. And the reasons for those wars will continue being determined 'by those that never suffer', John said.

Point men tended to be privates. And as the war rumbled on, they came and went. Kenny stopped counting after the twentieth point man died in Helmand.

While the privates fought, the politicians honoured their valour and made promises they later broke. The General Election had introduced the Coalition government and among David Cameron's first pledges was to enshrine in law the military covenant, the promise of a duty of care in return for sacrifices made. The prime minister pledged formal commitments like education for military children and better care for injured troops. But the government's armed forces bill, unveiled months later, included no such thing. Not a single reference to duty of care could be found. It even neglected to define the covenant. Only a campaign by the Royal British Legion forced a rethink.

The prime minister also promised as a 'priority' to commission a wide-ranging review of the help needed for the thousands of traumatised soldiers who ended up in prison. The results, virtually ignored when they were discreetly published during the Conservative Party's first conference after returning to power, resulted in the MoD allocating £150,000 to help former personnel with acute psychological issues – barely sufficient to rehabilitate the numbers of Bait Platoon.

Kenny and John expressed little surprise over the government's disregarded promises. It would happen again, they said, just like the inevitability of new wars and the certainty that more Meighans would follow them into battle. Kenny's cousin Thomas had already followed him to Helmand, part of the Scots battalion that helped liberate Musa Qala three months after Kenny left the adjoining valley, thirty months before Hardy died on its northern outskirts. Thomas had followed his elder brother, John, into the Argyll and Southern Highlanders.

But the younger John became another Meighan who saw too much. During the battalion's tour in Iraq in 2004 he witnessed a friend accidentally shot in the face at close range with a British machine gun. Shortly afterwards came the event that tipped him over the edge. A grenade was flung at his unit during a patrol in Maysan province. The bomb rolled along the ground, stopping beside his boot. 'He looked down to see what it was and thought that's it, game over. He thought of all the things he had never done and waited to die. But it never went off. It was a dud. He's never been the same, you don't come back from that,' said Kenny. The scene traumatised the twenty-five-year-old to the point where the army granted him a medical discharge. The last Kenny and John heard was that he was hitting the drink, but the updates were becoming less frequent. Already others were queuing up to take his place. Kenny's cousin, George 'Pudgy' Meighan, aged twenty-one, had recently joined the Territorial Army and begun preparing for his debut tour in Helmand.

'It seems to me that the younger generation will never learn, no matter what happened to those before them. They think it'll be different, but it's the same fucking number,' said John. Kenny had ignored the suffering of his dad, who in turn had overlooked the agony of the war wounds that killed his grandpa. 'The way I see it,' said Kenny, one afternoon in Colchester before heading to the bus depot, 'is that Afghanistan will be forgotten quickly. Everyone still talks about the Second World War because the whole country was involved, but Afghanistan affected no one but us. Soon there'll be another war for the next generation to fight and they'll go through their own shit before they learn, the same way as me and my dad. But you can't tell them because they won't listen.'

It was the best Christmas they could remember. Kenny

bought Sam a new pair of Ugg boots and received his customary ticket for the next Tottenham Hotspur home game. John was on good form, sipping mineral water as he ceremoniously read out cracker jokes while they waited for the film to start. One half of the room wanted *Bridge Over the River Kwai*; apparently it got better with the sixtieth viewing. Sam and Karen were angling for a rom-com featuring Jude Law and it seemed they might prevail.

On the carpet by the fire, beneath the pictures of John and Kenny in their combats and the watchful eye of Tia the dog, Cayden was playing intently on his own. In his chubby hands he gripped a toy figurine, a British infantryman.

Acknowledgements

Sincere thanks to the Meighan family, 1st Battalion the Royal Anglian regiment, Combat Stress and Preston Crown Court. Huge thanks also to my agent Ivan Mulcahy and of course Faber and Faber, in particular Kate Murray-Browne and Neil Belton.

ff

Faber and Faber is one of the great independent publishing houses. We were established in 1929 by Geoffrey Faber with T. S. Eliot as one of our first editors. We are proud to publish award-winning fiction and non-fiction, as well as an unrivalled list of poets and playwrights. Among our list of writers we have five Booker Prize winners and twelve Nobel Laureates, and we continue to seek out the most exciting and innovative writers at work today.

Find out more about our authors and books
faber.co.uk

Read our blog for insight and opinion on books and the arts
thethoughtfox.co.uk

Follow news and conversation
twitter.com/faberbooks

Watch readings and interviews
youtube.com/faberandfaber

Connect with other readers
facebook.com/faberandfaber

Explore our archive
flickr.com/faberandfaber